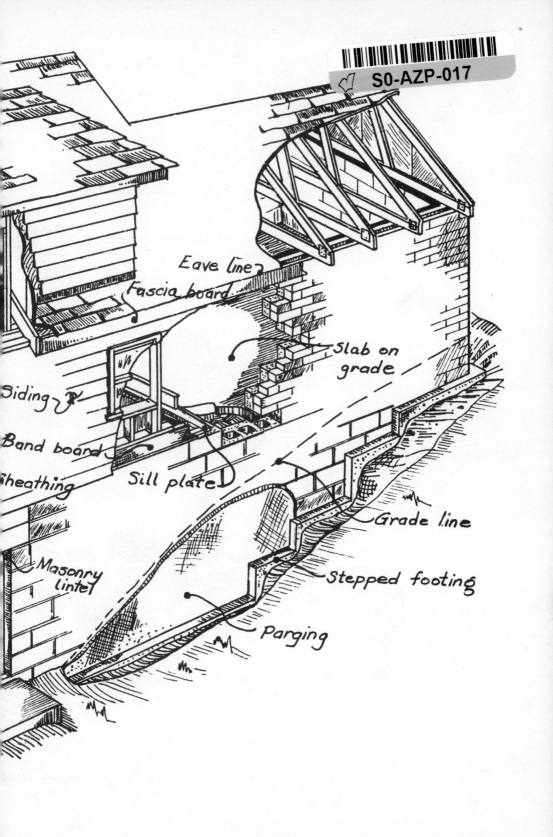

Eave line

Fascia board

Siding

Band board

Sheathing

Sill plate

Masonry lintel

Slab on grade

Grade line

Stepped footing

Parging

DIAGNOSING AND REPAIRING HOUSE STRUCTURE PROBLEMS

DIAGNOSING AND REPAIRING HOUSE STRUCTURE PROBLEMS

Edgar O. Seaquist, Jr., Ph.D., P.E.

McGraw-Hill Book Company

New York   St. Louis   San Francisco   Aukland
Bogotá   Singapore   Johannesburg   London
Madrid   Mexico   Montreal   New Delhi
Panama   São Paulo   Hamburg
Sydney   Tokyo   Paris
Toronto

Library of Congress Cataloging in Publication Data

Seaquist, Edgar Oliver, 1933-
  Diagnosing and repairing house structure problems.

  Includes index.
  1. Dwellings—Maintenance and repair.   I. Title.
TH4817.S43   643'.7   79-22905
ISBN   0-07-056013-7

1 2 3 4 5 6 7 8 9 0   KPKP   8 9 8 7 6 5 4 3 2 1 0

The editors for this book were Jeremy Robinson and
Christine M. Ulwick, the designer was Mark E. Safran, and
the production supervisor was Sally Fliess. Art and
photography by Edgar O. Seaquist. It was set in Baskerville
by Waldman Graphics.

Printed and bound by Kingsport Press.

To my wife, Carol,
and son, Carl

CONTENTS

PREFACE

The details of the average residential structure are built according to a very limited number of accepted standards—standards that are mandated by local building codes and that have hardly varied for hundreds of years. Once a house is complete the responsibility for interpreting the meaning of any damage and deterioration is left to the owners. Designers and builders rarely revisit the buildings they have helped to create, and even when they do they seldom know the building's entire history. As the years pass and owners come and go, the perspective of a continuity in time of the building is lost, for no one is left who can remember the details of construction or the sequence of any repairs. Thus, the diagnosis of distress and deterioration of residential buildings is a random process, far more subject to chance than to reason.

Once in a while prospective home buyers require that a building-design professional survey a structure before purchase, and while any damage is easily identified and remedies proposed, it is slightly embarrassing if the client asks for a reference as documentation for any conclusions. Either there are no complete references, or what does exist is in the form of a technical paper covering a very limited subject. In practically every other field of technology there are a number of well-established authorities and references, but in the case of residential buildings the most satisfactory means of establishing credibility is to return to fundamental principles and argue from these. This is a fine approach if everyone involved is an engineer or architect, but it simply is not practical for the nonprofessional.

This book catalogs and describes damage and deterioration patterns in residential buildings and, in addition, it presents a method of logic that enables an observer to reason out the causes of the distress. Many distress patterns, even though caused by very different phenomena, differ only slightly in appearance. The explanation of the cause cannot be simply codified into some indexed table from which cause, effect, and remedy can be easily related. Thus, the only way to arrive at the correct explanation of the cause is to understand some of the logic that goes into the diagnosis, and, in turn, to understand that such logic necessarily requires a general appreciation of the mechanism causing the distress and some modest understanding of certain material properties. Throughout the text there are simple, nontechnical explanations of how various building components function and how materials fail.

The importance and consequence of any damage is presented, and acceptable repairs are outlined. As part of the analysis of some failures, typically encountered repair techniques are assessed as to their relative value.

Having examined several hundred houses, I have seen patterns of distress that have had several unusual ingredients. First, it was obvious that much of the distress was not anticipated by the original designers and builders. Many distress patterns developed which, had they been foreseen in any way, could have been rectified simply by a change of some standard detail or building sequence. Second, much of the damage developed apparently contrary to conventional logic and standards. Finally, the typical distress patterns became more and more predictable based on age, generic type of house, location, and past history. Having been presented with this information, and aware of the scarcity of references on residential building distress, I began compiling files that evolved, ultimately, into this book.

Acknowledgments

I am indebted to a number of individuals and organizations for providing the modification, help, and opportunity to acquire the information to prepare this book. Most of all I must thank my wife and son, Carol and Carl, for not only originally encouraging me to write this book but also living through the years of my grumpiness as I worked on it. I must give special thanks to Carol, for it was she who untangled my unintelligible sentence structure, corrected my spelling, and continually reminded me that the English language can be used explicitly and concisely to convey information.

My colleagues at Greene and Seaquist Engineers, Inc., and Universal Associates, Inc., have been helpful in providing much of the opportunity for me to gather information for this book. As a consulting engineer I had a perspective on new buildings from having designed them; however, until several years ago I had only examined older buildings in connection with restoration projects and the occasional homeowner who had a particularly severe problem and needed professional advice. More recently, as a consultant to two insurers of large, municipal public works projects, I have had a rather unique opportunity to examine hundreds of residential buildings that were built over a two-hundred-year span; buildings that range in quality from slum to mansion, are distributed over several-hundred square miles of grossly varying topography, and cover every conceivable level of past maintenance and present condition. I therefore express my thanks to Kemper and Argonaut Insurance Companies and to their staffs, who have been so very helpful.

Edgar O. Seaquist, Jr.
Annapolis, Maryland

DIAGNOSING AND REPAIRING HOUSE STRUCTURE PROBLEMS

IDENTIFYING PROBLEMS AND REPAIRS

The largest single economic investment the average American ever makes is the purchase of a home. In initially selecting and later protecting the future value of this investment, however, people often understand little about the physical "condition" of their home. It is common practice for a person to speak of a used car in "good condition." While there is no absolute definition of exactly what this means, most people have an intuitive understanding of what "good condition" signifies. In buying a used car people check for the telltale signs of repaired accident damage—the slightly rippled sheet metal surface, uneven paint color, or irregularly fitting parts. It is surprising how sophisticated even a nonmechanical buyer becomes in evaluating condition of tires, drive train, and engine. The same process occurs when automobile owners consider when and how to spend their maintenance dollar in order to optimize the eventual resale value of the car. Drivers ponder long and hard over such issues as whether to replace brake linings immediately or wait until spring and run the risk of damaged drums or . . ., ad infinitum.

Such considerations are commonplace in relation to maintaining a car that initially costs one-tenth the price of a house and that all too quickly dwindles to being worthless. A house not only costs much more initially than an automobile but also has greatly increased in value in recent years, sometimes doubling in price in the same amount of time that a new car becomes valueless. While all this is true, too few homeowners can accurately identify simple distress in their home. Even when a problem area is noticed, fewer still know the cause and significance of the problem and when and how to make repairs.

It is interesting to compare the maintenance of houses with that of mass-produced appliances. Most appliances come with fairly detailed specifications and maintenance instructions; and when repairs are needed, well-trained repair specialists are readily available to do the job. In the extreme, small products can be returned to the manufacturer for service and repair. Most houses, on the other hand, are one-of-a-kind items. True, mass subdivisions have produced houses with repetitive floor plans and exterior appearance; but since most houses are built individually, there are invariably significant variations among even these houses. Materials vary, the sequence and time of construction is never constant, and services such as plumbing and electrical wiring are often positioned and attached differently in each house. Even on the assumption that a group of houses were "exactly alike," it would be difficult to find out about many of the construction details, sequence of construction, and materials. Such variability makes it almost impossible to know all the details concerning the construction of an individual house.

The very fact that houses are so individual with respect to original design details, construction methods, and maintenance history leads to a language problem in describing houses in general and building distress in particular. Since there are few absolutes associated with residential buildings, many descriptive statements must be qualified with words such as *generally, typically, often,* or *on the average.* Repetitive use of such qualifying words may not only become extremely boring to readers but also lead eventually to the conclusion that, there being so few absolutes and facts, it is irrelevant to try to understand the problems. On the other hand, without such qualifiers and some recognition of the variability of residential buildings, a reader might draw erroneous conclusions leading to unnecessary or incorrect repairs. Thus, it is simply unavoidable sometimes to use these qualifying terms; however, when they are not used it should be understood that unless specifically stated otherwise, any description or observations relating to residential buildings should be interpreted as extremely common.

Another set of terms commonly used to describe the conditions of buildings may, at first, seem somewhat redundant or ambiguous. The words *distress, damage,* and *deterioration* are used throughout in describing the condition of buildings. The word *distress,* as it is used in this book, will refer to the general class of miscellaneous and relatively minor irregularities from any cause. On the other hand, the word *damage* will be used in reference to major irregularities and in particular to those that have resulted from some overt action. Finally, *deterioration* is meant to refer to any problems that are more or less inevitable or unavoidable functions of time.

Thus, for example, random hairline cracks in a plaster wall might be referred to as a "plaster distress," while a broken door frame resulting from the wind slamming the door closed would be spoken of as "damage." Finally, a wood support member that has deformed with age might be said to have "deteriorated." Certainly, there is no universal agreement on the use of these words; however, the use as described above seems to be fairly common and certainly leads to understanding, the ultimate bases for judgment of any word usage.

As mentioned earlier, not knowing certain details of construction can hinder a homeowner's understanding of any distress in the home. This is minor, however, compared with the problem of accurately judging the significance and remedies of any building distress. For some mysterious reason the building trade in general, and the residential trade in particular, is and always has been surrounded by a certain aura of witchcraft. The most preposterous explanations are often given for otherwise simple propositions, and incredible repair solutions are suggested. Leaky basement walls are "waterproofed" by locating active drain systems on the inside of the walls—a solution that literally encourages water to flow through the wall. Rotten wood is sealed with paint that in turn prevents drying and accelerates the decay process. Support structure is removed and never replaced. All these things and more are done to houses in the name of "reasoned" repairs. For many homeowners there are few places to turn to for information.

Reasonableness of thought should become an essential part of any homeowner's repertoire in dealing with identification of problems and repairs to the home. There is nothing involving the average home that cannot be thoroughly understood by the average homeowner. Furthermore, the things that happen to houses, in general, are a result of fairly simple mechanisms. Demand a rational, reasonable explanation of any problem. If an explanation does not make sense to you, chances are that there is little or no meaning to it and you should go elsewhere for a diagnosis.

As always, there is the old problem of language. Like any specialty operations, the building trades have their own language, with particular words and ways of expressing things. Masons talk about "fat mortar"; carpenters refer to "green lumber," when visually it is a yellow-brown color; some parts of buildings are referred to by different names according to regional jargon, while other parts have uniform names. There is a glossary of words commonly used in the house-building trades at the end of this book. The endpapers are a cutaway sketch of a house, not only showing some of the construction details but also giving the names of building components.

In using this book and in discussions with construction trades people, architects, and engineers, always remember that many terms used in residential construction are either vague, inconsistent, or contradictory; in short, the terminology is rarely universal. For example, such terms as "rafters," "joists," "beams," and "purlins" are often used almost interchangeably to describe the primary structural support members for floors and roofs. In many cases the name is not overly important; on the other hand, it never hurts to have a vocabulary of a few proper terms in dealing with repair people. Describing something as a "thing-a-ma-bob" can be a signal to unscrupulous repair people that any explanation will be admissible and, correspondingly, that the cost will not be questioned.

Finally, it is hoped that this book will help the average homeowner to understand, identify, and make a determination of the significance of any distress. Furthermore, generalized procedures for remedial steps will be discussed.

Old versus New Homes

Following World War II, Americans have developed a mobile lifestyle that has gone beyond merely the long-distance, daily commute. Almost 10 percent of our population moves annually, and of this number roughly half moves 500 miles or more. A family, leaving a relatively new house in New England to buy another in one of the western Sun Belt states, will find a house constructed of almost exactly the same materials, with similar details and methods of construction. It is true that the house in the Southwest may have a stucco front instead of a New England–style brick veneer. The heating equipment may vary, but beyond such minor differences the two houses, at the extremes of our country from both a geographic and a climatic standpoint, are almost indistinguishable.

Such universality of house construction has not always been so. In fact, generic home types have been described by the section of the country in which they originated. There was the "Southern bungalow," as contrasted to the "Florida cottage." Both were one story, but here the similarity ended. The Southern bungalow was typically wood-frame construction set on individual masonry piers above a deep crawl space. Conversely, the Florida house was of masonry set directly on grade. Materials were different, the methods of construction had little similarity, and in particular the types of distress and deterioration of the two houses were totally different. These kinds of differences have existed among the houses of every major region.

A number of factors have contributed to the national standardization of house construction. As more of the materials in houses become factory made, manufacturers become bigger and more likely to distribute nationwide. Building products move transcontinentally to optimize supply variations and costs. Thus, for example, a house framed with Douglas fir lumber from Oregon is as likely to exist in Virginia as one having Southern pine from the Carolinas. Similar examples can be found for almost all building components.

Some building trades have, for all practical purposes, ceased to exist and have been supplanted by a nationally distributed product. Fifty years ago interior wall surfaces were often plaster-on-wood lath. This wall finish generally was used only in areas where the materials were available locally. In Southwestern states where wood was relatively less available, stucco was used on the interior as well as exterior of houses as a common wall finish. In any event, as panelized plaster wallboard became more common, fewer plasterers worked, until today almost all residential buildings have walls of panelized plasterboard.

Building codes and the Federal Housing Authority (FHA) also have contributed to the national similarity of houses. Not only are the same codes used in various regions, but even in different building codes the requirements are so similar that standardization is further promoted. The FHA and other federal agencies set minimum requirements as prerequisites for certain loan guarantees. These eventually evolved into almost minimum standards for all but the most expensively built houses. The result of these code- and standard-induced similarities among houses is that for houses built during the past twenty years or so there is little need to differentiate on a regional basis.

On the other hand, much older houses, and particularly those built prior to the 1940s, differ so much from region to region that it is often difficult to generalize about the type of construction, detailing, and typical distress patterns. This is really no great problem, however, since so few of these houses still remain. Prior to the middle of the nineteenth century houses were restricted to the Eastern seaboard, with a smattering of frontier houses leading into the Ohio Valley and the specialized Spanish settlements in the Southwest. Accurate counts of the numbers of houses surviving from this period are not available; however, a reasonable estimate can be developed by simply examining population figures. In 1850 the United States population was roughly 23 million. Family units averaged slightly over six members. Thus it can be inferred that there were approximately 4 million single-family homes of all classes in the United States by midcentury. Fire, decay, and renewal have taken their toll, with the result that less than 2 million houses survive from this period.

By 1940 the population had risen to 132 million with an estimated 35 million households, while in the intervening years the population climbed to over 200 million with 73 million households. The number of individual houses (not necessarily single-family) is roughly 50 million. Thus, more than half of all houses in the United States have been built since the mid-1930s, and of the remaining number roughly 4 percent were built before the midnineteenth century. Incidentally, the figures summarized above seem oddly inconsistent, but they reflect three dominant characteristics of our history: the switch from a rural to an urban society, the decrease in family-unit size, and the transitory nature of the early westward expansion. In any event, the easiest characterization of house types is by age rather than by geographic location.

Historically there have been periods during which identifiably different construction techniques and materials were used. These periods do not necessarily correspond to the changes in architectural style which are, of course, identifiable in their own right. Thus, throughout this book references will be made to some generic characteristics of construction or distress patterns that are common to one of these given periods. For example, from early in this century to the late 1940s a significant number of houses incorporated a certain plaster detail more or less unique to this period. In such houses certain characteristic plaster distresses usually will have developed. If homeowners can identify their houses as having various characteristics common to a particular generic type, they can more easily understand and rectify certain distress problems.

Environmental Factors

Every homeowner should be aware of another important distinction among older houses which involves their climatic or perhaps environmental history—the thermal and moisture cycles of the buildings. Recognizing that the three dominant external parameters that affect a building structure are *time, temperature,* and *moisture,* it follows that the latter two are those that could produce significant variations between houses (for we have no control over time). Consider, for example, a house sealed in a constant temperature and constant moisture environment. How much would such a building deteriorate? The answer is—very little! A consideration of various artifacts from ancient Egypt demonstrates this phenomenon. Examples exist of four-thousand-year-old wood, metal, plaster, stucco, and ceramic work, all of which have deteriorated far less than similar objects from, say, the early Christian era. Why? The answer is, because Egypt in general and the storage chambers of objects in particular were very nearly constant in temperature and moisture.

The immediate conclusion should not be that it is necessarily desirable to have particularly high temperatures and low moisture, but rather that the more important consideration is uniform conditions or, at most, slow cycling of these parameters.

A counterexample to the desirability of low moisture is illustrated in the case of certain pieces of oriental furniture. Prior to the early 1950s, many items of oriental furniture were brought into the United States, largely by military people who had been stationed in the Far East. Surprisingly, little survived the transition from the relatively humid conditions of coastal mainland China to the dry, temperate climate of American winters. Glue joints failed, dowels shrank and could not be reglued, and wood split. Most of this furniture was relatively old and had existed in a damp environment for a long time. In recent years the newly made oriental imports do not appear to be particularly vulnerable to climatic changes. Even though they are constructed of the same woods and in general are structurally detailed in the same way as the old oriental furniture, they remain sound because they stay in a moist environment for only a short time before they are exported.

The issue here, of course, is that both moisture and temperature cause dimensional changes or cycles that generate damage. It is desirable to have uniform cyclic patterns, not just on a year-to-year basis but also over the total life of a building. If a structure starts out with a certain set of temperature and moisture conditions, changes will often lead to a new class of distress.

A number of examples illustrate the importance of these phenomena. One of the most dramatic involves the humidification of houses during the winter months. People have observed that during the winter, as the interior moisture content of the air decreases, wood dries and shrinks, and subsequently plaster cracks. People have concluded that in addition to the physiological advantages to the occupants, it would be desirable to add moisture to the interior atmosphere in order to minimize this drying process. In the case of new construction, humidification is a reasonable procedure, but it can cause gross damage in older homes that have never before been humidified. First, it represents a change in environment for old houses. Second, many older houses lack a vapor barrier near the inside wall surface, which can prevent the migration of water (vapor) through the wall. Third, the crack pattern in these homes has been established already from a particular combination of temperature and moisture conditions. Once these conditions change, as happens when older houses are humidified for the first time, a new set of cracks may appear.

Everyone is aware that the use of central heat in residential buildings is comparatively recent in origin. Most rural houses built well before the turn of this century had individual stoves in each room. Actually, one of the dominant constraints of the floor plan was to allow access to chimneys for these stoves. The next time you drive through a rural area note the plan geometry of houses. Those built more or less prior to the 1920s are almost invariably linear, that is, one room deep. This geometry was required so that rooms could easily share chimneys. Following this period, you will notice houses changed abruptly to a more nearly square geometry, reflecting not only the lack of dependence on chimneys but also the distribution system from a central-heating furnace.

There is a delightful account of a week-long soiree at Charles Carroll's mansion, Homewood, in Baltimore, Maryland. The houseguests were provided with only two heated rooms, and when it came time for bed, greatcoats were put on and a rush was made to get under the down comforters before permanent frostbite set in. Thus Homewood, like the rest of early American houses, was rarely heated throughout during the winter. Whatever distress this environment allows, it differs from that caused by the conditions of a house heated uniformly during the winter.

Occupants who are new to a relatively modern house can produce a new set of distress patterns. It is not at all uncommon for a house that has had, for example, a limited number of plaster cracks, to develop a new set after the first year or so of a new occupancy. Not only do people vary the temperature at which they maintain a house, but also such variables as number of occupants, age of occupants, and cooking habits can grossly alter the moisture conditions within a house.

We have spoken here about temperature and moisture conditions affecting the condition of a building. While it is not necessary to know the exact mechanisms of the movement within houses, a few simple examples should be kept in mind, particularly with respect to the movement of wood. The first consideration is to appreciate the directional characteristics of wood. Everyone is familiar with how a tree grows in annual growth rings. The grain of the wood runs in the height direction of the tree and the radial and tangential directions are defined as shown in the sketch, Figure 1-1. Almost all the properties of wood differ rather significantly with respect to the direction of grain. Roughly, the strength properties are four to five times greater in the direction of the grain than in the direction perpendicular to the grain, that is, either radial or tangential, or a combination of both. So far as the change in length with the change in temperature (thermal expansion) is concerned, wood will shrink or expand in the direction of the grain between 5 and 10 percent the amount perpendicular to the grain. Similarly, wood will change length (shrink) as it dries; but here again the larger movement is in the

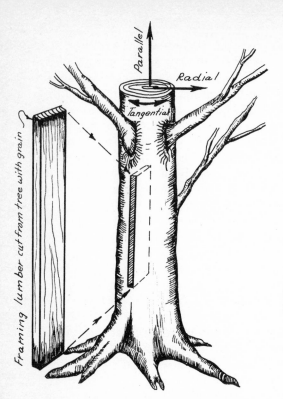

Fig. 1-1 Grain direction relationship between lumber and tree.

direction perpendicular to the grain, with the shrinkage parallel to the grain
being roughly 2 percent of the movement in the other directions. Thus, as
a general rule, the movements due to temperature and moisture are *not*
particularly significant in the direction of the grain. Since the structural lumber in a house runs in the direction of the grain, the movements in the length
of a floor or overall height of a wall can be neglected, particularly those due
to moisture changes.

Now consider the actual magnitude of some of these changes. Rather than
continue to use the terms "parallel" and "perpendicular" to grain it is easier
simply to think in terms of the *length* of a board as being parallel to the grain
and the *width* as being perpendicular. As stated above, the major dimensional
changes due to temperature and moisture occur in the *width* of the board.
The temperature range of wood in the average residence is roughly 20°F for
interior framing and woodwork and 40°F for exterior framing, that is, wood
within exterior walls. Exterior window parts may change in temperature as
much as 100°F. Throughout this book the effects and relative significance of
these movements will be discussed, but for the present it is worthwhile to
understand that a gradual change of ⅟32 inch in most building materials is
not too significant and at most will cause cracking and separation at paint
joints. On the other hand, ⅙ inch is significant and accounts for some splitting
and cracking around exterior exposed wood. One further characteristic of

thermal expansion of wood should be noted. Since the percentage expansion in the length direction is 5 to 10 percent the expansion rate in the width direction, and since many wood pieces in a house are roughly ten to twenty times as long as they are wide, the *total* expansion or contraction of a typical piece of wood is roughly the same in the length as in the width direction.

Next comes the problem of dealing with changes in wood dimension with the change in moisture conditions. Wood will expand as its moisture content (expressed as a percentage by weight) increases up to approximately 28 percent moisture content, a point called the "fiber saturation point" of wood. At higher moisture content wood will not change its properties significantly. In general, wood elements in residential structures rarely exceed moisture contents of 20 percent, so the upper limits of moisture content are not of too much importance insofar as they affect house components. Houses differ significantly in their moisture environment, but a rough rule of thumb is that a piece of wood in a house may cycle yearly through an 8 percent difference in moisture content. Thus a 10-inch-wide board could change in the extremes by almost ½ inch and on a yearly cyclic basis by ⅛ to ¼ inch. Since in the length direction the expansion rate is only 2 percent of that in the width direction, the total changes in a board twenty times longer than it is wide are roughly one-third these quantities and can often be neglected.

Thus we see that moisture change is one of the dominant parameters causing movement to the wood components of a residential building. Oddly enough, dimensional changes due to moisture also occur in brick, concrete, and many other building materials. Unfortunately, the extent of movement differs with each material and it is this variation that leads to much damage and distress.

In summary, we have found that the easiest method of categorizing houses is by age, while the principal distinguishing parameters among houses involve the thermal and moisture environment that the buildings have experienced. Of course, many errors and potential problems were literally built into houses, but there seems to be no more likelihood of having a "built-in" problem in a new house than in one built one hundred years ago. One of the singularly most common expressions of anyone involved with residential buildings is, "They don't build them as good as they used to." Certainly, houses are built far differently today than one hundred years ago: designs have greatly changed, materials are different, and certain aspects of craftsperson expertise have changed. In many respects, however, the average house built today is far better than that built in the past. Throughout this book many examples of relative value between new and old houses will be made, and the final appraisal will be left to the reader.

Building Codes

Most communities require that a building permit be issued for each new residential unit being constructed. It is often little more than a formality, and it is sometimes difficult to suppose that the permit process is anything other than another means of taxation. Indeed, the permit is in one real sense the first step in taxation, for an application for a permit generally includes the dollar value of the home, which eventually becomes the basis for a property tax. Beyond this, permits are a method of controlling certain regulations and enforcing minimum building requirements. The simplest requirements involve fire-prevention measures, regulation of plumbing and electrical components, and finally specification of all aspects of the house as they involve safety and general durability. Such a specification generally takes the form of a *building code.* The permit requirement eventually evolves into a stipulation that the house be built in accordance with the local *business code.*

Such codes become long and involved technical documents; and while many major cities and a few states have written and published their own codes, most jurisdictions have simply adopted one of the several standard building codes. The procedure is to adopt a code and then amend or supplement the code to suit local requirements and needs.

The most widely used standard codes include:

- BOCA—Basic Building Code
- National Building Code
- Southern Standard Building Code
- One- and Two-Family Dwelling Code

Building codes are generally on sale at the office where building permits are issued.

In addition to these standard codes, which specify or restrict most aspects of buildings, there are several supplemental codes that are sometimes made part of the building requirements by having been referred to in one of the standard codes. These supplemental codes cover one specific aspect and are generally more detailed and restrictive than the general building codes. Some important supplement codes are:

- Safety Code for Building Construction (ASA A10.2–1944)
- National Electric Code (NFiPA No. 70–1968)
- National Plumbing Code (ASA A40.8–1955)
- Standard Requirements for Masonry (ASA A41.1–1953)
- BOCA Supplementary Codes
- American Society of Testing Materials (ASTM) Standards

It is certainly not necessary for the average homeowner to own or even be particularly familiar with these codes; in fact, it should be clearly understood that just because a community adopts a code does not mean that all houses in the community must meet the code requirements. With the possible exception of certain fire, electrical, and plumbing requirements, the codes are mostly applicable only to new construction. The codes themselves do, however, stipulate under what circumstances they are applicable and when repairs and remodeling must meet code requirements. In any event, since the codes do specify standards and stipulate minimum building requirements, they are excellent reference documents; moreover, when any remodeling or even extensive repairs are made, the local building code should be consulted.

In the process of making repairs there are three other extremely important reasons for consulting the building codes. The first is for insurance purposes. Under the terms of some homeowners' insurance policies, coverage may not extend to repairs and modifications made that violate the local building codes. This is most true in connection with fire requirements, but it also includes structural damage and life safety as a result of any building code violations.

Under certain circumstances the violation of code requirements is a violation of the law, with accompanying penalties. As a practical matter this rarely presents a serious problem other than to those associated with the denial of insurance coverage and possibly the guarantee of loan commitments.

The codes become extremely useful in the remodeling process as a means of verifying building contractors' proposals and recommendations. Certainly under no circumstances should any contract be let without a rigorous stipulation (with penalties for nonconformance) to the effect that any repairs, modifications, or remodeling must meet all the appropriate requirements of the local building code.

Finally, a peripheral word of caution is needed in connection with building permits. Permits invariably cost money, and one of the standard justifications for the cost is that some form of inspection is provided by the issuing agency. Many people assume that the inspection carries with it some guarantee that the work has been done correctly; and the added inference is that if errors and omissions come to light in the future, there will be some recourse to the inspection agency. Not so! The vast majority of governmental inspections involve little more than perfunctory visits to the job site; if either omissions or commissions of inspection are made, literally no benefit accrues to the owner. This is not to say that such inspection is valueless, for inspectors consistently spot errors and conscientiously review corrective work. The problem is that the inspection carries with it no guarantees of completeness or accuracy. If an owner wishes inspection that is more complete and essentially has some guarantee, he or she should contact a registered architect or engineer for such services.

FOUNDATIONS

Foundations are, of course, a building's support to the earth. The two most often encountered types are "spread footings" (sometimes called "contact footings") and, less common, "deep foundations" such as piles. A variety of parameters, including supporting soil conditions, building weight and rigidity, conventional building practices, cost, and material availability, combine to dictate the particular selection and design of foundations. Because of their relative inaccessibility, building foundations pose special problems when repairs are needed. Repairs are not only expensive and time-consuming but also often beyond the expertise of the average home builder, thus requiring special contractors and attendant special costs. Designers often emphasize this to clients by telling them that the foundations should be the last item on which to compromise or economize.

Foundation Materials

The introduction of different types of contact foundations (footings) in the course of American building history seems to be largely a function of material and labor availability. From the colonial period until late into the nineteenth century when concrete became readily available, buildings with masonry foundation walls of either stone or brick were simply founded directly on the ground. To accommodate heavier buildings requiring a larger contact area with the earth to support the load, the foundation walls were widened at the base and allowed to narrow, or corbel, as they rose above the foundation line. Thus the foundation was simply a continuation, albeit modified, of the foundation wall. This practice contrasts to our more modern method of having a distinctly different element, or footing, as the building foundation. Here a slight matter of semantics arises. It is not uncommon to hear people refer to a brick (or stone) wall "founded" directly on the earth, as a wall without a foundation. Of course, there is a foundation consisting of the wall base. What is perhaps meant is that there is no individual "footing" or different and distinct foundation element other than the wall.

Very shortly after the introduction of brick as a building material it must have been realized that there were certain disadvantages to brick-masonry foundations. To begin with, colonial bricks were almost invariably a local product, often made directly at the building site. Not only was the selection of materials random, but the firing of the bricks was a sometime thing—sometimes right, and sometimes wrong. The net result was a brick of generally

13

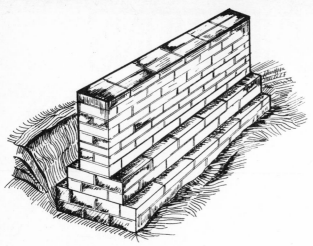

Fig. 2-1 Corbelled masonry wall footing.

poor quality. Brick masonry of any kind, and soft, underfired bricks in particular, react with salts and acids in the soils, causing the brick and mortar to deteriorate. Recognizing this deficiency in brick foundations, builders constructed finer homes on stone foundation walls, walls that widen at the base to provide the actual foundation to the soil, as shown in Figure 2-1. Both brick- and wood-frame buildings were constructed on these stone walls.

One type of foundation that has been used for the entire 350 years of American building experience is wood. Originally a log was placed in a trench and the house founded on this log. Intuitively it would seem that wood would be a poor choice of materials for a foundation—a material vulnerable to rot and insect infestation. As it turns out, wood is a reasonably good footing material provided certain constraints are adhered to in its use. For example, untreated wood is relatively long lasting if it is either kept dry or restricted from oxygen when it is in a water environment. Also, if wood is buried at proper depths in the soils, insects will not attack it. One should not assume, however, that wood is an ideal, free-from-distress material for foundations—it is not. On the other hand, it does have certain advantages; even today wood is sometimes selected as the preferred foundation material.

Today wood can be injected with chemicals that minimize the effects of both rot and insect infestation. Such pressure-treated wood foundations have certain cost advantages and are a particularly good thermal barrier to the cool temperatures of the ground.

For the vast majority of homes built today the most common foundation is the poured-concrete spread footing, shown in Figure 2-2. A concrete "beam" is poured on the ground. Thicknesses typically range from 8 to 12 inches and widths can easily be varied to reduce the bearing pressures on the soils—widths of 16 to 36 inches are common for residential buildings. Ideally, steel bars are placed in such footings for reinforcement and as a help to prevent cracking.

Fig. 2-2   Concrete spread footing.

Deep foundations such as piles are invariably more expensive than contact foundations, but they may be the only alternative where soils are poor or the potential exists for such phenomena as water undermining. Pile foundations are commonly found along the coastal areas of the United States. In some cases the house designs reflect such deep foundations, as in the so-called pole buildings, but there are many homes founded on piles that are conventional in every other way.

While piles can be of wood (timbers), steel, or concrete, residential buildings on deep foundations most often utilize wood pilings. Timber poles literally are hammered down into the earth and building structure rests on top of these. Often a concrete beam spans from pile to pile (see Figure 2-3). Timber pile lengths vary from a few feet to 50 and 60 feet long.

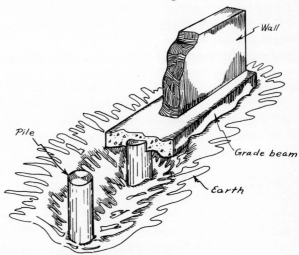

Fig. 2-3   Grade beam on pile foundation.

Fig. 2-4　Pad or mat foundation.

Most owners who have houses founded on piles will know it—it is a special feature that is generally brought to the attention of a buyer. Also, houses requiring pile foundations tend to be pretty much grouped together, as at a coast, and it is extremely unlikely for an owner to be unaware that his or her house has a pile foundation.

One final type of foundation deserves consideration: the so-called mat, pad, or slab foundation (see Figure 2-4). In warm, dry sections of the country a concrete slab the full size of a house can serve both as foundation and ground floor. For the most part such a detail is found only in the Deep South or in the Southwest. Since the exposed edge is generally visible at the grade line, it is easy to identify such foundations.

Foundation Requirements

The most essential function of a building foundation is to distribute the building weight on soil material of sufficient strength to resist these loads. To appreciate this requirement a modest understanding of some of the characteristics of soil as a building material is useful. Soils engineers, in moments of either frustration or candor, often say that the first rule of soils mechanics (the study of the "mechanical" properties of soil) is that there are no rules. Soil is such a variable, nonhomogeneous material that only generalized statements, representing average conditions, can be made. Practically speaking, however, the primary parameter in dealing with soils as they affect residential buildings involves settlements (or vertical movement). Several types of settlements are important: *initial* settlements; and *long-term* settlements, which include both *uniform* and *differential,* that is, *nonuniform,* settlements.

Initial Settlements

The average house with a basement weighs considerably less than the earth that has been removed for the basement. Thus, if the building loads are reasonably distributed and the ground was originally stable, very little movement of the soils should occur. Yet, independent of the actual loads, the earth below the house has been disturbed. First, it was unloaded by removing the earth to form the basement; as a result the ground literally rebounded, or moved upward. Next, local excavations were made for footings and sewer lines. Inevitably, the soils in the vicinity of such locations were loosened. Finally, as the house was built and the "dead load" (or building weight without the "live load" of people) was applied, there was some slight settlement. These are the soil movements that are almost inevitable, and they occur more or less independently of the type, condition, or strength of the soil. Furthermore, they generally occur in a relatively short time, a period of a few months at most. Such settlements are typical of all building construction, and since the majority of such movements occur as the building weight is added, any effects of these movements can be more or less compensated for, or built into the house. These initial settlements typically range up to ½ inch. Perhaps the most immediate effect of initial settlement is movement at the various service lines entering and leaving a house. For example, sewer pipes are generally installed in the early stages of construction. Any settlement of the house can tend to strain or shear such piping; thus it is not uncommon to have minor plumbing supply problems shortly after a house is occupied. In any event, exclusive of such problems, initial or primary soil settlements rarely have any long-term effects on a house. Instead, it is long-term soil settlements that lead to most of the foundation problems in residences.

Long-Term Settlements

Uniform Settlements. In considering long-term settlements it is important to make a distinction between uniform and nonuniform (or differential) building settlements. If a house moves downward uniformly in all directions, as shown in Figure 2-5, there is little or no effect on the house per se. No cracking occurs; furthermore, an occupant inside the house cannot be aware

Fig. 2-5   Uniform vertical settlement.

of uniform settlement movements. Uniform settlement can cause service supply lines to rupture because they literally are bent as the house moves downward. Also, any appendages to the house such as outside stairs, adjoining walkways, and exterior walls may crack and be dislocated. One important caution in evaluating such uniform settlement is not to confuse it with "foundation fill" settlement.

Foundation Fill Settlement.   In the process of building there is a trench created around the entire perimeter of the outside wall. This excavation must be filled (backfilled) and, unfortunately, it is rarely done with optimum care. The result is that the backfill is not compacted, or densified, as much as the surrounding earth. Over a long period of time this fill material gradually settles as it compacts, and a depression is left all around the house. Obviously, to the casual observer such fill settlement would look the same as uniform building settlement. There are several ways to distinguish easily between these phenomena. First, fill settlement generally starts to occur shortly after a house is built and continues for several years thereafter. Because the soils surrounding the foundation wall are loose and thus are easily invaded by water, fill settlement is often accompanied by foundation water problems. The next distinguishing factor is one of magnitude. Obvious fill settlements can be slight, but it is not uncommon to see surface soil movements of several inches. On the other hand, except in extreme circumstances, long-term, uniform house settlements rarely exceed the ½- to 1-inch range. Finally, if there is a serious question about the possibility of settlement, the movement can actually be measured with respect to a fixed object.

Such measuring is not as easy as it sounds, particularly if the settlement has already occurred, in which case it is almost impossible to determine. Making an absolute measurement of settlement is difficult also because it involves a small enough dimension that fairly accurate instrumentation is required—generally involving the equipment of a land surveyor. Finally, the problem of finding a fixed reference point is no easy task. The earth at and near the surface moves up and down by as much as ¼ inch, more or less on a yearly cycle. Except for structures founded 15 to 20 feet below the surface, many buildings have similar fluctuation in elevation. In residential areas, therefore, truly stationary buildings are rare, and establishing absolute, uniform settlements may be impractical.

Tipping Settlements.   While the problems caused by uniform settlement, both long and short term, rarely produce serious residential building distresses, the same is not true in the case of nonuniform (or differential) settlement. Several types of nonuniform settlements can occur. Each is accompanied by certain characteristic distress patterns and each has its own remedy. The least common nonuniform settlement condition is one that might best be described as a constant "tipping" of an entire building; that is, all straight lines in the building remain straight, but originally horizontal lines are no longer horizontal. Such movement is sometimes referred to as "linear settlement." Tipping-type settlements most often occur in houses built on unstable, relatively steep hillsides. Settlements of 4 and 5 inches in a 30-foot house sometimes occur without any cracking or other visual damage to the building. Unlike uniform settlement, an inch or more tipping in 10 feet can certainly be noticed by an observer in or outside the house. However, beyond the possible problems with any service lines and the possible psychological discomfort, tipped houses, from a structural standpoint, are not overly worrisome. The biggest single problem and one with which the owners of such houses *must* concern themselves is the possibility that the tipping will progress. The very nature of the most common cause of such movement, namely, unstable, moving hillside soils, would suggest that it is a more or less continuing problem. There are several blocks of houses in one Eastern city that have been tipping at a relatively uniform rate for the fifty years of their existence. The owners have progressively made repairs that compensate for the movement, and the houses are still perfectly serviceable. In fact, owing to their desirable location, these houses continue to demand a high resale value.

Fig. 2-6   Uniform tipped settlement.

The question of the stability of hillsides is extremely complex because it involves so many poorly defined parameters. However, probably the two most significant external factors (that is, exclusive of local soil characteristics) affecting hillside stability are first, whether the slope is natural or synthetic, and second, how water moves out of the face of the hillside. In general, natural, dry slopes tend to be more stable. If owners are faced with a problem of stability and the hill is synthetic and wet either on the surface or out of the face of the hill, they should consult a technical professional *and* keep in mind the earlier admonition that both the explanation and the remedy should be reasonable and understandable.

Differential Settlements.   By far the most common type of settlement, and unfortunately the one that produces the most extensive distress, is differential settlement. Differential settlement is sometimes referred to as being non-uniform or, perhaps more descriptively, "non-straight line." Literally, such settlement occurs when the soils below a building develop into some curved shape. When the building can no longer conform to such a shape, some failure occurs. In dealing with differential settlement four steps should be followed: (1) establish that there is settlement and identify the nature of such settlement; (2) appraise the consequences; (3) decide whether remedial steps are required; and (4) determine what remedies to apply. Something should

Fig. 2-7 Single crack pattern due to differential settlement.

be understood at the outset in dealing with this class of settlement problems: Actual foundation repairs can be so extremely expensive and can so often lead to other problems that any repairs to the actual foundation should be undertaken almost as a last resort and then only after exploring every alternative.

The process of clearly identifying differential foundation settlement is a relatively easy proposition. By simply sighting along normally straight building lines such as floor lines, masonry joints, or various fenestration, abrupt changes can generally be detected. There is a typical foundation wall crack that is regularly attributed to foundation movement but that is actually associated with concrete-block shrinkage. This will be discussed in more detail in the following chapter, but for the present a sufficient criterion for identifying settlements on the basis of wall cracks can be established by considering the following general rules. First, soil settlements are rarely abrupt; they tend to be somewhat gradual. (The most common exceptions to this rule are settlements associated with earthwork around sewer and other utility lines.) Thus, crack distress due to ground settlements tends to be shaped somewhat like the crack shown in Figure 2-7 that is, wider at the top and diminishing to near zero at the footing line. Masonry walls can sometimes be deceptive with regard to this crack pattern. The crack, as it moves up in a wall, will oftentimes separate along mortar joint lines and fan out into several cracks. It is the sum of these cracks that gives the clue to the extent and magnitude of the settlement movement. Figure 2-8 shows such a fan pattern of cracks,

Fig. 2-8 Multiple crack pattern due to differential settlement.

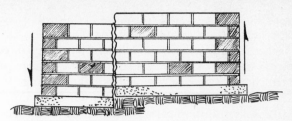

Fig. 2-9   Shear translation due to differential settlement.

and it should be evident that the sum of the cracks d1, d2, and d3, at the top of the wall are analogous to the single opening, c, in Figure 2-7.

Abrupt soil settlements can cause the so-called shear-type failure pattern, in which one element of a wall simply moves down vertically with respect to an adjacent part, without any rotation of either element (Figure 2-9). Such movement most often occurs at locations in a house where some abrupt building change takes place; for example, where a single room protrudes beyond the main house.

The discussion of building settlement has thus far concentrated on foundation movements parallel to the direction of the foundation. An equally common settlement condition, and one that can eventually lead to extreme building distress, involves movements *perpendicular* to a building wall and foundation. Such movements can cause the wall to tip outward, as shown in Figure 2-10. While it may be rather shocking to see a house wall tipped 1 or 2 inches in its height, the tip per se may not be the most critical problem as a result of this class of movement. As shown in the sketch (Figure 2-10), floor and roof joists can slide on their bearing surfaces, with obviously dramatic consequences. Rarely are soils naturally so abruptly variable as to produce this type of differential settlement in the relatively narrow width (typically

Fig. 2-10 Tipped wall due to differential settlement.

1½ to 2 feet) of wall footings. The two most common causes of this type of settlement are related to (1) excavations made at the footings during construction and subsequently improperly backfilled, and (2) water-service lines, that is, water-supply and sewer and drainage pipes, which may rupture and discharge water on one side of the footing. It is not uncommon to find a water line broken in two places. One opening discharges water that scours the soils and then carries them away in the second, downstream break. This is actually one of the problems that can develop as a result of an improperly installed foundation drain system. Many building codes require that a perforated drain line be installed near the foundation elevation. In some cases this drain discharges into a "sump" (drainage pit) on the inside of the building. It is then pumped out to a storm sewer or to an outfall away from the house. It should be obvious that such a system can literally encourage water to flow around the foundation line by providing the easiest discharge path for the water. Properly installed, well above the footing elevation, such a drainage system can prevent basement water problems. On the other hand, poorly located, it can allow scouring action in the soil immediately around the footing and eventually lead to settlements, the most common of which is wall tipping. If you think you may have problems with such a drain, simply check the bottom of the sump pump pit. If it is full of fine-grain soil (silts), your drainage system may actually be removing earth near the foundation line. Clean the pit thoroughly and see how long it takes to refill. If in one or two heavy rains several inches of silt accumulate, you should investigate the source of this material *and* try to determine how high above the actual footing the drain line runs. If the foundation drain is 12 to 24 inches above the bottom of the footing, it is unlikely that any scouring will affect the footing stability.

Many houses, in addition to bearing on walls for support, bear on beams that eventually rest on columns or piers. The foundations of such columns are as vulnerable to settlement as are wall foundations. Most important, perhaps, is the potential for differential settlement between any load-bearing wall footings and column footings. Probably such a difference in settlement potential is amplified by the type of loads applied to interior column footings as compared with exterior, load-bearing masonry wall footings. The interior column often supports the wooden floor and interior partitions, both of which are relatively lightweight, perhaps as little as 8 to 16 pounds per square foot of projected area. Still, these column footings must be initially sized to carry not only the dead weight of the building but also the live weight of the occupants. This live-weight code requirement is often 40 pounds per square foot or as much as five times the dead load. Thus, the column footing exists for most of its life with one-sixth its design load on the soils. Contrast this situation with exterior masonry wall footings that must continuously support the heavy masonry walls and yet oftentimes have little or even no requirement for carrying any live load. Under such circumstances it is possible to have a wall footing designed to be continuously loaded exactly at its limit with respect to soil bearing. It should therefore not be surprising that differential settlement often develops between column and wall footings.

Following this line of reasoning, it generally would be anticipated that the exterior masonry walls, with their continuously applied load, would settle more than column or pier footings, with their low applied-load potential. In general this is the case. The net result is a "bump" up through the entire house that is reflected in floors out of level and in walls cracking. The really surprising phenomenon is that in many cases the reverse is true; namely, the column footings settle more than the exterior wall footings. The explanation is generally that the footings simply are undersized. In pretwentieth-century dwellings, before the widespread use of concrete, interior column footings were often simply slabs of stone. Apparently these slabs came in limited sizes; in any event, there was the practical limitation of handling a large, heavy slab of stone—the result was random sizing of column footing, without much regard for the load distribution or settlement potential.

In one city in a 10-square-block area a standard row house was built repetitively block after block shortly after World War I. The area encompasses relatively variable soil conditions, yet from one end of this development to the other the interior columns have settled by as much as 2½ inches. Whatever the error in footing sizing, it must have been properly identified after eight or ten years, because around the periphery of this area houses built at a slightly later date do not seem to suffer this problem. In any event, the beam line supports a partition that extends up through the house alongside the stair corridor. In every house where the settlement has occurred you step off the stairs and then walk "downhill" to adjacent rooms.

One note of caution should be taken in identifying interior column footing settlement: Almost exactly the same distress pattern often develops as a result of either a shrinkage phenomenon or inadequate framing around stair openings. Since each phenomenon requires a completely different remedy, it is important to distinguish between them. Column footing settlement can most easily be identified by checking the levelness (or out-of-levelness) of the beams intersecting on a column. Normal construction tolerances may allow ¼ to ½ inch differences to occur between bearing points; however, any more than this can be attributed generally to column settlement.

Crack Development and Settlement

Once a crack pattern has been identified as being due to earth settlements, the next step is to determine whether the crack is moving and therefore whether the settlement is continuing. If the surface surrounding the crack is smooth, like plaster for example, an easy method of monitoring the crack movement is simply to scribe a gauge mark on both sides of the crack, measure the distance between these marks, and record right on the wall the dimension and the date (Figure 2-11). Later check the measurement and compare the two to determine the movement. Incidentally, movements on the order of magnitude of ¹⁄₁₆ inch are important and measurement accuracy should take this into account.

It is hoped that no movement will be recorded, in which case the conclusion

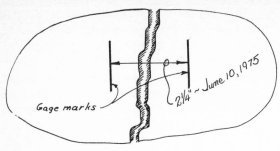

Fig. 2-11 Wall-crack monitoring.

will necessarily be that the settlement occurred early in the building's life and therefore is unlikely to reoccur. Under such circumstances the remedial work would most likely involve cosmetically covering the crack damage. If floors are sloping objectionably, they can be leveled simply by nailing tapered battens to the existing floor surface and affixing a completely new floor deck on top. Battens 1 inch wide located 16 inches on center are satisfactory, and the actual floor decks should be ½ inch plywood as a minimum. Finally, the floor surface, of wood, tile, or carpeting, can be applied on top of the plywood.

If, as a result of crack monitoring, movements on the order of magnitude of 1/16 to 1/8 inch are detected in a six- to twelve-month period, an owner may be fairly certain that long-term, continuing settlements are occurring. Remember that the *magnitude* of the crack movement may not be the same as the actual settlement. As a first step it is generally sufficient to know that significant movement is occurring and not necessarily how much. Probably the most practical next step is to take a walk around your neighborhood. Look for signs of settlement in nearby houses and if possible discuss the problem with neighbors. Some people may not be overly inclined to tell anyone that their house is settling, and certainly a little prudence must be exercised in telling someone else about either your problems or the possibility of their house settling—property values and friendships may be affected. The point is that poor soil conditions leading to building settlement are often extensive enough to encompass several houses or even an entire community. If there is a near duplicate of your house close by, you should make a special point of trying to examine the section of the duplicate corresponding to your area of distress. In older neighborhoods signs of earth subsidence often show up in irregular street and sidewalk surfaces. In addition, look for new repairs to roads, curbs, and nearby houses.

The objective of such a comparative survey, is, of course, to try to determine the consequences of any settlement. In this regard a variety of parameters can become important, including:

• Probable cause
• Permissible magnitude of settlement
• Time sequence
• Extent of distress

- Structural implications (particularly as they relate to life safety)
- Possible methods of repair
- Cost of repair
- Property-value changes
- Insurance coverage
- Mortgage commitments

Probable Cause   It is rarely necessary to know all the mechanisms that can contribute to soil subsidence and consequent foundation settlements. However, there should be a clear distinction made between two somewhat generic types—types that might best be characterized as those that can be mitigated in some fashion, that is, either controlled or stopped, and those that from a practical standpoint are almost inevitable and over which there is very little control. Do not be alarmed by assuming that if the subsidence causing your settlement condition is of the second class, all is lost and you must either move your house or abandon it. There are many reasonable ways to modify a house in such a way that even relatively gross earth movements can be accommodated. The reason for distinguishing between these types of subsidence is so that homeowners can know where to direct their attack—specifically, the soils in the first case, and the house in the second.

In the absence of some external phenomena, the earth near the surface is a relatively stable or perhaps benign material. Obviously anything that literally has been "lying around" since geological times should have reached some state of equilibrium. The few exceptions to this are various classes of somewhat unique soils that are particularly pressure and moisture sensitive and subject to volume changes. Fortunately, such materials are more often the exception than the rule; moreover, in the normal building process they generally would be identified and therefore excluded from the admissible building sites. These materials are characterized by unusually fine and uniform grain (particle) size of the silt and clay types.

The external phenomena most likely to contribute to ground-settlement conditions are water, slopes (hillsides), and earth voids. The last phenomenon is almost exclusively restricted to those parts of the country where limestone caves are prevalent or where there has been extensive mining. Most owners in these restricted locales are aware of the potential problems and can easily identify settlements associated with voids.

The other two settlement generators, water and slopes, are common to almost every area of the country and are those most likely to be encountered. If your house is built at or near a slope, it will certainly come as no surprise; and when faced with a settlement condition, you can reasonably assume that the hill is the cause. Hillsides with a slope of less than two horizontal units to one vertical unit (2 to 1) generally are relatively stable; however, extensive regrading over old, higher slopes may cause lower-angle hills to move.

For unstable hillsides the question invariably arises as to whether to stop the hill or stop the house and let the hill move under the house. Both approaches have been successfully utilized; however, the details are sufficiently involved that an engineer or experienced builder should be consulted. A few words to the wise: Retaining unstable hillsides or houses on such hills involves relatively high forces, certainly higher than those encountered in the average house. As a rough rule of thumb, retaining earth pressures are between one-half to one those of water pressure; that is, the earth exerts an equivalent fluid pressure against a wall of between 30 to 60 pounds per square foot per foot of depth. For example, if a 40-foot-wide house were buried 8 feet into a hill on one side, there would be between 20 to 40 tons of force pushing the house down the hill. It is not expected that the average owner know exactly what will resist forces of this magnitude; on the other hand, common sense should provide an intuitive feel for the problem. The biggest highway trucks weigh this much, and think what would be involved in attaching a big dump truck by means of a pulley to your house—that is the amount of force tending to push such a hillside house down the hill (see Figure 2-12). The point is that relatively more complex and substantial structures are required for such retaining than are typical of residential buildings. Necessarily the costs are high, and errors can be painfully expensive. Some of the methods used to retain houses on hillsides are various types of anchors installed deep in the hillside, retaining walls, and earth "feet" or wall projections buried deep in the hill.

Another common cause of extensive, damaging settlement is water. The mechanisms by which water in soil can lead to settlements are varied. Water can actually wash out soil materials at various depths below the surface; permeate the soil and cause consolidation, hydraulic uplift, and allow soil density changes. A walk around the neighborhood, as recommended, can often provide clues concerning subsurface water flow. The house in Figure

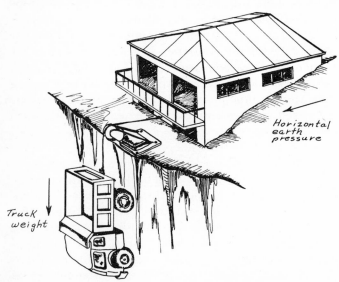

Fig. 2-12   Truck weight equivalent to hillside earth force.

Fig. 2-13 Differentially settled house wall.

2-13 has settled differentially by 4 and 5 inches. It was built in the mid-1950s over an old swale or drainage contour. Local regrading, streets, and other houses in the area have obscured the fact that the house is actually located atop an old drain path; but the water has continued to flow in the soil below the houses and literally has undermined the entire foundation.

Solutions for subsurface water conditions generally involve some form of "dewatering," but whether this is an active or passive process is important. Extensive pumping can be a relatively small but continuing expense; furthermore, in many situations pumping can effectively "encourage" the water to undermine a foundation. One new homeowner, faced with a minor settlement problem and a basement water problem, tried to solve them both by installing an interior drain system below the basement slab. The drain was connected to a sump pump that eventually discharged the water several hundred feet away. The problem became acute when it was discovered that the system was actually drawing additional water from the surrounding soil and below the wall footings. This water flow was washing out the fine-grain soil materials and leading to more settlement.

Permissible Magnitude of Settlement   How much settlement can be tolerated? Obviously, part of the answer is to know how much damage can be tolerated. Wall cracks and similar distress can be regularly patched, slopes in floors can be tolerated, and as long as the building is safe for occupancy settlements of fairly severe amounts can be endured. It is not uncommon to see people living more or less unaware of 1-inch-floor-elevation change. On the other hand, as movements reach the range of 2 inches or more it becomes a problem more serious to ignore. Resale opportunities diminish, and structures are no longer unaffected. Thus, if in some way an owner can conclude that settlements will remain below the range of 1 to 1½ inches, at least in the foreseeable future, then it may be most prudent for the owner to simply live with the settlement and the accompanying periodic repairs. Above this range something almost invariably must be done.

Time Sequence Several methods are available for predicting the probable time sequence of any settlement condition. Probably the most practical method is comparison: If a situation can be identified at one location for which the time sequence is clearly known, then the timing of similar settlements at another site can be established. Another satisfactory approach to predicting the relation of time and settlement is to measure the settlement periodically and plot the curve on a graph comparing time and movement. Except for seasonal variations the time-displacement relation of settlement tends to be a fairly smooth curve. Figure 2-14 shows several different settlement curves. The three most common are: the *linear* movement, which simply indicates that every year there will be a constant settlement and that it will go on and on; the *decreasing-to-zero* type, which indicates that at some time in the future the settlement will actually stop; and, as curve #3 indicates, as time passes the yearly amount will *increase*. Often after only three or four data points are taken at six-month intervals, for example, the shape of the curve can be sufficiently defined so that one of the three types (as represented in Figure 2-14 by curves #1, #2, and #3) can be identified.

It should be clear that there are a number of reasons for knowing a priori the probable history of any settlement condition. Obviously, if it can be established that the movement will more or less stop within a reasonable time period, repairs can be postponed accordingly. Knowing the ultimate magnitude of deformation can also dictate the type and extent of repairs.

It should not necessarily be assumed that a short-term settlement is to be preferred to a long-term condition. Most building materials are relatively more brittle than ductile; that is, when they are highly loaded, they will break or rupture rather than deform. For example, compare a steel cookie sheet (ductile material) and a glass windowpane (brittle material) of comparable size. Under the action of low loads both will bend and then return to their original shapes when unloaded. This phenomenon is called their "elastic property." Even if the experiment has not actually been performed, everyone is familiar with the fact that the cookie sheet can eventually be bent out of shape whereas the pane of glass will break *before* it can be deformed into a

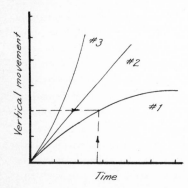

Fig. 2-14 Curves showing time-displacement relation of settlement.

Fig. 2-15 A line of old, differentially settled buildings.

different shape. These properties are called, respectively, their "ductile" or "plastic" (for steel) and "brittle" (for glass) characteristics.

Glass, plaster, brick, stone, and concrete are examples of brittle materials. The experiment just described provides a means of distinguishing among various materials *provided* the time of loading and unloading is relatively short. On the other hand, when loading times become long—perhaps measured in years rather than days—many brittle materials react as ductile materials. Under short-time loading, stone is an extremely brittle material and would normally be expected to break before it deforms significantly. If a permanent load is applied to a stone beam, for example, for an extremely long period of time, even though the load is far less than the breaking load, it may plastically deform. The material characteristic whereby an otherwise brittle material will act like a ductile or plastic material during long-term loading is called "creep."

Thus, if settlement takes place for a long enough period of time, a building will deform to accommodate the settlement, without cracking. Often such gradual deformation causes negligible structural damage even though the amount of movement would be considered catastrophic if it were to occur rapidly. Figure 2-15 shows a line of old buildings that have deformed more than a foot in their width and yet whose basic structure has been harmed very little. In certain cases such deformities are considered attractive and may actually enhance the value of a building.

In any event, the important issue is that in considering the time sequence of settlement a value judgment cannot necessarily be made to favor short-term over long-term settlements. Each individual case must be considered separately with respect to its own unique requirements. An important consideration is that continuous movements on the order of 1 inch in ten years will almost certainly generate crack damage and deteriorate the structural integrity of a building. Conversely, movements of 2 or 3 inches in a sixty- or seventy-year time frame generally allow the creep phenomenon to occur with little damage that requires repair.

One word of caution: Once in a while an owner will acquire an old house that has settled grossly over a number of years. The irregularities in mortar joints and floor lines are disquieting and the owner decides to "jack up the house" to correct the distortions. This is fine, provided he or she takes one hundred years to jack it back to its original shape. Otherwise, the owner can expect all the cracks and distress anticipated with short-term settlement to occur in reverse.

Extent of Distress and Structural Implications   The ultimate decision concerning which remedies to apply to correct settlement problems must include a consideration of the structural penalties to the building. The final judgment must be based, of course, on whether the building is safe. Fortunately, most settlement movements occur slowly enough so that owners are warned of any really serious problem; furthermore, rarely does an abrupt, catastrophic failure occur as a result of earth movement. Certainly if owners are in the least apprehensive about the structural integrity of their homes, they should consult an engineer experienced in building problems.

Probably the two most common, but by no means only, structural problems generated by earth-movement phenomena are: (1) the loss of sufficient bearing (end support) for structural members such as joists, beams, and trusses; and (2) the loss of earth-retaining capacity of below-grade foundation walls (see Chapter 3). In the first case a simple visual inspection of joist ends is sufficient to determine the extent of any problem. Bearing lengths (i.e., the lengths of structural members resting on walls) are typically in the 3- to 4-inch range, dimensions that allow a good margin of safety against failure. Slight deviations, say, of ½ to ¼ inch, are admissible and rarely can be said to diminish the structural integrity. When movements approach one-half the original bearing length, however, some remedial action is almost mandatory.

Possible Methods of Repair   Because the number of possible alternatives is so great, it is difficult to generalize in recommending repair methods for settlement conditions. The earlier-stated criterion of reasonableness should still hold, but perhaps more important are several precautions in relation to repairs of settlements.

A standard recommendation for restoring a house to its presettlement condition is to jack it back up. If a home is of wood-frame construction and the settlements have occurred rather quickly in recent years, this is not an unreasonable approach. If any different conditions exist, however, proceed with caution when it comes to jacking. For a number of reasons, building deformations are "one-directional"; that is, they do not work the same way going up as coming down. The creep problem associated with brittle-material deformation has already been discussed, but a more common problem associated with jacking buildings is the way any opening develops. For example, cracks in masonry generally are accompanied by a crumbling of surrounding mortar and brick. The particles fall into the crack and actually jam it open. If an attempt is made to close such a crack by jacking, the debris in the crack resists closing and the result is a similar crack in the opposite direction to accommodate the movement. When structural framing members move, similar conditions develop. Not only can debris fall into a space and block the return of a joist, but the very nature of nailing is directional and nailed members often can be taken apart in only one direction. Thus, it is often necessary to remove nails in joists and similar members before jacking. An analogous problem that can be extremely disconcerting often develops during a jacking operation; specifically, an end of a joist different from the one that moved during settling may move during jacking. From this type of problem comes the first rule of jacking a building—*account for all movement.* Too often people watch, expectantly awaiting a particular crack to close or a structural member to shift back into position and continue jacking, without giving much thought to what *is* moving. For every turn of the jack screw a corresponding movement should be identified and actually recorded.

If jacking is inevitable and due consideration has been given to the possible alternatives, there are several other precautions. Your building took months or perhaps even years to arrive at its final, settled condition. While it would obviously be impractical to take a similar amount of time to restore the structure to its original position, the slower the jacking, the better. In many cases, particularly in extremely old houses, the procedure is literally to make one turn of the screw per day. In terms of movement this might correspond to $\frac{1}{16}$ inch per day. During such an operation cracks should regularly be checked and cleared of any loose debris and all movement should be accounted for. The most satisfactory method of clearing a masonry crack is to blow it clean with compressed air.

A common remedy to settlement is to replace or enlarge the foundation size. While this procedure cannot return a building to its original position, it can, in some cases, stop the settlement process. Reworking a building foundation is not only a costly operation but also relatively more complex than the average home construction technology. Thus, while it can cure settlement problems, it can also generate new ones—not only a different class of settlement but also groundwater problems. Any time excavations are undertaken around foundations lines, conditions exist to allow different drainage patterns. Thus, if exterior excavation is part of a foundation enlargement, the normal precautions used in new construction of waterproofing and drainage should be incorporated as part of the work.

In the case of tipped footings, discussed earlier, "underpinning" or extending the footing width is often part of a remedial program. If, however, the cause of the tipping, such as a broken water line, has been discovered and corrected, it may be unnecessary to go to the extreme of widening the footing. If the argument is advanced that the tipped wall produces uneven bearing pressures (which of course it does) and these *differential* soil pressures will in turn allow further tipping, there are still other alternatives that may be cheaper and actually better to prevent further movements. One reasonable way to decrease the adverse effects of tipping walls is to provide an anchor through the walls at each floor level, one which actually ties the wall to the floor. The equivalent of this floor tie is a steel rod running completely through the house at the floor line, anchoring one wall to another. You may have noticed metal stars on the walls of old buildings. These are cast-iron "washers" for rods actually tying walls to floors or walls to walls. They were once generally installed after the house was completed and it was discovered that the walls were bowing outward. There are several phenomena that can lead to wall bowing, one of which is the tipping action due to foundation failure. Before you embark on any corrective program for tipping or bowing walls, make sure you have identified the correct cause.

One of the few types of settlement that can be solved rather unilaterally by some type of underpinning or footing extension is the settlement at individual column footings in a residential building basement. Generally, such footings are fairly accessible and only a few inches below the basement floor; furthermore, the necessarily symmetric nature of a footing extension that surrounds a column footing to form a sort of "square donut" tends to minimize any asymmetric settlements that accompany one-sided footing extensions.

Since interior column footings rarely support any masonry, it is not unreasonable to consider some jacking to restore original floor levels. Some plaster cracking should be anticipated, particularly in the vicinity of cracks, caused by the original settlement, that have been patched. Floor-high screw jacks are readily available at hardware and lumber stores, and the only precaution the owner should take is to be sure to release any anchors between beams and footings, for example, bolts securing a beam to a column. Occasionally a homeowner takes very seriously the admonition about jacking slowly and advances the screw only one-quarter turn per week. The results are that at this low rate of re-straining the building, few if any new distress problems develop.

In Brief

With care in observing, and thought about alternative solutions, many of the settlement problems encountered in the average residence can be solved by owners acting on their own. In some cases, mainly distinguished by degree and complexity of solution, professional advice should be sought. Under such circumstances the rule of reasonableness still holds. All the evidence of extent of distress should be presented to you, the need for remedial work should be clearly demonstrated with some criteria of quantitative measurements, and finally, the method of repair must meet the judgment of cost consistent with the house value. Remember that rarely are building settlements a rapid process, and you generally have enough time to go slowly and consider all the factors.

FOUNDATION WALLS

3

Like so many other terms in building construction, the term "foundation walls" does not have a definition upon which all agree. Certainly the term refers to walls that start at the footing or foundation. Beyond that, however, it is a matter of contention as to the point at which the walls cease to be foundation walls per se as they rise. Some people wish to restrict the term to that portion of walls between the foundation and whatever floor level is directly above. By this definition, however, below-grade, basement walls would not be *foundation* walls, and only that portion of the walls *below* the basement floor level could be considered as such. For our purposes, however, the definition of foundation walls will include walls extending from the foundation up to the first-floor level above the exterior grade elevation. Thus, what is commonly referred to as a "basement wall" would also be a foundation wall. The reason for this is that, for the class of walls defined in this manner, there is a generic class of distress and damage and, concomitantly, repair methods unique to this type of wall.

Service Requirement

The service requirements for foundation walls are: (1) that they sustain the vertical load of the building; (2) that where applicable they retain (or support) the horizontal earth and water pressure; and (3) that when they are basement foundation walls they must stop water intrusion into a basement space.

The manner in which foundation walls retain the earth requires a little understanding in order to appreciate some of the repair constraints. A basement retaining wall acts as a beam in exactly the same manner as does a floor joist, the only difference being that the wall is a vertical beam whereas the floor joist is a horizontal beam. The earth presses horizontally against this "wall beam" and these forces are "reacted" at the top and bottom of the wall, just as the joist is reacted at either end where it bears on the wall. The only difference between the two examples is that the earth pressure, similar to water pressure, is "hydraulic" in the sense that the pressure increases as the depth below grade increases. Figure 3-1 shows the analogous loads on joist and wall, in which the small arrows represent the resistive (reaction) forces. In the case of the basement wall, the lower reaction is against the concrete floor slab while the upper reaction exerts a force on the floor.

The magnitude of the horizontal earth pressure is an extremely variable item. We have already touched on the lack of consistency and general perversity of soils, and these very inconsistencies often lead to serious misunderstanding and eventually to damage in regard to basement walls. There are some soils, notably clays, which, if maintained completely dry, can be cut absolutely vertically and remain completely stable. This characteristic is strikingly illustrated in many old buildings that have had a shallow basement space excavated to form a normal-height basement. Figure 3-2 illustrates such a basement. Clay walls have been cut straight down 5 feet to create a normal-height basement space. So long as the soils are kept dry these vertical soil walls will continue to stand. In the illustration, the excavations were made shortly after the turn of the century, and so far no distress has developed. On the other hand, everyone is familiar with what happens to certain soils when they become wet. The clay hills of the South and unstable (when wet) slopes in south central California give ample evidence of the instability of some wet soils. Granular soils like sand and gravel would never tolerate a vertical cut and would always slide to some natural slope.

These examples illustrate some of the extremes in horizontal earth pressure against a basement retaining wall. The dry clay can stand and produce no force whatever, while the same material when saturated with water can literally push a wall completely in. Furthermore, the amount of water in the surrounding soils can create a hydrostatic force that can be even more devastating than soil pressures.

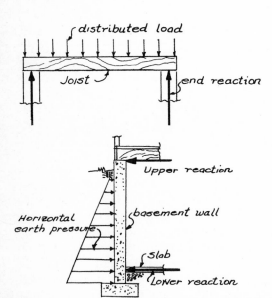

Fig. 3-1 Horizontal earth pressure on a foundation wall.

Fig. 3-2 Vertically cut earth "basement walls."

Water Retention

Just as earth-retention characteristics are quite variable as a result of different soil conditions, so can basement wall water retention be equally variable. Not only are exterior soil conditions important, but the quantity of water actually allowed to flow near a basement wall also is dependent on surface drainage contours, overall elevation of the building lot, roof drain discharge locations, and foundation drain details.

Basement foundation walls are rarely constructed in a manner that can prevent water intrusion. While the individual materials such as brick, block, and concrete could, with care, be used to build a water-impregnable "tank," the necessary construction techniques would be excessively expensive and impractical in the average residence. Instead, the outside of the basement wall is coated with a water-resistant membrane. The two most commonly used waterproofing materials are a cement stucco or parge, and tar or asphalt compounds. Sometimes the builder decides that if one is good, two must be better, and therefore applies a combination of cement parge and asphaltic paints. Such an approach to waterproofing does have some merits, but all too often neither coating is applied optimally and as a result water leaks through the foundation wall. Thus the generic defect with all parging materials relates not so much to the materials themselves as to the technique of application.

Foundation Wall Materials

All the common masonry materials, including stone, brick, and concrete block, have been used for the construction of foundation walls. Since early in this century concrete has been used for such walls in some sections of the Middle West and now is being used increasingly for this purpose elsewhere as well. In the 1920s and 1930s a common foundation wall material was a hollow, fired-clay tile block that was particularly suitable for basement wall construction not only because it was extremely durable, but also because it had relatively better insulating properties than most other materials. Less common, except in extreme Northern regions, is the use of heavy wood timbers. Such wood walls must be constructed of timbers treated to resist insect infestation and rot. In dry, cold climates wood may be the best alternative today because of its good insulating characteristics.

Mortar Strength

Necessary in any masonry wall is mortar to hold the units together. As a general rule this mortar is the weak link in the masonry system. Most foundation wall distress patterns can be detected first along and in the mortar joints. Actually, the mortar can be weak in a number of different ways; it is not necessarily true that any particular mortar is consistently weak in all possible ways. For example, one property of mortar is its crushing or compressive strength. While it is extremely rare that a residential building wall would fail as a result of excessive vertical loads, the most likely element to fail in this way is the mortar. Compression failures in mortar are dramatic and absolute, for the crushed mortar literally flows out of the joints like sand. This is rare and should not be confused with the deteriorating mortar condition often found in extremely old brick-masonry walls.

In addition to compression strength, mortar possesses a "bond strength," or the property of adhering to the masonry units. Bond strength is not only a mortar property but also a variable that depends on certain conditions of the brick or block surface to which it is to adhere, specifically, the porosity and moisture characteristics. It is in this mortar bond joint that most wall failures originate.

In certain situations it may be useful to know fairly accurately some of the properties of the mortar in a wall. Samples can be collected, tested, and analyzed by a testing laboratory. Unfortunately, the results may be discouraging when compared with supposed modern standards. The problem with such an approach to attempt to establish a quality of mortar is that there are simply no conventional standards for mortar as it exists in a wall at a building site. All the standards refer to laboratory-mixed, -applied, and -tested mortar. Really, a more appropriate method of making a judgment on mortar quality is to compare the mortar properties of a damaged wall with those of an undamaged wall. Obviously, comparative laboratory tests of both walls can be made; however, for the average homeowner some rough rules of thumb may provide an adequate means of evaluating mortar quality. A measure of the compressive strength of mortar may be obtained by simply driving a nail into the mortar. A "hard nail" or masonry nail should certainly penetrate into average-strength mortar when driven with a normal-weight hammer. Check to make sure that the nail is actually piercing the mortar and not just fracturing or spalling out large chunks. As the practical upper limits of mortar strengths are reached, it becomes more and more difficult to drive in a hard nail or even the shorter, hand-driven, "ram-set"–type nail. Finally, it is literally impossible to drive a nail by hand into some mortars for any appreciable depth. Unfortunately, such extremely high-strength mortar may not always be desirable, and for most applications the average-strength mortar as defined above is perhaps the optimum. Another way of identifying this average-strength mortar is to try to insert a carpentry nail, say, an 8-penny nail. In well-cured mortar, six months old or more, an 8-penny nail should not penetrate more than just below the surface and should simply bend over when driven harder. (Incidentally, watch your fingers in attempting this experiment!) If a carpentry nail easily penetrates full depth into a mortar joint, chances are the mortar has marginal strength properties. Be sure to repeat this experiment at several locations in a wall to assure yourself that you have not inadvertently selected an abnormally weak spot. Finally, if you have doubts about the amount of driving effort required or the objectivity of your technique, repeat the process on a wall you know to be particularly sound. At the extreme lower end of mortar strength is the type that can easily be raked out of the joint with a steel tool such as a nail or a pocketknife.

Mortar takes a relatively long time to reach its full strength or "cure," and any of the experiments described are only valid on mortar at least several months old. Sometimes in masonry laid in the winter the mortar will actually freeze, and while this is never desirable, it may have deteriorated only the surface and not the body of mortar. Thus, the test of raking out mortar should not necessarily be considered an indication of poor-quality mortar if it is restricted to the surface, perhaps the first ⅛ to ¼ inch.

A rough judgment of the bond strength between the masonry unit and the mortar can be established if a mortar joint is more or less exposed. A poorly bonded mortar can be "popped" off the brick surface by a relatively light hammer blow. On the other hand, a really superior bond literally cannot be hammered off; either the mortar or the surface of the masonry unit will fail in crushing before the bond joint fails.

Earlier it was mentioned that extremely high-strength mortar is not necessarily optimum. The issue is more accurately stated by stipulating that the mortar strength and the masonry-unit strength should be consistent. High-strength masonry units should have relatively higher-strength mortar and vice versa. The reason for this is far more than just a dogma of orderliness. In walls laid with compatible mortar and bricks the load will be relatively more uniformly distributed, with a resulting net increase in overall wall strength. The explanation for this phenomenon can be explained briefly as follows: As mortar-strength properties increase, the mortar also increases in stiffness; that is, it does not deform as much under load. This can be visualized more clearly by considering two elastic rubber bands. Suppose it takes exactly the same force to actually break them, but one stretches twice as far as the other when pulled with a force of the same magnitude. We would say that they are the same strength but one is twice as *stiff* as the other. In general, mortar does not work this way. As the strength increases, the stiffness increases. Thus, in a wall with variable-strength mortar or where a gross inconsistency exists between mortar and masonry units, there are literally "hard spots" in the wall; and at these points the loads are concentrated in such a way as to cause failure. Actually, there are other, somewhat more complex, incentives for this consistency requirement, but it may simply be stated that the more uniform the mechanical properties within a masonry wall, the higher the strength of the wall.

In any event, this principle implies that with a soft brick a relatively weak (and therefore soft mortar) is desirable, while with an extremely hard masonry unit, such as a sand-aggregate concrete block, a relatively higher-strength mortar should be used.

Masonry walls can be constructed with steel reinforcement. In hollow-core units, steel bars can be inserted in the cavities and encased in concrete (Figure 3-3) or (less desirably) mortar. Generally, such a detail is only used in very special cases where loads are particularly high; however, a far more common method of reinforcing masonry walls consists of laying a patented reinforcing wire horizontally in the mortar joints. Such reinforcing not only adds to the overall strength of the wall but also serves as an excellent crack stopper or a device to limit the propagation of a vertical wall crack.

There are several slightly differently designed commercial wall-reinforcing

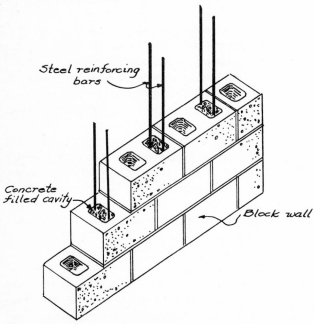

Fig. 3-3   Vertically reinforced CMU wall.

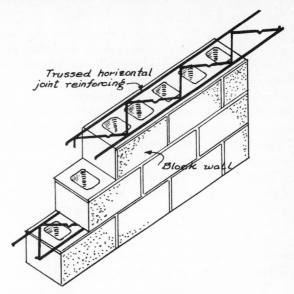

Fig. 3-4   Horizontal joint reinforcement.

products available, but one in particular has gained such wide usage that the product name has become almost synonymous with this type of wall reinforcing. Thus, the term "Dur-o-wall" reinforcing, which is technically called "trussed horizontal wall joint reinforcing," (Figure 3-4) is used as the generic name (much as *Kleenex* is used to describe paper tissues). In any event, the presence of this type of reinforcing in a wall is significant because it will change distress patterns, and because the choice of corrections for distressed walls is often contingent on whether Dur-o-wall is present in the wall. Reinforced masonry walls are a relatively new phenomenon and are unlikely to be found in a wall more than around thirty years old.

If the question arises as to whether a particular wall is reinforced with horizontal joint reinforcing, it is not too difficult to find the answer. The edge of the wire can generally be exposed by digging out some of the mortar to a depth of ½ to ¾ inch. In foundation walls the reinforcing occurs 8 to 16 inches apart, and therefore two successive mortar joints should be checked. With care, the steel can be detected with a magnetic stud finder or, according to the direction of the wall (not east–west), a compass.

Thus, the most common foundation wall material is masonry, and not only is the particular type of masonry unit important, but insofar as distress and potential damage to a wall are concerned, equally important are the mortar and any steel reinforcing. Since the nature and patterns of wall cracking are so dependent on wall materials, a homeowner should first identify the materials before reaching any conclusions with respect to wall distress. Furthermore, if there are any questions as to which materials exist in a wall, any mason should be able to help in the identifying process.

Foundation Wall Distress

Since the observer of any distress is necessarily presented with the *effect* of distress, it would at first seem logical to relate the effect (or crack pattern) directly to the cause. Unfortunately, this approach poses other problems because there are so many combinations of damage, wall movement, and crack patterns, each of which adds relatively subtle nuances that provide the necessary body of information to define the actual cause of the distress. In addition, the question of time enters into the diagnosis of the distress in several ways. Not only is *when* the crack appeared important, but also *how long* it took for the crack to develop and *how* the crack was related to other events such as construction sequence and time of year are important factors. Many observers try to make up rules that relate one particular crack pattern to a specific cause. Invariably, as a rule appears to be yielding consistent results, a gross exception is encountered. Thus, rather than reason from the standpoint of *effect to cause,* more consistent results can be obtained by defining the various causes and describing the effects most generally encountered, that is, from *cause to effect.*

The observer must develop certain information to perform this analysis and then proceed to relate this information to the possible patterns of distress associated with each of these causes.

This information should include:

1 Wall material—masonry-unit type, mortar, reinforcing
2 Wall history—e.g., age, repairs, previous distress, change in environment
3 Wall elevation crack geometry—a sketch to see whether particular patterns exist and whether overall movement can be inferred
4 Wall thickness crack geometry—questions concerning whether the crack is uniform in the width of the wall or wider on the interior, etc.
5 Additional indications of movement elsewhere in the building—including basement slab, upper walls, and at floor lines
6 Related factors—how the crack is related to water retention, etc.

While all masonry materials share common ailments, there are certain problems more or less unique to each material. Thus, an appropriate categorization of foundation wall distress is by wall materials. Furthermore, since most of the concerns involve not only foundation walls but rather that special class, namely, basement walls, the following discussion will concentrate on basement walls of particular materials.

Concrete Masonry Unit Walls

By far the most common contemporary foundation wall material is the concrete masonry unit (CMU). The typical CMU block is 8 × 16 inches (Figure 3-5). Completely solid blocks are available, but more commonly cavities or cores are cast into the block—either two or three per 16-inch length. According to the particular constituent materials, which, incidentally, vary from one section of the country to another with the availability and cost of these materials, the blocks vary from a rather coarse or porous appearance to an extremely smooth one, like a fine-grain limestone. The appearance has little to do with the quality and physical properties of blocks, and most are manufactured according to a rigid standard set by the American Society of Testing Materials (ASTM). In this regard probably the greatest variation between CMU walls is not the basic block material but the condition of the blocks at the time they are laid and the way they are laid. People regularly refer to this material as "cement blocks" or "cinder blocks." Actually, these terms are inappropriate because they actually refer to two products that are seldom used today. Until the mid-1950s a block was manufactured with an aggregate (the noncement, mineral constituent of blocks) of cinders from the residue of the steel manufacturing process. This was not an altogether satisfactory material for several reasons, and by the late 1950s it was actually outlawed in many areas. The principal problem was that there were small pieces of iron mixed in with the cinders, and of course these particles eventually wound up in the cinder blocks. If any moisture got into the block (an almost inevitable situation), the iron particles would expand and literally cause the block to explode. Not only was it disturbing to hear the periodic popping sounds from the basement, but occasionally people were actually injured by flying particles. Fortunately, the tendency of iron particles to expand and explode lasted only a year or two, and so the houses built with cinder-block basement walls are by now safe and *soundless.*

The term cement block is loosely used to refer to a block unit composed of more or less conventional concrete products, that is, a small-stone aggregate, sand, and portland cement. Such blocks are much heavier than the more conventional CMU products and generally have smooth surfaces. In the 1920s and 1930s they were very commonly used as a basement wall material and left exposed above grade. The exposed blocks were often formed to look like cut stone, as in Figure 3-6. Generally these blocks are extremely hard and for several reasons are less subject to wall distress problems than are the con-

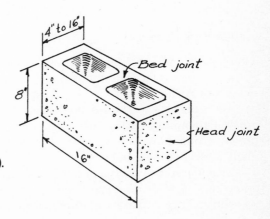

Fig. 3-5   Concrete masonry unit (CMU).

Fig. 3-6 "Cement" block with cut stone shape face.

ventional CMUs. In any event, because of their higher cost they are seldom made or used today. The most similar product we have today is the so-called sand-aggregate block, found in the Southeast.

The principal causes of distress in CMU walls are:

1   Block shrinkage due to moisture drying immediately following construction

2   Thermal and moisture expansion and contraction in normal service

3   Earth-retaining failure, either bending failure or support failure at the top or bottom

4   Foundation settlements, either vertical settlements or foundation tipping (see Chapter 2)

5   Damage during backfilling and heavy-equipment overloads

6   Water leakage

Concrete-Block Shrinkage

There are two phenomena involving CMU shrinkage that are associated with common distress in foundation walls. All concrete products shrink in the process of curing, that is, in the process of going from the semiliquid state of "wet" concrete to the finished "hard" or cured product. Although the greatest amount of curing shrinkage occurs within the first two months, this process (commonly called "drying" or "initial shrinkage") continues indefinitely in decreasing amounts.

The initial shrinkage is a one-time movement and is not reversible. On the other hand, CMUs undergo another movement, due to moisture, which is reversible. They expand with increase in moisture and contract with loss of moisture. The magnitude of both these types of shrinkage is dependent on a number of factors including the constituent materials, the way these materials are assembled and mixed, and the curing conditions. Unfortunately, all these factors are extremely variable, and it is not uncommon for the shrinkage to differ by as much as three to four times from one group of tests to another.

In any event, a mason has very little control over the initial shrinkage; and, in fact, the only precaution that can be used to minimize the adverse effects is simply to wait as long as possible after manufacture before installing the blocks to assure that the maximum amount of curing has taken place.

A more insidious problem involves the reversible moisture shrinkage phenomena. The in-service moisture content of a CMU installed in a dry, heated basement may be only a small percentage. During erection an air-dried block may retain as much as 20 percent moisture, while a completely saturated block can retain 40 percent moisture by weight. Thus, the potential for shrinkage exists and dimensional changes corresponding to these changes in moisture can be substantial—and disastrous—in terms of a potential for cracks. For example, a 30-foot-long basement wall may have to accommodate over ¼-inch shrinkage due to relatively average drying conditions. In the extreme, of course, this could result in a ¼-inch crack in the basement wall. Ideally, the individual block should be dried to approximately the average moisture condition to which the finished walls will be exposed in service. Regrettably, this is almost never done. To make matters even worse, blocks are sometimes actually moistened before laying as a result of the mistaken assumption that blocks, like fired-brick products, should be wet before laying. Thus, the average CMU wall must accommodate some decrease in length and an attendant potential for cracking.

To distinguish the cracking owing to moisture movements in a block wall requires a very simple understanding of the geometry of a shrunken and unshrunken wall. Let us consider a wall which, owing to moisture loss, has the potential for shrinkage cracking. How is it most likely to crack? A simple way to envision this process is to think of the shrunken (or shortened) wall as having to be "stretched" to fit into the space of the original, unshrunken wall (Figure 3-7). Recall that masonry walls are relatively weak when pulled apart, that is, when they are in *tension*. The wall must be stretched to fit into the original space of the end walls, the footing along the lower edge, and the floor structure along the top. Thus, forces must be applied at each one of these surfaces in order to stretch the wall back into shape. When the wall is fitted back together in this way, it is in continuous contact with the relatively strong footing just as it actually was when it was first laid on the footing. The wall can crack in two ways: (1) a continuous one, running completely along the footing and up each side wall, as in Figure 3-8*a;* or (2) a *minimum* of one crack that is wider at the top and decreases to nothing at the footing, as in Figure 3-8*b*. Of course, the wall in Figure 3-8*b* will still be strained at some locations, but it is "easier" if the wall has this one crack and some strain than if it has a crack around the edges, as in Figure 3-8*a*. It should be understood

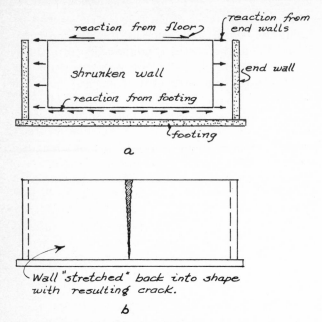

reaction from floor ⌐reaction from end walls

shrunken wall ⟶ ⟵ end wall

⌐reaction from footing

⌐footing

a

Wall "stretched" back into shape with resulting crack.

b

Fig. 3-7 Diagram of CMU wall shrinkage.

that this is a somewhat simplified, analogous way of reasoning about how a shrinkage in a wall could produce a certain geometry of cracking, and it depends on the relative strength of the various constraining elements. Still, it is a useful method of reasoning and one that will lead to some consistent conclusions. In any event, the first type or mode of shrinkage cracking is a single, more or less vertical crack at the center of a shrunken wall, generally wider at the top and decreasing in width toward the bottom.

Discussed earlier were the relative strengths of mortar and block and the bond strength of the mortar as often the weak element in a wall. According to the various strengths of the block, mortar, and mortar bond to the block, the central vertical crack can develop in alternative patterns. A common pattern is the "step crack," where the crack follows a path *along* mortar joints and not *through* any block units. The increase in crack width with height still exists, as in Figure 3-8a. Oftentimes the crack will divide into two cracks, as in Figure 3-8b. The actual movement, however, will remain the same, and the sum of the two cracks will equal the one in Figure 3-8a.

So far a very idealized wall has been considered, specifically one that is uniform in material properties and shrinkage-age potential. In practice things are seldom this simple, and it is the accounting for the nonuniformity that often obscures the actual motion. For example, any opening such as a window or doorway necessarily produces a weak section in the wall; thus, cracks often occur adjacent to doors and windows. Also, if several weak places exist, the single cracks may develop as multiple cracks at all these locations. Barring openings, however, shrinkage cracks rarely develop toward the ends of walls and are more generally found in the middle third of a wall. This is one of the primary distinctions between shrinkage cracks and wall cracks resulting from settlement in foundation walls, as illustrated in Figure 2-8. A common dilemma occurs in distinguishing between such settlement-induced cracking and those due to shrinkage. In the final analysis the only absolute distinction between the cause of such cracks is whether the foundation is cracked. If the crack continues into the footing, it is almost certainly associated with settlement; otherwise, shrinkage is the reason. Of course, it is often difficult to get a clear view of a wall footing, so generally part of the slab must be cut away to allow an examination.

Still another useful parameter in diagnosing shrinkage cracking is the time-sequencing of the cracks. As a practical matter, after the initial drying process occurs following construction, the moisture content of masonry in basement walls does not vary sufficiently to cause significant cracking. It is true that once in a while a house will experience some unusual moisture condition, such as a flooded basement or a prolonged breakdown in dehumidifying equipment during a damp summer. Following such occurrences, shrinkage cracks can and often do develop. On the other hand, the vast majority of shrinkage cracking occurs in the first year or two in the occupied life of a building. Toward the end of winter is generally the time that individual building components are driest, and it is at this time that cracks start to develop. Such cracking is rarely abrupt, simply because the shrinkage is a relatively gradual process; and the crack will first appear as a hairline and gradually enlarge over a period of several weeks.

Crack patterns from shrinkage can be rather significantly altered when horizontal joint reinforcing such as Dur-o-wall is used. Such reinforcing does not eliminate shrinkage cracking; instead, it distributes the stresses, with the result that many small, distributed cracks are allowed to develop instead of a few large ones.

As in all building distress there are exceptions to the crack patterns asso-

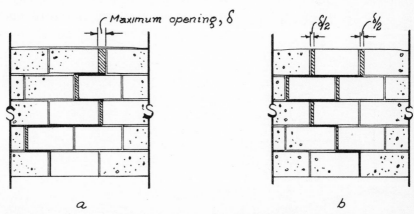

Fig. 3-8 (*a*) Single, stepped mortar joint crack. (*b*) Dividing or multiple stepped mortar joint crack.

ciated with moisture shrinkage of CMU basement walls. Nevertheless, there are a few fairly constant rules for identifying such cracking. They are:

1 Cracks that appear in the first one to two years following construction
2 Crack patterns that are generally wider at the top than at the bottom
3 Vertical and step cracks that are more or less centered in the wall unless there are windows and door openings elsewhere
4 Cracks that do not continue into the footing
5 Cracks that represent only horizontal movement without differential vertical (across the crack) movement

The remedies for shrinkage cracks generally involve three considerations: (1) the decrease in structural integrity of the wall; (2) loss of water-retention capabilities; and (3) unsightliness. As explained earlier, basement walls act as beams in the vertical direction and, therefore, vertical cracks may not compromise the wall structure. On the other hand, step cracks that have long horizontal runs near the midheight of the wall may significantly weaken the wall. In many houses such cracking occurs, no repairs are ever made, and the wall stands and functions for the remaining life of the house. If the cracks continue to grow or if a house is in a region of high groundwater or high soil pressure, then remedial corrections should be undertaken. The first recommendation is a "don't"—do not try to ram a small amount of mortar into the cracks. This may solve the cosmetic problem, but from a structural standpoint a little loose mortar on the inside mortar joint is of no consequence. Of course, in the extreme the house can be shored up and the walls taken down and rebuilt; however, this is rarely necessary or advisable. Instead, one of three methods is often used to restore the structural integrity of cracked CMU walls.

1 A block buttress exactly analogous to the "flying buttress" of a Gothic cathedral can be installed on the inside of the wall opposite some of the more severe cracks. Such a buttress may consist of 8- or 12-inch blocks, 16 to 32 inches deep, similar to the detail shown in Figure 3-9. Often people incorporate shelf supports on two such piers and get double service.

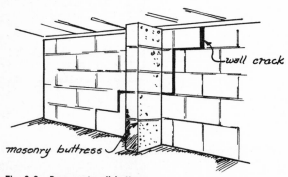

Fig. 3-9 Basement wall buttress.

The limitation on the adaptability of this correction is most often the foundation for such a pier. If it cannot be demonstrated that the basement concrete slab is adequate to sustain the load, a portion of the slab must be removed and a proper wall footing installed below the slab.

2 The block cavities adjacent to the cracking can be filled with concrete. This is easier said than done and takes some special precautions to achieve a really worthwhile job. Often it is possible to break into the cavity of the top-course block. Through this opening a fairly wet (but rich in cement) mix can be rammed. The problem is making sure the concrete flows all the way to the bottom. The cavity of the bottom block can be broken open, and when the concrete flows out, the entire cavity height should be filled. Sometimes it is necessary to cut a small hole in the floor above and ram the concrete down with a steel reinforcement bar, say, ½ inch in diameter. If such a procedure is used, the final step is to push the bar completely into the filled cavity and thereby have a reinforced wall.

3 The third option is to pressure-inject a concrete grout into cracks. This operation requires special equipment but is particularly effective if epoxy concrete grout is used. This is a relatively fine-grain concrete with an epoxy binder-agent added.

The advantage of a grouting repair technique is that it generally restores both the structural properties as well as the water integrity of a wall. Unfortunately, it is not always applicable, because some blocks have irregularly shaped ends (head joints) and the grout works its way back into the hollow cavities rather than into the cracks.

In-service Thermal and Moisture Movements

The thermal and moisture environment of below-grade basement walls is relatively constant: the earth on one side maintains a steady temperature in the 60°F (16°C) range, while the interior of most houses fluctuates no more than 10°F (6°C) either side of 75°F (24°C). Except for extremely humid southern and coastal areas, more or less the same is true with regard to variations in air moisture content. In some situations the largest variations in moisture are more artificial than natural, that is, when a forced drying procedure (dehumidification) is utilized in the summer and, conversely, when humidification is added in the winter. Incidentally, the order of magnitude of thermal expansion in concrete masonry is considerably less than that for typical moisture movements, and corresponding to the extremes of ¼-inch movement in a 30-foot wall mentioned earlier, comparable movements due to temperature changes might be on the order of ⅟₃₂ inch for a 20°F (11°C) change. In any event, in *average* basement walls it is uncommon to find significant distress due to thermal movements and moisture-induced movements after the initial drying has occurred.

It is the special case or nonaverage wall in which the effects of temperature and moisture movements are most noticeable. Specifically, such atypical situations include unusually long walls, say, greater than 80 to 100 feet; walls with abrupt changes in cross section, as at doors and windows or at a transition point between a two-story wall and a one-story wall; and at abrupt turns or jogs in relatively long walls, as at chimneys. The key elements for being atypical are length and abrupt change.

Probably there is no more common distress pattern in a block basement wall than a step crack at a door lintel, particularly in a door near the end of a long basement wall. Such cracks are almost inevitable when special precautions have not been taken in the original construction. If such a crack does occur at a doorway, there is generally no earth retention on the outside; and assuming the crack remains in the size range of $\frac{1}{16}$ to $\frac{1}{8}$ inch, there is really little cause for alarm. The only incentive for repair in such a situation is appearance only, and in such cases simply filling the crack with a mortar mix should be sufficient. Do not, however, be surprised if the crack reopens— chances are it will. The one precaution is to try to grout the crack at its extreme open position. This way, if the crack reappears, it will be at the same location and not further along the wall.

The in-service moisture and thermal environment of a wall is cyclic, with a more or less annual period to the cycle. The corresponding movements of the wall are also cyclic, but unfortunately the crack movement does not always follow this yearly cycle. Some cracks literally open and close with the seasons, particularly those in wood and plaster walls above grade. As cracks develop in masonry walls, hard particles of mortar and masonry tend to break off and filter down in the crack space. Such debris literally jams the crack open so that it cannot close during a shrinkage period. During the next expansion period the crack opens further, more debris falls into the opening, and the crack continues to grow annually. Thus, from a process that can produce only a relatively small opening during any one cycle, a much larger crack can ultimately develop. This phenomenon often leads to incorrect identification of thermal- and moisture-induced cracking. Observers at first find it difficult

Fig. 3-10 Lintel step crack in exterior wall.

to explain how a ¼-inch-wide crack can be attributed to thermal expansion when it can easily be demonstrated that the maximum thermal movement is measured as being only a few hundredths of an inch. At first there seems to be an anomaly at work, but the key to the process is not only that the crack is jammed open and thus prevented from closing, but also that masonry is much stronger in compression than in tension. If, associated with the failure of masonry products, there were such a phenomenon as a "compression crack" or a narrow band of material that compressed to nothing as the wall expanded, then the process would be completely reversible even if the crack did fill. Of course, this is not the case, and thus, since the failure mode of masonry is not reversible, crack development becomes nonreversible if the normal mechanism is somehow interrupted.

A modest understanding of this mechanism is more than just of academic interest, because this same mechanism can influence repair methods and sequencing. Thus, if patched cracks continually reopen, and particularly if they even grow larger, some thought should be given to alternative repair techniques. For such situations the best solution may be to create a so-called control joint—literally, an opening that will allow movement and yet be cosmetically acceptable and serviceable to the extent that it stops water and weather intrusion. Certainly the easiest control-joint repair technique is to fill a joist with a completely flexible material that can tolerate the extremes in movement without rupturing. The generic name for such material is "caulking." Today there are a number of commercial products for such purposes, but a word of caution is advisable concerning the selection of the optimum material. Some caulking materials are expressly restricted to interior use, some cannot tolerate continuous exposure to sunlight, and some are most adaptable to filling narrow openings. Read the instructions and limitations before buying such a product. Incidentally, one of the best joint-filling materials still is natural tar pitch. In many areas it is difficult to obtain, and manufactured substitutes are recommended as being comparable.

Earth-Retaining Failure

At the beginning of this chapter the mechanism of earth retention was discussed, and it was noted that below-grade basement walls resist the earth pressure exactly analogously to the way a floor beam supports a load—there are reactions at each end and the wall is "bending" in its height. Following the analogy one would guess that a wall, when overloaded owing to excessive horizontal earth pressure, could fail in several ways. It could fail in bending or "breaking" toward the middle, or it could fail at either the upper or lower supports, that is, at the basement slab line or at the floor structure above. As a practical matter, walls that are restrained at the bottom by a concrete slab rarely have lower-reaction failures. Thus, it is the bending and top-reaction failures that are of most concern.

A basement wall bending failure is characterized by a long, horizontal crack, almost always in the mortar joint. As the crack approaches the end walls it decreases and eventually vanishes simply because the end walls offer horizontal support and at the ends the wall is not loaded in bending. A bending-failure crack, as seen in the exaggerated sketch of Figure 3-11, is wider on the inside of the wall and still tight on the outside. This variation in crack width *through* the wall is different from the other types of cracks that have been considered and is, in part, the key to identifying such a failure.

Wall cracks resulting from a bending failure of the wall are serious and should never be treated lightly or disregarded. Technically, as soon as the crack opens the wall has *failed*—but it has not yet collapsed. Once in a while people tend to take a rather cavalier attitude to such cracks and argue that they know of such cracks having existed in buildings for many years, without ill effects. It is true that, depending on the amount of vertical load, the wall can continue to resist *some* amount of horizontal earth. For example, think of taking two blocks of wood and pushing them together end to end. The two blocks can support some load in bending, that is, a load at right angles to the pushing forces. Furthermore, intuitively one would suppose that there is some point at which a crack could be permitted in the butt joint and still just *balance* the load. It is literally a balancing act, and the wall, just as the two blocks of wood, could collapse abruptly with the slightest variation of any of the forces. Such a wall collapse would be catastrophic and should not be knowingly allowed.

If such a crack can be identified in time, the wall shored, and corrective action taken, the problems are not insurmountable. The remedies may not, however, be within the expertise of the average do-it-yourselfer. Obviously, any correction should be made on the basis of two conditions: one, whether the wall is sufficiently strong to resist "normal" earth pressures, and two, whether normal earth pressure has developed as a unique, one-time situation. Probably the two principal causes of abnormal earth pressures are water-saturated soils caused by unusually heavy rains and heavy equipment driving too close to the wall. In the second case trucks and cars should be kept away from foundation walls, especially for any prolonged period. If it can be determined that the load condition is a unique occurrence, unlikely to ever

Fig. 3-11 Basement wall bending failure.

reoccur, then the remedy is simply a matter of repairing the wall; otherwise, provisions should be taken to reduce the external load and simultaneously increase the wall strength.

Not all houses or yards can accommodate a lowering of the exterior grade elevation, but if this can be done without a change in drainage patterns, then an easy way to reduce soil pressures is simply to remove 1 or 2 feet of earth. Since the forces on the wall are proportional to the depth of fill squared, lowering the grade 2 out of 8 feet is very significant—reducing the load almost by half. Obviously, directing any excess water away from a wall is also beneficial; however, beyond these two measures little else can be done to reduce soil-pressure loads.

Corrective action for a failed (cracked) retaining wall is very similar to the techniques used for repairing shrinkage-cracked walls, namely, buttresses, concrete-filled cavities, and pressure-injected concrete grout. In using the last remedy it is generally worthwhile to try to jack the wall back into position. Because of the external resistance of the earth, the jacking operation should be carried out progressively over a period of several days to allow the earth to yield back. Furthermore, grouting is almost exclusively restricted to solid (rather than hollow) CMUs and therefore is only applicable in restricted cases.

One further correction is sometimes applicable for strengthening a CMU basement-retaining wall. The wall can literally be tied to the earth by means of a steel bar driven into the earth and secured to an anchor. The details and adaptability of this approach should be confirmed by an engineer, because there are certain exceptions. Nonetheless, the general method is to break out one block and drill a hole 3 or 4 inches in diameter into the earth. A steel rod with a hinged anchor is pushed back into the hole and the "wings" of the anchor are set by drawing the rod forward again. The rod is then secured to the wall and the block replaced.

Another mode of wall failure, in addition to a bending failure, is due to inadequate support at the top of the wall, or top-reaction failure. In the construction process some attachment system typically is provided between the top of the wall and the floor construction. Usually a bolt is cemented into several of the block cavities and subsequently attached to a wood timber or "sill plate." Even assuming that such anchors are provided, this method of top support often proves inadequate for several reasons. Oftentimes not enough anchors are provided, since the typical 6- and 8-feet-on-centers specified in many codes are not adequate for marginal soils conditions. Furthermore, the method of cementing the anchors into the block cavities is seldom as complete as it might be. Finally, the details of the anchors between the sill plate and floor construction are often left more to chance than to any positive act. The result is that many residential buildings suffer some degree of failure at the upper wall support. In extreme cases walls actually push in and collapse. More commonly they push in a few inches and then wedge themselves tightly against some other member. Such a failure as this is easily identified by observing how the various building elements misalign. Corrective measures can include jacking the wall back into position, but this must be done with

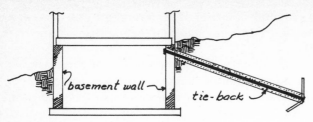

Fig. 3-12   Basement wall "tie-back" anchor.

care as in any jacking operation. Motions of this type tend to be "one-way" in the sense that nails can sometimes pull out but not be easily pushed back. Thus, every connector should be completely freed and if possible the floor construction should be slightly strained upward before an attempt is made to push the wall back to its original position.

Once the wall head is in its final position, the methods of correcting the inadequate anchorage can be carried out. Remember that not only must the sill plate be anchored to the wall, but also the sill must in turn be anchored to the floor construction. If the floor joists are resting on the failed wall, a good approach is to use a lag screw to attach a continuous piece of framing lumber, say, a 3×6, to the underside of the joists and tightly against the wall. This will transfer the wall load directly into the floor joists.

This mode of failure often occurs on non-load-bearing walls or walls parallel to the floor joists. A detail similar to the 3×6 block can be installed on several rows of solid "bridging" or framing lumber the same depth as the floor joists and installed at right angles to the joist and extending several joist-rows back.

A very common failure of this type is often encountered in older row houses where there is a narrow walkway between buildings. If even relatively small amounts of water settle in this passageway and then freeze, the expanded soils will tend to push the walls in. The result is often a strange overhang at the transition between the upper framing and the foundation wall. In such situations water should be eliminated from the soils in the passageway by such means as installing drain tiles and paving the walkway. Furthermore, it is often wise to dig down a few feet along the side of the

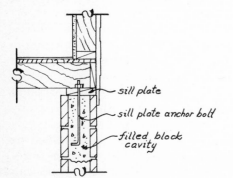

sill plate

sill plate anchor bolt

filled block cavity

Fig. 3-13   Sill plate anchor.

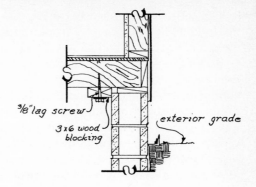

Fig. 3-14 Wall thrust anchor detail.

walls and install a layer of a compressible material between the earth and wall. A 1-inch-thick by 2-feet-deep piece of Styrofoam insulation board is suitable. If moisture does permeate the earth, freeze, and expand, it then will simply compress this material rather than push against the wall.

Damage to Foundation Walls during Construction

In many situations the most severe loads a foundation wall will ever experience are those that occur during construction. At that time not only are foundation walls more exposed to the hazards of weather, such as freezing, but also

Fig. 3-15 Foundation wall at passageway pushed in by expanded, frozen earth.

certain construction practices can produce loads on walls that they were simply not intended to support. Improper backfilling procedures and heavy-equipment loads are the chief causes of wall distress during construction.

Backfilling errors most often involve filling the void on the outside between the wall and earth either before (1) the wall reaches its full strength; (2) the basement slab is installed and therefore no base horizontal support exists; or (3) the floor structure is installed to prevent the wall being pushed in at the top. Obviously, if really extreme damage is caused during backfilling, it is repaired, and the eventual owner never is aware of any problem. In some cases, however, odd irregularities in walls can be explained only on the basis of backfilling errors. It is not too uncommon to find walls that are deformed into a bowed arc in the length direction. Since walls are rarely laid up with such a distortion, the conclusion is that the movement occurred during backfilling. A similar logic explains walls that are slightly tipped inward at the top and yet have adequate horizontal support from the floor joist. As a practical matter such distortions may not have much significance other than from an aesthetic standpoint; and short of the rather impractical solution of complete removal, there is little that can be done to correct such distortions. The important issue is to be able to distinguish between such a built-in distortion and some ongoing distress that could lead to a failure; for example, you should not confuse a backfill–induced wall tipping with an actual retaining failure. The distinguishing characteristic of such movement is that there are almost inevitably telltale signs to provide clues to the sequence between the movement and construction. For example, if the basement slab is uniformly tight against a wall bowed in its length, then the bowing must have occurred prior to the installation of the slab.

Either during backfilling or some other phase of construction heavy construction equipment such as trucks and tractors often are run near a foundation wall. The increase in horizontal earth pressure owing to the added weight of the equipment can trigger a retaining type of failure. It is to be hoped that such damage is immediately identified and repaired, but sometimes it is left for the first owner to discover. Here again the dilemma is to distinguish such early damage from an existing problem. Since retaining-type failures require immediate action, the question is not one of when to repair, but of what might have been the cause. The answer to this latter question can alter the repair procedure. Thus, if you are aware of foundation wall retaining failures in your very new house, you should give some consideration to the possibility that the failure was induced during construction by heavy equipment operating too close to the wall.

Foundation Wall Water Leakage

Water intrusion is perhaps the single biggest complaint people voice about foundation walls. The causes are generally obvious, and yet some of the most preposterous solutions are proposed and actually carried out. People pay hundreds of dollars to waterproofing contractors for work that often worsens the water problem and in a surprising number of cases actually collapses foundation walls. This certainly solves the water problem, for it is the classic example of throwing the baby out with the bath water.

The normal design and construction methods of foundation walls are adequate to limit leakage for an *average* water condition. Literally no conventional residential wall would be sufficient to act as a reverse "swimming pool," that is, to resist water pressure equivalent to a few feet or more. The standard methods of restricting water penetration are to have a water-resistant membrane on the outside of the wall, and various combinations of exterior and interior foundation drain systems to direct the water away from the wall.

The most typical explanations for basement wall leakage are:

1 Surface water
   a Natural drainage
   b Poorly directed roof drains
2 Subsurface water
   a Natural groundwater conditions
   b Broken utility supply lines
   c Damaged or blocked subsurface drain system
3 Uniquely permeable soils around the foundation wall

A special consideration that should be examined and clearly understood before attempting either a diagnosis or a remedy to leakage problems is that while many of the construction and correction procedures are designed principally with natural subsurface groundwater in mind, this is very rarely a real problem. Common sense would dissuade most people from founding a basement below natural groundwater level. If common sense does not apply, then the almost insurmountable problems of trying to build a house below groundwater level limits even further the number of basements likely to be located below water level. Most jurisdictions have laws and codes that rarely permit a house to be founded with a basement near groundwater level. Finally, if a house actually were sited with the basement into groundwater, the leakage through the floor slab and around the slab edge would be equal to or more than that which would penetrate the walls. Thus, it is extremely unlikely that a wall leak is a result of the natural groundwater level actually being above the basement slab level. The surprising thing is that many of the supposed water-prevention solutions make this assumption and are most applicable to this condition. At issue here is the following situation: Once it is established that the water against a foundation wall does *not* come from below, that is, that the basement is actually above the natural groundwater level (③ in Figure 3-16), then deep drain systems near the foundation elevation may actually *encourage* water to penetrate down along the side of the wall. It is true that ideally such a drainage system would prevent a water-pressure buildup against a wall; but such a buildup would generally involve so much more water than is likely to accumulate near a house that it is of debatable value from this standpoint. Some building regulations even require that not only an exterior system be installed but also an interior perimeter drain be placed under the basement slab. Such drain systems are often connected to a pit dug through the basement floor (a sump pit), and any water accumulation is then pumped out to be discharged away from the house. Understand, such a system is certainly preferable to having a flooded basement, but it is only valid in certain situations and in some cases may be more hindrance than help.

The two most likely sources of water against a foundation wall are from surface water filtering down and impregnating the soils adjacent to the foundation, and from roof drains discharging too near the wall. Examine the surface contours surrounding your house. If a large area (several thousand square feet or more) drains to a low point at or within 10 to 15 feet of the wall, this may well be the source of your water problem. While it is true that water can enter the surface further away and flow horizontally along water-resistent strata to a foundation wall, such conditions tend to be more the exception than the rule. Low points within the 10- to 15-foot range are most often the critical collection points.

The second source to consider is water from roof drains. Obviously, when drains discharge onto concrete splash blocks that direct the water only a few feet away, a significant amount of water can easily flow back around the basement wall. Far more insidious are the drains that are carefully directed into an underground drain system. Such piping not only can become blocked with debris but also often deteriorates and collapses with time. Some modern builders argue a unique theory that allows such drains to terminate underground in what is called a "drain field," which is, in reality, a pile of several cubic feet of stone. The almost inevitable result of such a system is that fine particles of soil and leaves collect between the stones, eventually block the water flow, and finally make the entire drainage system useless. Such an

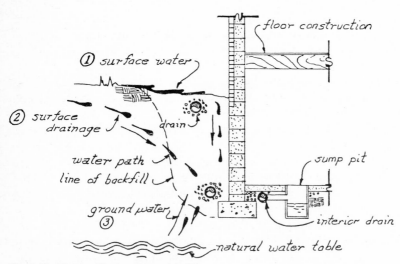

Fig. 3-16 Water paths to a basement wall.

underground drain system to receive roof water is really only practical when the water can be discharged to a point below the basement level.

Piping material for underground drains includes terra cotta, cast iron, and various cement and plastic products. Since the early 1970s a standard underground water drain has been a corrugated, flexible plastic material with slot perforations along the length to receive the water. This is widely used because it is flexible and can be bent easily around turns without special fittings. Unfortunately, this piping is not as durable as the more rigid products, and in many applications it has collapsed and blocked water flow. In any event, one of the first steps in solving a basement water problem is to determine whether underground piping receiving roof water is clear and free flowing. This may take some standing in the rain to determine, or a simple test with a hose may maintain your neighbors' opinion of your sanity. All but the plastic products are amenable to snaking out any blockage.

There have already been several references made to the method and quality of foundation wall backfill—the material that is used to fill the void between the earth and foundation wall when the house is first built. Again the details of the backfill become important, because in many cases it is through these backfill materials that water flows to the foundation wall. Two common maladies of the backfill are that (1) the excavation becomes a convenient disposal location for general building rubble and debris; and (2) even when clean earth is used as fill, it is casually thrown into the hole and not compacted enough to limit water flowing through it. Thus, in a very literal sense many houses are built with a sponge surrounding the basement wall. Couple this condition with surface drainage in the general area, and leaky basement walls result.

What are the remedies? The first rule is to not do something foolish just for the sake of doing something. Like all building repairs, first try to ferret out the cause. Examine the drainage near walls and try to see if the leak is associated with a particular type of rain, that is, long, soaking rain, which generally implies deeper water from further away, or short, intense rain, which produces more surface flow and roof drain overflow. Experiment around the foundation by hosing it down and try to determine if there is a unique path for the water flow. Finally, if the flow is steady, investigate both water supply and sewage hookups to the house to make sure there are no broken mains.

One thing that will certainly be true of any basement leak is that there will be exactly as many solutions suggested as solicited. The owner of a leaky basement should be aware of some of the possibilities that may be suggested. A relatively standard recommendation is to inject a "filler" material into the soils adjacent to the foundation. Most commonly this consists of a fine-grain material that, it is hoped, will fill all the voids in the earth surrounding the wall, densify the soil, and make it less permeable to water. In theory this is a fine idea, and if it could be done precisely, it might well minimize water intrusion. Unfortunately, there are several pitfalls. The first is that by densifying the soils, the earth pressure increases on the wall and in the extreme can cause a retaining failure. Another problem with this procedure is that since it is done remotely, no one is ever quite sure exactly where these grout materials go. They can flow uniformly against the wall, irregularly to actually form new water paths, or into the foundation drain system and block the pipes completely. They have even been known to work their way into sewer lines, flow hundreds of feet, and block the entire system. Thus, soil fillers or grouts should only be used with extreme caution.

Another correction is to dig up the entire perimeter, install additional drains, and reinstall new backfill. Again, this *may* be a reasonable solution. On the other hand, it may actually encourage the water to flow through poorly installed new backfill and into the new drainage system. Still another common remedy is to cut away the basement slab for a few feet at the wall line, dig out the earth down to the footing, install a perimeter drainpipe that feeds into a sump, break holes through the foundation wall, and finally reinstall the slab. This method is guaranteed to draw water not only to the foundation wall but also through the soils below the footing. Now you have the option of a collapsed wall or a settlement failure!

If these remedies sound discouraging, what are the best solutions? The best solution is to intercept the water before it gets to the wall. Sometimes modest regrading of surface contours around the house will direct the water away from the walls. Another method is to install a high drain field several feet away from the wall. Of course, this is a reasonable solution only if there is some place to run the water to, a lower place away from the house or a storm-drain system. Farm supply houses have a piping called "agricultural tile" that is very good for this purpose. Finally, if it can be determined that the water enters the earth very close to the house, a good solution is to create a "spillway" or "flashing" detail against the wall. This consists of digging down alongside the wall for a foot or so and then down at an angle away from the wall. Then a sheet of waterproof paper like roofing felt is laid in the hole and up along the wall for 8 to 10 inches, as shown in Figure 3-17. This lap is cemented to the wall with a bituminous material like roofing tar (or pitch). Finally, the earth is backfilled over this barrier.

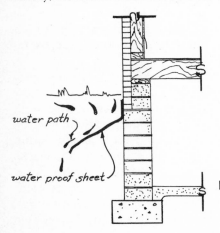

Fig. 3-17 Surface water deflecting sheet.

Fig. 3-18 Spillway at base of wall.

Similar results can be obtained by installing a concrete or brick path around the house that will keep surface water away from the wall. Many people object to this solution because it prevents planting close to the house, yet properly done it can actually be attractive. For example, many homes in colonial times had no gutters and the water ran directly off the roof into a brick spillway. Today in many restored homes and in such places as Colonial Williamsburg this detail is followed with pleasing results, as shown in Figure 3-18.

Every hardware and building supply store has a line of paints that are alternately referred to as "masonry paints," "cement paints," "waterproofing," or "damp-proofing coat." The idea is to paint the inside of a leaking wall and seal it against water intrusion. For modest exterior water pressures this can be a very satisfactory solution, particularly in the case of just a general damp area. An application of such a product must be complete, and it generally involves trying to seal the joint between the wall and basement slab to be effective. The biggest precaution is to prepare the wall exactly as recommended, for sometimes there is no second chance.

The best advice for limiting water intrusion through basement walls is, of course, to do it right originally. For owners of existing houses this is rather a gratuitous observation, but for those people lucky enough to be starting fresh with new-house construction there are several simple rules.

1 Provide a complete exterior waterproof membrane on the exterior of the wall.

2 Grade the surface to direct water flow as far as possible away from walls.

3 Pipe roof drainage to a low area well removed from the house.

4 Allow no debris and rubble to be installed in the backfill.

5 Install exterior foundation drains of a cement or fired-clay material near both the top and bottom of the wall and discharge these drains by gravity flow as far from the house as possible.

6 Install a backfill material that can be consolidated to prevent water intrusion. In some sections of the country this actually may require material to be brought in from off the building site. It would probably be best to check with a local engineer or building department for a description of the best local soil for this purpose.

7 Avoid having large plants and trees close to the foundation walls.

8 Install in the basement floor a drain attached to the sanitary system if local codes permit.

9 Finally, even the most nearly optimum foundation wall may leak once or twice in the life of a building following a record rainfall. On the basis of one incident do not begin a remedial program; rather, wait and see whether the leak is a recurring phenomenon.

Foundation Wall Earth-Settlement Distress

In Chapter 2 the relation between earth movements and building distress was discussed. Perhaps the most common diagnosis of minor cracking in foundation walls is—settlement. Surprisingly, settlement is rarely the cause; moreover, as a general rule, when settlement does occur, the wall distress is gross and *very* apparent. For example, the wall-cracking in Figure 3-19 is a result of settlement. Not only is it extensive, but also the geometry of movement is quite apparent; namely, the soils below the foundation near the end of the wall moved down vertically, and this movement extended for 10 feet or so along the wall. When relatively small cracks, from the so-called hairline size to $\frac{1}{16}$ inch in width occur, the corresponding movements to the wall must be on the same order of magnitude. Earth movements of $\frac{1}{16}$ inch are certainly to be expected, but remember that they must be differential (i.e., changing) to cause cracking, and they must occur relatively quickly. Concrete masonry walls are relatively strong as a beam in the direction of the wall, and, therefore, they can span or bridge minor voids caused by local earth movements. Furthermore, since earth settlement generally is a relatively slow process, the wall can deform plastically.

In Figure 3-19 the way the wall has bridged the void is very apparent—almost as if someone had purposely built an opening (the lower collapsed section) over the earth void. Another example of how settlements, because they are typically slow in development, allow plastic (creep) movement of otherwise brittle masonry can be seen in Figure 3-20. Although this is a brick *garden* wall, it illustrates two phenomena common to masonry wall foundation failure distress. First, note that the bricks in the lower part of the wall have

Fig. 3-19   Cracked wall caused by earth settlement.

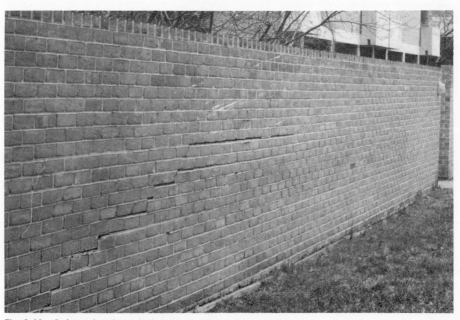

Fig. 3-20   Deformed and cracked wall caused by earth settlement.

deformed 6 inches or more without cracking. Secondly, note the spanning action of the wall above the crack. The explanation of exactly where this horizontal crack will occur is rather complicated and involves such parameters as the time history of the settlement, the relative strength of the masonry and mortar, and the length of the earth settlement. In any event, Figures 3-19 and 3-20 are more typical, both in extent and geometry, of earth settlements than are light vertical cracks along a wall.

Brick-Masonry Foundation Walls

Brick masonry is rarely used today as a foundation wall material. Most examples of such walls, therefore, will be found in dwellings built prior to the 1940s. The high cost of brick masonry is certainly an important factor in the discontinuation of brick as a foundation wall material. Brick has the disadvantage of being not as good an insulator as block; on the other hand, brick masonry can typically sustain much higher loads than the commonly used hollow CMUs.

Deteriorating Brick

Many of the distress patterns that occur in CMU walls also develop in brick foundation walls; however, there are some damage phenomena unique to brick masonry. In older brick-masonry foundation walls, one of the more common types of distress is characterized by flaking or what is sometimes described as "decomposition" of the brick and mortar. Literally, the brick surface sluffs off in the form of a fine dust. At the base of walls where such decomposition exists there is a pile of red dust, and it is not uncommon to be able to rake out with a pencil sections of both brick and mortar several inches deep. The explanation of the exact mechanism that causes this deterioration is, unfortunately, not well documented. The general consensus is that the brick deteriorates as a result of salts and acids in solution in groundwater being drawn up into the masonry by capillary action. One thing is certainly true, and that is that all bricks do not decompose in this fashion. The phenomenon is restricted either to brick that was originally relatively soft or to so-called underfired brick. It is not uncommon to see basement walls several hundred years old with different types of brick of more or less the same age as, for example, in old homes that have extensions built within a few years of the original construction. The decomposition starts and stops abruptly at the lines of changing brick, while all other variables remain the same.

This particular phenomenon should not be confused with another failure mechanism common to soft brick. Often on the exterior of old buildings along the grade line the brick and particularly the mortar is spalled and damaged for the first several feet above grade. This is often a failure mechanism associated with freeze damage to the brick. Water penetrates the surfaces, freezes, and pushes the surface layer off. There are several ways to distinguish this failure from that caused by salt decomposition. Generally the freeze damaged brick surface breaks off in large chunks, ranging up to several square inches in area, whereas the salt-decomposition failure is a flaking of the brick particles into a dust. The surface below the freeze-damaged brick is hard, while in the other case the decomposition continues into the body of the brick. Finally, since the salts are drawn up from the earth, the damage caused by the reaction of the salts with the brick is restricted to several feet above the grade line. Freeze-damaged brick, while particularly common near the base of an exterior wall subject to splashing and poor drainage, also can occur higher up in the wall where the brick is unusually wet. On the interior surface of roof parapet walls or at downspouts that are damaged or regularly overflow, evidence of freeze damage is common.

There is some evidence that the origin of the problem, namely uninterrupted contact with the earth, was identified at least toward the end of the nineteenth century. In brick foundation walls built in this period masons sometimes installed pieces of slate in the mortar joints at several points in the height of the wall (see Figure 3-21). Presumably the slate acted as a barrier to the migration of the salts. This solution seems to have been at least partially successful, for above each layer of slate there is a marked decrease in the extent of deterioration.

The remedies for this problem are somewhat difficult to generalize. Several things, however, seem to be clear and rather absolute about any correction. Any covering or sealant applied to the wall exacerbates the deterioration. A vivid illustration of this situation occurs where a part of an old wall has been

Fig. 3-21 Slate barrier in masonry wall.

plastered or stuccoed. When the covering is removed the wall is significantly more damaged than at the uncovered portion. Apparently the free surface not only allows more drying but also decreases the capillary action whereby the moist solution is drawn up in the wall. Silicone wall sealants and other surfacing compounds that form vapor barriers seem to function much like plaster and therefore should not be applied to walls with this type of damage.

One obvious solution to spalling and flaking brick masonry is to dig out the damaged bricks and replace them with modern bricks and mortar. Earlier in this text the idea of the desirability of uniformity of masonry walls was discussed. Patches and infilling should be made with compatible masonry, that is, with material of similar stiffness. Since the very cause of this deterioration is initially soft brick, and since the decomposition process further softens the brick, comparable masonry certainly does not strengthen the wall. The only solution is to remove and replace relatively extensive panels of the damaged wall, enough so that points of concentrated load do not exist as a result of the variable stiffness of the wall. Certainly, one absolute rule is to never remove just one withe (i.e., one brick width) of brick. Such a repair procedure almost inevitably results in a seriously bowed wall.

Crack Distress in Brick Walls

Although brick masonry expands and shrinks with changes in moisture in the same way as do walls of CMUs, the order of magnitude is far less. Also, the minimum dimension in some brick does not occur at zero moisture but at a modest moisture content. Partially for this reason and partially to allow better mortar-to-brick bonding, bricks are actually moistened before laying.

The coefficient of thermal expansion of brick is almost the same as that of concrete. Since basement walls are fairly uniform in temperature, excessive shrinkage distress in brick-masonry foundation walls is rare.

Given any set of strain patterns from shrinkage, soil pressures (retaining), or settlement, a block wall may crack randomly through the mortar joint, the block, or both, according to the relative strengths of block and mortar. Furthermore, cracks in block walls commonly divide into several paths to pass along successive mortar joints. Thus, a simple wide crack is not as likely to occur as a series of relatively smaller cracks. Somewhat the reverse is true in brick foundation walls. Essentially the wall is more homogeneous, or uniform. Partially owing to the fact that brick walls are at least two bricks wide (i.e., an 8-inch wall) and partially because the mortar path is much more tortuous for a crack to advance in, cracks in brick masonry tend to be single, large cracks and tend to follow the maximum-strain path. For this reason cracks in brick walls often look much more dramatic than comparable cracks from the same cause in block work.

Because brick-masonry walls have very few voids, crack-repair techniques using a pressure-injected cementitious grout are particularly adaptable. This may be impractical, because it involves special equipment that for a small job may be too expensive or unavailable in all parts of the country. One thing is very clear, and that is that if a wall crack *needs* filling to assure structural integrity, then it needs relatively complete filling and not a narrow band of mortar just at the surface of a crack. The problem is, of course, how to work the mortar well into the joint. There is a tendency to add water to the mortar mix and try to make it flow into the crack. This simply will not work, because any tool like a trowel or knife will cut through the soft, liquid mortar and not drive it back into the crack. The answer is to use a very dry mortar mix. Such a mix can be rammed well into the crack with a blunt-edged tool slightly more narrow than the width of the crack. Roughly estimate the volume of the crack and try to ram or "dry-pack," as it is sometimes called, a comparable volume of mortar into the joint.

For some cracks in brick masonry the recommended repair is made with a flexible grout or caulking material. This procedure is applicable when the crack has not jeopardized the structural or water-retention characteristics of the wall and when further movement across the crack is anticipated. For example, a crack that has been demonstrated to cycle with the seasons and that is nearly vertical need not be filled with a rigid grout. Most caulking materials are available in dispensers that allow a modest pressure injection. In using such "caulking guns," however, remember to keep the nozzle small and inserted as deeply as possible into the crack so that a narrow band of caulk is injected.

Concrete Foundation Walls

Even though concrete has been widely used as a wall material in commercial buildings since the turn of the century, it has only been in relatively recent years that large numbers of residential buildings have had concrete basement walls. Without the availability of reusable forms in which to place the concrete, the cost would be prohibitive.

In recent years a variety of so-called patented forms have been available that can be reused for hundreds of walls. While it is possible to insert steel rods into concrete walls and have truly *reinforced concrete walls,* the typical residential concrete wall is, technically speaking, a plain concrete wall even though it may have several horizontal steel bars. Such reinforcing is provided as a sort of "crack stopper," designed to minimize cracks due to shrinkage and temperature dimensional changes.

Concrete foundation walls are obviously an ideal basement wall material from the standpoint of creating a more or less continuous membrane barrier against water intrusion. Properly installed concrete has equal or better strength characteristics than most masonry walls. The biggest single problem with such walls is that the shrinkage process associated with concrete curing must be accommodated. This implies that in a 30-foot wall, up to ¼-inch movement in the length may occur; and without certain precautions, a crack of this magnitude may develop. These precautions are generally beyond the control of a home buyer, because not only do they generally occur before the actual purchase, but even for the owner-builder they require a confrontation with "the concrete worker"—a formidable emotional experience for the average person. Central to the minimization of the crack are precautions taken in the composition and placing of the concrete; the single most important precaution is to make sure that the concrete is not *too wet* (i.e., containing excessive water) when placed.

The most common crack patterns that develop in plain concrete foundation walls are relatively narrow (hairline to $\frac{1}{32}$ inch), nearly vertical cracks. Such cracks often originate at the corners of windows and other openings or near the middle third of a wall. Cracks of this type are most commonly caused by the curing and moisture shrinkage of concrete and will develop between the first several months following construction up to two years. Cracks that develop much after two years are probably due to other causes; that is, they are thermally induced or caused by earth movements.

Most of the techniques applicable to brick can be used in the repair of concrete-wall cracks. If there are a large number of extensive cracks to be filled, the mobilization costs of a professional with pressure-injection equipment can often be tolerated and certainly should be considered.

In addition to various crack patterns that might signal distress in concrete walls is a somewhat more subtle problem. Once in a great while concrete walls are built with inadequate-strength concrete. There are a variety of reasons for this, but the most common is excessive water in the concrete mix. Of course, the problem with a wall of inadequate-strength concrete is that it generally *looks* like any other wall. Perhaps the surface will flake somewhat or the color will be an unusual gray, but more typically there is no visual difference. The simple nail test described in Chapter 1 will give a rough indication of inadequate strength—specifically, a hard nail should be able to be driven into the wall only with considerable difficulty. If a nail goes full depth easily, you probably have a wall with weak concrete.

Just because a concrete wall has lower strength than originally intended does not necessarily mean the strength is inadequate for the particular service application. Absolute strength is not the only important characteristic of concrete in foundation walls. Durability and water retention are equally vital; unfortunately, these characteristics decrease with decreased strength and particularly with decreased strength owing to excessive water in the original liquid concrete mix. If you suspect that you have an understrength concrete basement wall, you should seek the advice of an expert, have the strength tested, and learn the possible consequences. Repairs for such a problem are quite variable and should be predicated on exactly what the strength turns out to be and what the service requirements are.

In Brief

There are other types of foundation wall materials and unique service applications that have not been considered. The most commonly encountered materials and situations have been discussed; nevertheless, the rationale behind potential distress and most repair techniques follows the same lines that have been discussed here. For problems much beyond the scope of this book, professional engineers or architects should be consulted. Remember, however, that the diagnosis, cause, and remedy must make sense. In the extreme, if conflicts do occur, a comparative method of analysis should be turned to; that is, in other walls of similar material, are distress patterns the same, and what have been the consequences of either neglect or repair?

EXTERIOR WALLS

4

In this chapter that part of exterior walls that rests on the foundation walls and extends up to the roofline will be considered. Since windows and doors are in these walls and in a sense form a part of them, they also will be discussed in this chapter. Foundation walls have been defined as walls extending from the foundation to the first-floor level above the exterior grade; thus, a foundation wall also might be included in a definition of exterior walls. There are, however, several important reasons for defining the walls in this way and considering them separately. Not only is there often a material change in the walls at the first-floor level above the exterior grade, but also the walls above and below this point are subject to grossly different environments and service requirements. Thus, a completely different set of distress and deterioration patterns develop that, in turn, dictate different repair methods.

The service requirements of exterior walls in residential buildings include:

• Support for any upper floors and roof
• A weatherproof surface to keep out wind, water, and sun
• Selectively letting in air and light through windows
• Egress through doors
• Providing some of the lateral (i.e., side-to-side) structural stability of the building against side loads, the principal one being wind
• An insulated barrier between the exterior and interior temperature differences
• Longevity with minimum maintenance
• Visually pleasing surface, texture, and composition

Exterior walls in residential buildings can logically be separated into two generic types: one in which the wall is more or less homogeneous and the exterior weatherproof surface is an integral part of the structure, such as in masonry walls; and the other in which the exterior surface is more or less independent of the structure, as in a stud wall system with a lightweight outer sheathing and siding. All the characteristics of walls, including deterioration,

69

TABLE 4-1 Exterior walls

MASONRY
  Solid—Single Material
  • Brick (fired clay)
  • Concrete masonry units (CMUs)
  • Concrete (poured in place)
  • Stone
  • Concrete brick
  Solid Combinations (2 wythes of different materials)
  • Brick + CMU
  • Brick + clay tile
  • Stucco + masonry
  • Concrete face brick + CMU
  • Stone + CMU
  Cavity (2 wythes separated by 2 to 3 inches)
  • Brick + brick
  • Brick + CMU
  • Brick + clay tile
  • Stone + CMU
  • Concrete face brick + CMU
STUD-FRAMED WALL CONSTRUCTION
  Stud Type
  • Wood
  • Aluminum
  • Steel
  Sheathing Types
  • Wood plank
  • Plywood
  • Wood-fiber composition board
  • Gypsum plaster board
  • Foam plastic board
  • Stucco on expanded metal lathe
  Siding Types
  • Wood plank
  • Plywood
  • Shingles
    -Asbestos cement
    -Wood
  • Stucco
  • Brick
  • Aluminum- plank
              - sheet
  • Wood-fiber composition board
  • Plastics
  Miscellaneous Exterior–Wall Materials
  • Logs
  • Half timber—wood timber with stucco fill-in
  • Metal panel
  • Precast concrete panels

differ between these two types; thus, the first step in evaluating the significance of any distress is to distinguish between these generic types.

The cutaway view shown on the endpapers will help the reader to understand some construction details. Any homeowner who thinks he or she may have a problem and yet is not overly familiar with how walls are constructed might visit a construction site where houses comparable to the homeowner's are being built.

The list in Table 4-1 gives most types of exterior walls and materials that are likely to be encountered. At first it seems surprising that there are so many combinations, and it may seem valid to ask about how successful these various materials have proven to be. For example, considering the differences in characteristics between lightweight aluminum siding applied in bands 8 to 10 inches high and a continuous cement stucco surface applied to heavy plywood, two inescapable questions are legitimate: first, why so many combinations; and second, do they all work equally as well? The answers to these questions are worth considering in that they have important ramifications for various distress patterns.

The principal judgments for determining exterior wall surface materials most often seem to be based on cost, availability of materials, labor skills, and appearance. It is obvious that several important service requirements of exterior walls are neglected when the above factors are the chief elements in the selection process. Where structural requirements are neglected, problems generally develop fairly quickly, and either the deficiency is corrected or the use of the material is abandoned. For example, in Chapter 3 cinder block was discussed as a foundation wall material. At first it was thought that cinder block would be an adequate exterior wall material. When the iron particles in the block rusted, expanded, and literally blew out chunks of the wall, however, it was apparent that an error had been made, and the use of this material in exterior walls was soon abandoned. Unfortunately, things are not always this simple, because it often takes years to discover that a building wall material is inadequate, and by then there may be thousands of homes built with a generic defect.

Some of the errors made in selecting wall materials involve a certain lack of appreciation of the effects of the environment to which the walls are subjected.

Exterior Wall Environmental Factors

Thermal effects, moisture, and load are the principal environmental factors that affect the serviceability of an exterior wall. With the exceptions of insect infestation in wooden walls and settlement-induced damage, almost all of the commonly encountered distress patterns can be associated with one or more of these factors.

While it is not necessary to understand all the details of these environmental factors, a modest understanding of the basic mechanisms will help in analyzing the cause of certain distress patterns as well as what remedies are most appropriate.

Thermal Effects

Heat is transferred in one of three ways: by "conduction" heat passes through a solid material; by "convection" heat is transferred or moved in a moving fluid; by "radiation" it is transmitted from one body to another in the form of electromagnetic waves. In each case a temperature difference must exist to allow the transfer of heat; furthermore, the amount of heat-energy transfer depends on these temperature differences and various physical properties of the materials involved. Heat can be stored in any material—the amount varies according to certain physical properties. Finally, heat takes time to be transferred.

With these ideas in mind consider the heat-transfer process through the wall of a house in winter. The inside wall surface receives heat by convection as the interior air currents flow past the wall. Thus, the interior wall surface will reach a temperature only a few degrees less than the room air temperature, say, 63°F (13°C) for an average house warmed to 68°F (20°C). Next, the heat is conducted through the wall, and the amount that is allowed to pass is a function of the "resistance" (the "R value" quoted for commercial home insulation). The greater the resistance (R value), the less heat passes through the wall. As the heat passes through the wall a temperature drop occurs, with the final exterior surface temperature a few degrees above the outside air temperature. Finally, the heat is carried away into the outside air by convection currents—the stronger the wind, the more exterior convection and the more heat loss to the outside air. Thus, on a cold, windy day your furnace will run much longer than on a still-air day of the same temperature.

When the sun strikes an exterior wall, it warms the surface and effectively pumps heat back into the house. Another way to think about it is to say that the sun helps by allowing less heat to escape through the outside wall.

So far, the heat-transfer mechanism has been described on the premise that any temperature changes have occurred relatively slowly. If any abrupt changes occur, for example, if the sun comes out from behind a cloud or the wind abruptly changes speed or direction, it will take some time for the wall to be affected and reach a condition of unchanging temperatures or "steady-state" condition. One important factor that governs the time it takes to reach a condition of equilibrium is the heat-storage capacity of the wall. This characteristic is sometimes referred to as the "thermal mass" of the wall, because a rough analogy can be made between (1) the heat-storage characteristics of a material related to heat-transfer durations and (2) the mass of a material as it relates to movements (i.e., the inertia principle). In general, heavier, more-dense materials can store more heat. A thick-walled, heavy cooking pot stays warm much longer than a lightweight, thin-walled pot, and intuitively we attribute this difference to the fact that the heavy pot can store more heat.

In a residential building, therefore, thin, lightweight walls will change temperature much more quickly than heavier ones. Extremely heavy masonry walls will store so much heat and allow such a slow transfer of heat that the heat absorbed during the day can actually be used to heat a house at night. This principle is being adapted in some modern residences in the form of so-called passive systems to bring about fuel savings. Conversely, houses in the hot Southwest desert areas for centuries have used heavy masonry walls to store the cool night air, or more accurately, to dissipate the heat stored during the day in the cooler nights.

The material characteristics that most affect solar-radiation heat transfer are certain surface properties related to the color and surface texture of a material. Everyone is familiar with how much hotter a black car gets than a white one. The same phenomenon occurs in houses where a light-colored house will reflect the sunlight while a darker house will absorb more heat energy. Do not rush out and paint your house black, hoping to save energy next winter. On the other hand, when you are contemplating new wall (and roof) colors, it is reasonable to at least consider the solar-radiation effects, particularly on a sunny wall (one facing south).

The effects of the thermal environment on a residential building wall are varied and have a great deal to do with the success or failure of a particular wall material. Obviously, a desirable exterior wall or method of construction is one with a high resistance to heat flow. As the resistance increases, the temperature differences between the inner and outer surfaces increase. Now, when any homogeneous or composite material has a temperature change through its thickness, it will tend to bow or warp as the hotter side expands and the cooler side contracts. Thus, the exterior walls of a house tend to bow

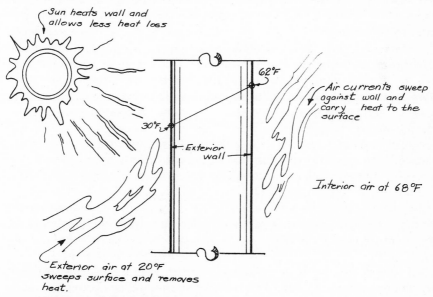

Fig. 4-1 Heat transfer through a house wall.

inward in the winter and outward in the summer. Considering that the temperature differences can be as much as 70°F (21°C) across the wall thickness in both summer and winter extremes, the bow could theoretically amount to ³⁄₈ inch or more for some material combinations. Do walls bow this much? The answer is generally no, because either the materials or their attachments are flexible and effectively allow the differential dimensions to exist without bowing. This is one of the many reasons that wood-plank siding is an assembly of individual boards lapped over one another. They can thus expand and contract relatively freely. Once in a while a builder overlooks this phenomenon and applies wood tightly butt-jointed. The results are disastrous. If the attachments are strong enough, the overall wall can actually bow; otherwise, the nails fail and the individual planks pop out of the stud supports.

Recall that this phenomenon is worsened as the temperature difference increases. In many old homes there was little or no insulation other than what would be provided by the wood siding. The temperature difference through the thickness of the wall, therefore, was not as great as in contemporary houses, and the tendency to bow was relatively slight. In the construction of Mount Vernon, for example, George Washington applied flush wood siding and stuccoed the exterior to simulate a stone surface. It certainly worked, but mostly because the walls were uninsulated and the nails allowed some movement between the siding and the studs.

This tendency to bow would suggest that in one way or another a wall-siding material should have some flexibility. There is another incentive for this that is associated with the heat-storage capabilities of a wall. Thin, lightweight walls that have very little heat-storage capacity will tend to heat up (or cool down) very quickly. For example, when the sun comes from behind a dark cloud and strikes the surface of a darkly colored, aluminum-sided house, the surface temperature can easily jump by 50 to 60°F (10 to 15°C) in a few minutes. Naturally, the interior of the wall cannot respond this quickly, and therefore it must accommodate rather gross differential movements. Fortunately, manufacturers of aluminum siding have recognized this problem and in the lap system and attachment fittings, provided for sufficient "play" to allow movement. Even so, many aluminum-sided houses make some popping noises and creaking sounds as the walls move to accommodate temperature changes.

A logical observation is that a masonry wall is certainly not very flexible and therefore may suffer from adverse effects of differential thermal movements. The fact is that many of the problems encountered in masonry walls, particularly older, solid walls, can be attributed to just this phenomenon. The saving grace with most masonry walls is that because of their mass and thermal properties, they tend to change temperature relatively slowly. Furthermore, as building materials go, masonry is a relatively poor insulator and therefore the temperature gradients are less likely to be as great as in modern, well-insulated, composite walls. Many modern masonry walls have cavities between layers or withes, and although with this system the wall is a better insulator, thus allowing larger temperature differences between the inner and outer surfaces to exist, it is relatively more flexible. This type of masonry wall, therefore, may well survive better than some other types of solid masonry.

Historically, new wall materials have been introduced, tried, and found wanting. One of the common reasons for this lack of success has been the inability of these new materials to withstand the thermal environment. From the preceding discussion, several basic rules governing the construction of successful wall combinations based on thermal properties can be derived. Roughly, the rules can be stated as follows: (1) If the wall materials are lightweight, with surfaces of relatively conductive materials, then it should be regularly "jointed" or utilized in relatively small, discontinuous pieces. The attachments should allow movement. Finally, such a material system is not very conducive to being part of the primary wall structure, and some other segment of the wall must provide the structure. (2) If the exterior surface of the wall is to be more or less continuous, and particularly if it is to be an active part of the structure, then it should be a relatively heavy material that can provide good "capacitance" against sudden temperature changes, and in general it should have intermediate values of thermal resistance.

Over the years, there have been several interesting violations of these rules—interesting in the sense of the type of distress that has developed. By analogy the understanding of these errors may either help in the diagnosis of other kinds of distress or, more profitably, dictate more prudent repair methods.

In the early 1950s the cost of stone and marble had increased so much that it was rarely used on houses. Partially as a cost-reduction technique and partially because new adhesives allowed seemingly satisfactory attachment details, very thin marble fascia paneling was produced. Buildings were clad with this material by means of relatively loose fittings. For several years all went well, but gradually the panels began to bow and warp. Coupled with this, the mastics began to fail. Needless to say, the results were disastrous. The long-term effects of some epoxy cements in contact with marble and stone have only recently become recognized. It has taken literally twenty to thirty years to learn that with time, the cements deteriorate from chemical reactions with the stones.

Almost simultaneous with these "experiments" in surface materials was the introduction of relatively large panels of factory precast concrete for exterior wall coverings. Because of relatively high cost this was never a particularly common residential wall material; nevertheless, it is interesting to know that there were several cases of wall panels being built with thin marble exterior surfaces. These worked and continue to work because the backing concrete provided the added mass to minimize thermal bowing and the bond between the concrete and stone was one that did not fail with time.

In addition to the problems that developed with thin stone surface materials, there are analogous problems with similar materials. For example, many houses built in the first half of the twentieth century had wood-stud exterior walls covered with stucco. Such walls worked relatively well in a variety of different climates, and while there are typical crack patterns common to "stucco-over-frame" houses, these houses have survived and offer few surprising developments. In many sections of the country this type of construction has lost popularity. It is more expensive than some of the other wall-clading materials, and it does not seem to fit some of the more popular styles. In areas where stucco has remained popular it is often applied over concrete masonry.

The original stucco-on-frame details were quite standard. Diagonal wood siding, ¾ inch thick, was nailed to the stud. Over this, heavy roofing (felt) paper provided a relatively secure moisture barrier. Next, expanded metal "wire" was nailed down and the first coat of stucco was applied. Within hours of application of the first coat, a second coat was added to bring the total thickness of the stucco to roughly ¾ inch. If all went well, the rest of the house was then completed, and the maximum delay period between the application of the second coat and the final, finish coat was allowed. The intent was to let the wood dry, shrink, and move as much as possible before the final coat was applied. The final coat was applied with a variety of finishes, and in these finishes the art of stucco appears. There is, of course, the most common smooth "sand" finish that is applied with a trowel and then "floated" with a wood board to achieve the sand texture. Also, there are various "struck" finishes, with a sort of roughly contoured surface with patches of smooth surfaces where the stucco has been struck with a steel-finish trowel. One of the most fascinating stucco finishes is the one that old-time craftspeople call "dribble" or perhaps "dabble" [sic] stucco. The surface is rough and gives the appearance of being a stucco with small pebbles embedded. Actually, these "pebbles" are runs and drips of an almost pure cement wash or slurry that has been flipped or dribbled on the surface with a small broom. In the Middle East, finish stucco of this type is applied with a little hand-operated dispensing machine that flips the cement slurry on the surface.

In the early 1970s, interest in stucco-on-frame construction revived. Many houses were built this way, and the stucco surface was sound and durable. Unfortunately, this construction caused problems in a significant number of houses, so much so that they were eventually reclad in other materials such as aluminum siding. What went wrong? So far as the installers were concerned, most of the details were the same, with the possible exception that the wood sheathing was of plywood rather than diagonal planks. Two other things changed, however. First, few builders either knew of or could afford the long wait during which the wood stabilized dimensionally. Second, and probably far more important, stud walls were packed with insulation. The stucco-on-wood had less mass, for often it was only a two-coat application, and the plywood was only ½ inch thick or even less. With the added insulation, the overall wall temperature gradient was grossly more, and the insulation literally isolated the outer surface from the inner and worsened the thermal-shock effects. The results were predictable. The overall wall moved owing to thermal changes and the stucco surface spalled off. The rules of a continuous, relatively stiff surface, thermally isolated without adequate mass, were violated.

There are many other examples of exterior-wall experiments which, largely owing to the effects of the thermal environment, have proven to be unsatisfactory. Various panelized metal houses, including those of steel and copper, have been tried. Many times economic factors prevent the wide acceptance of these "system" house walls, but surprisingly often it is their inability to meet the thermal service requirements that foretells their doom.

Moisture Effects

Obviously, the exterior wall of a house can be wet by rain and snow. There is another source of water that in many respects can be more troublesome and eventually cause more wall distress. This is the water that is literally pumped through the walls as a consequence of the "water-vapor pressure" difference between inside and outside. Most people are generally familiar with the idea of relative humidity. Specifically, air at any given temperature can allow a certain amount of water to be mixed or dispersed in the air. The air can hold only so much water vapor, and if more is supplied than the air can hold, it simply precipitates or rains out. The relative humidity is a statement of what percentage of the maximum allowable water exists in the air at any given time. Now, corresponding to any given temperature and quantity of water, there is a certain pressure of the water vapor. If a different *vapor pressure* exists between the outside and the inside of a wall, then the water vapor is pushed through the wall in an attempt to equalize the pressure. While the differences in vapor pressure are extremely small with respect to, say, the hydrostatic water pressure that could build up against a basement wall, time is on the side of water movement due to differential vapor pressure. Thus, even though the pressure differences are small, they may exist for days at a time or long enough to allow the migration of water. An analogy might be helpful in understanding this phenomenon. If a large, shallow cookie sheet were filled with water, there would be a pressure difference across the bottom, that is, between the bottom of the water and the outside bottom of the sheet. Of course, the pressure is a result of the weight of the water. If a hole were drilled in the bottom of the cookie sheet, the pressure would force the water out through the hole. As the hole got smaller the water would continue to flow out—it just would take longer. The holes in the wall of a house are small, but on the days that the pressure difference exists, water can still run through.

There are a myriad of consequences to water vapor passing through a wall. Perhaps the most severe result is that the vapor will condense partway in its passage through a wall. Just as water vapor condenses on a glass of ice water, water vapor within a wall may condense if the air and wall temperatures fall below a certain value called the "dew point." Generally speaking, the most severe vapor-pressure differences exist during the winter months, and the moisture movement is from inside to outside the house. An easy way to remember this is that the water flow is *from* the hot side *toward* the cold side. In the summer, under certain conditions, there are exceptions to this rule, but in any case the results are rarely as significant, and it is invariably the wintertime conditions that are most troublesome and cause the greatest damage.

There are more or less two choices to prevent condensation in the middle of a wall. One option is to provide an impervious barrier at or near the inside surface. Metal and some of the dense, hard plastics are really impervious to water flow; however, some of the softer plastics and even a few paints provide reasonably good resistance to moisture migration. Unfortunately, just as in the analogy of the water on the cookie sheet, one hole, no matter how small, will still allow the movement of water, given enough time. Thus, barriers such as the aluminum surface on fiberglass insulation should be carefully taped at all joints and breaks.

The second alternative to avoid condensation in the middle of a wall is hardly admissible in terms of modern ideas about energy conservation. It involves having an extremely poorly insulated wall plus a well-ventilated wall. For a number of years this approach was the norm for residential framed wall construction, that is, to not insulate and to leave the stud space open so that air could circulate between the inside and outside wall surfaces. The idea was rather crude, but reasonably effective insofar as moisture buildup in a wall was concerned. With an uninsulated wall, the temperature difference through the wall is slight. If the dew point occurred within the wall, it would at least be near or in the surface materials, and the interior air circulation could carry off any excess moisture.

As walls become more insulated and exterior surfaces become better sealed against air leakage, the problems of vapor condensation become more severe. In some experimental homes so much water has vaporized within the wall that water literally runs out through the floor.

The general classes of distress that can be attributed to the moisture environment of an exterior wall are relatively obvious and include the following: paint deterioration, rust, rot, expansion and contraction of wood, decrease in insulating characteristics, and mildew. Another important distress phenomenon due to moisture is the damage to exterior surfaces that are subjected to freezing temperatures. No damage will occur to a dry brick wall as it falls below freezing; however, if the brick is wet, particularly near the surface, the surface can literally be blown off if the moisture in the brick freezes and expands. Analogous damage can occur even in wood, in which case paint can be made to spall off the surface during freezing. Included in the effects of the moisture environment, therefore, are the effects of freezing.

Load Environment

The exterior wall load environment can be divided practically into the vertical loads that include the live (people) and dead (material) weights of everything supported above; and the lateral or horizontal loads including primarily wind but also earthquake and some live, or people-induced, lateral loads.

In typical residences, the total *uniformly* distributed vertical loads range from a few hundred pounds per (linear) foot of wall to extremes of a few thousand pounds for heavy walls that support several floors and a roof. Except in very unusual cases, these loads are really not particularly large in terms of conventional building materials and details, and thus have little significance in relation to building distress. More significant than uniformly distributed loads are concentrated or point loads that occur in load-carrying walls. For example, adjacent to any discontinuity in the wall such as a window, door, or abrupt change in direction, concentrated loads will occur. If a relatively average, uniform load of 2,000 pounds per foot exists above a wide window or door, say, 6 feet wide, then two concentrated forces of $\frac{1}{2}(6) \times 2000 = 6000$ pounds will occur at both ends of the opening. Forces of this magnitude can be significant, if not in terms of producing distress, then at least in relation to repair procedures.

In most areas of the country codes and common practice require that exterior wall surfaces be capable of withstanding horizontal wind forces of 15 to 20 pounds per square foot. Again, these are not abnormally high loads in terms of what can easily be carried in conventional wall construction. While code requirements are somewhat variable, these lateral-load requirements must be carried in both the inner and outer direction. This is a recognition that wind pressures can create suctions as well as positive or "external push" on walls. Not all walls meet these requirements, and the consequences of this may be evidenced in a variety of distress patterns.

Exterior Wall Distress Patterns

The most practical way to classify exterior wall damage and deterioration is to consider individually the two most common generic wall types, masonry and framed. Not only are the classes of distress patterns totally different, but remedial procedures are applicable to only one or the other of these wall types. There is one hybrid—a combination of both—that has become extremely common in the last forty to fifty years, and that is the brick-veneer, wood-stud construction. Because of the frequency of this type wall, it will be considered as a separate type.

Framed Walls

Structural Stud System The exact details of construction of the standard stud system for a framed wall may vary slightly among different regions and different carpenters. The general arrangement of the studs is shown in the cutaway sketch of Figure 4-2. Studs, until recent years, have been wood framing lumber, generally 2 × 4s and occasionally 2 × 6s. At various times in the past twenty-five years metal studs, prefabricated from galvanized sheet steel or aluminum, have been used with almost exactly the same detailing as wood studs. Rather than attach the various parts with nails, carpenters use either rivets or screws. There are several advantages to metal studding; however, its higher cost has most often restricted its use to extremely repetitive mass construction where the studs can be precut and at least part of the wall preassembled. Fewer carpenters are familiar with metal studs, and they tend to be relatively more difficult to cut and specially adjust for the numerous variations and special cases that inevitably occur in residential construction.

The standard and certainly the most common stud is the 2×4—framing lumber that measures $1\frac{1}{2}$ inches $\times$ $3\frac{1}{2}$ inches. The discrepancy between the name and the actual dimension is not an advertising gimmick meant to deceive anyone. The 2×4 designation was originally the dimension of the "green" lumber (i.e., newly cut and wet) in the rough-sawed condition before its final dressing or milling to a smooth finish. Many old houses often have larger studs, because lumber standards have varied slightly over the years and because studs were very often not dressed. Once in a while an owner will discover rough-sawed lumber and in a fit of nostalgia conclude that it is superior to modern, dressed (mill-finished) lumber. Actually, the reverse is true. The problem is associated with the way lumber is "graded," or rated. This rating process is primarily a visual inspection to determine grain geometry, knot frequency, and any other irregularities. In rough-sawed lumber the surface is obscured, with the result that knots, checks, and defects cannot be easily detected and certainly cannot be graded by modern criteria. Another problem with undressed lumber is that with a rough, spiny sort of surface, it can be ignited much more easily than can modern, fully dressed lumber with its smooth, continuous surface. This is rarely an important consideration, but in the case of exposed framing it may be important.

Stud walls, being wood, are subject to insect infestation and rot or decay. The factors that govern the various decay mechanisms are complicated and not always understood. A homeowner has very little control over many of the factors, for they include such things as the manner of felling and seasoning the wood, and some of the growing conditions. For example, the season when

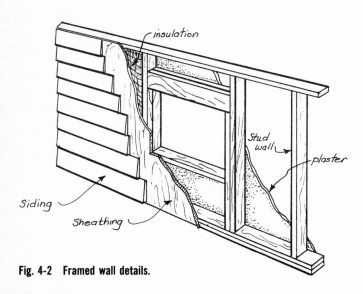

Fig. 4-2 Framed wall details.

the tree was originally felled is important because at certain times of the year, principally spring and late summer, the sapwoods contain an abundance of moisture. This moisture contains excessive starches and sugar compounds that eventually hasten the decay process. For practical purposes the three conditions most likely to encourage the decay process are moisture, lack of ventilation, and moderate warmth. The terms *dry rot* and *wet rot* are often used to differentiate between two different decay processes. These are actually very precise terms, but are often very imprecisely used. "Dry rot" refers to a fermentation and breaking down of the chemical compounds of wood when a certain fungus exists in the presence of moderate moisture. Literally, the organism's excretion dissolves part of the cell structure and the wood powders or crumbles. The process requires some moisture, but probably the reason for the name is more related to the results than the cause. Dry-rotted lumber when touched will crumble away in a powdery dust—it appears dry— and hence the name. The growth of the fungus is stimulated by moderate temperatures in the 90 to 120°F range, some moisture, and lack of ventilation. This requirement of lack of ventilation can be both the clue to where dry rot may exist and a means of slowing or reducing the continuation of the process. Dry rot is relatively more common in floor- and roof-framing members than in walls, because in the older walls with little if any insulation in the space between the inner and outer surfaces, air can circulate relatively freely, thus providing the necessary ventilation. In addition, the nature of wood sheathing and siding generally allows some air leakage—a situation not conducive to energy conservation, but certainly a dry-rot inhibitor. The dry-rot phenomenon is one of the several reasons why old houses should be insulated and re-sided with extreme caution. Both operations tend to restrict air flow and generally increase the moisture and temperature of the wall—all the necessary ingredients for dry rot.

The complete decomposition of wood is, of course, the final result of dry rot, and at this stage the damage has been done and the only recourse is to replace the wood *in toto*. Wood in the process of dry-rot decay is often indicated by a swelling of the lumber, or perhaps a more apt description would be a "puffiness." Often the color changes to a reddish one, although interior dry rot may not affect the surface. If the suspect area can be inspected without disturbing the air, a musty odor can sometimes be detected around dry-rotted lumber, although small, confined sections of decay will simply not emit enough odor to be noticeable.

Dry rot, when once established, is difficult to eradicate. There are chemical poisons available that will disinfect the wood, provided it actually contacts the distressed particles. Since dry rot often exists well within the interior of a heavy piece of timber, it is difficult to develop the required contact without some individual-timber-injection process. The only absolute remedy is to simply remove the decayed wood.

It is difficult to predict the rate of advancement of dry rot, but before undertaking any major rehabilitation of a dry-rotted stud wall, some modest monitoring should be done to determine the rate of progression. In some cases, the fungus has been introduced early in the life of the building, perhaps from unseasoned or untreated wood, and the damage is confined and advancing at an extremely slow rate. The one treatment for dry rot that should absolutely *never* be allowed is to paint or tar the surface. This will seal in the organisms and almost guarantee a rapid advancement of the decay.

"Wet rot" is a process initiated by organisms in the wood that act like catalysts for producing chemicals which, in the presence of moisture, dissolve out the cell walls of sapwood and cause the decay of lumber. A yellowish color generally accompanies wet rot, and the amount of water required for continuation of the process generally is enough to actually keep the lumber damp. At the base of studs where water continually runs down from a leak, the wood is apt to be wet-rotted. The wood eventually becomes spongy and appears to be actually dissolving.

Recall that well-seasoned wood, properly treated to poison bacteria and in a uniform state of either moisture or dryness, should never decay. Timbers kept constantly immersed may weaken but will not decay. All over Western Europe modern construction-project crews are forever encountering timber piles that were installed by Roman military engineers. Many buildings on the Continent and in England are built on foundations of Roman buildings— buildings that were founded on timber piles. The point is that moisture alone is not to blame, but the combination of moisture, lack of ventilation, and moderate temperatures will almost invariably allow rot to develop.

There are a number of worms, beetles, bees, and of course the ever-present termites that attack wood. Some actually eat the wood, some only bore into it to create a living and nesting space, while others secrete chemicals that react with the wood structure. The details of the habits of the various insects, how they attack wood, the types of damage they do, and finally the methods of treatment are extensive and involved. If insects of any sort exist in or near wood, a qualified exterminator should be consulted. Often the extent and cost of treatment seems disproportionate to the distress, but the argument goes that the progress of insect distress is unpredictable and the ultimate consequences ruinous. While this is certainly true, it is not a justification for pumping a house and the surrounding yard full of poisons and making it a wasteland for every type of insect. Everyone has come to realize that there is some equitable balance and that some insects are beneficial. If all the spiders in and around a house are killed, the number of "nuisance" bugs will increase dramatically.

University extension and farm bureau services are relatively accessible in most communities. Both these groups have good information on harmful insects, and in many cases they can be consulted about the specifics of insect damage in residential buildings. They can thus provide a useful means of confirming the diagnosis and treatment recommended by exterminators.

Load Environment   The other major distress condition that develops in exterior stud walls is a result of the load environment. Repeatedly the desirability of uniformity in material properties, environmental factors, and structural geometry has been emphasized. The geometric discontinuity in stud walls occurs at windows and doors, and it is precisely in the structure around these openings that structural damage, if it develops, will first occur. To appreciate some of the problems, the details of the framing at an opening, and particularly at the lintel (or structural top support) must be reviewed (see Figure 4-2). Some of the information from Chapter 1 concerning wood properties must also be reexamined. Recall that wood properties, in this particular case strength and expansion characteristics, are largely dependent on the orientation of the wood grain. Wood is one-fourth to one-third weaker in compression in the direction perpendicular to the grain, that is, across the grain in the normal timber plank, than in the length direction, that is, in the direction parallel to the grain. Also, wood shrinks and expands owing to temperature and moisture changes, and here again the properties vary with the direction of the grain. Owing to moisture changes wood will shrink one-tenth to one-twentieth as much in the length direction as in the width direction, that is, parallel and perpendicular to the grain, respectively. Now consider the details of framing of lintels above openings in stud walls.

Obviously, at the ends of the lintel, loads (reactions) are concentrated and almost inevitably are higher than elsewhere in a continuous line of uniformly spaced and loaded studs. The conventional means of support for the lintel is a stud (often called a "jack stud") inserted directly below the bearing ends. As the width of the opening increases and the loads correspondingly become greater, additional jack studs can be added to carry the added load. Unfortunately, this is an often overlooked addition. The result is that a "bearing failure" occurs in the timber lintel. This is a crushing of the grain accompanied by a downward movement of the lintel. Such an overstressed condition rarely if ever leads to a collapse type of failure, for apparently the load-carrying capacity of the wood increases as the wood compresses and densifies. Furthermore, the movements are generally restricted to ⅛ to ¼ inch, an amount that often is accommodated in relatively minor cracking and joint separation.

The most common distress patterns that develop as a result of lintel end-bearing-crushing is interior plaster cracking or various joint separations at

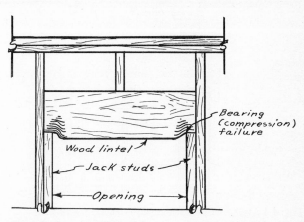

Fig. 4-3 Door lintel failed in compression at bearing ends.

the exterior woodwork around the windows. None of this is particularly serious, and in the majority of situations in which the crushing and deflection are one-time occurrences, conventional patching techniques should be adequate.

A far more frustrating distortion problem that because of its cyclic nature makes repairs complicated, can develop at wood lintels. All wood in a house varies in moisture content throughout the year. In many exterior walls, particularly well-insulated ones, the changes in moisture content of wood within the wall are apt to cause dimensional changes of 3 and 4 percent in the course of a year. For a typical 8-inch-deep lintel, this can amount to more than ¼ inch change in dimension. A very characteristic crack develops above windows and doors as a result of this movement, a crack pattern that actually silhouettes the lintel and often continues irregularly to the ceiling, as illustrated in Figure 4-4. Since the movement is cyclic, any patching is particularly difficult.

One of the remarkable things about this particular crack mechanism is its variability. In row houses that have been built simultaneously of essentially the same materials by the same craftspeople, some houses develop this crack pattern in *every* window, others have such cracks only on one wall, while still others have totally uncracked walls. The differences are, of course, due to slight, subtle variations in construction sequence that allow one house to dry out slightly more than another before the interior plaster wall finish has been installed. In addition, some occupants generate more moisture that continually gets transmitted to the lintels. As explained earlier, higher interior temperatures create high vapor pressures. Some people actively supply additional moisture to the interior air by means of humidification, while others do it inadvertently by different cooking and bathing habits. For example, in raising the temperature from 65 to 85°F (18 to 30°C), the practical extremes of typical interior winter temperatures, the interior vapor pressure doubles while the pressure difference across the wall, the critical factor for vapor migration, may actually increase by a factor of 4. Such vapor-pressure dif-

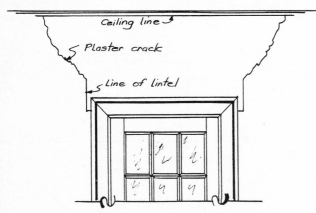

Fig. 4-4   Typical lintel crack in plaster above window.

ferences correspond roughly to moisture accumulations on the same order of magnitude that, in turn, allow wood expansions several times greater in one house than in another.

Stud Wall Surface Materials Deterioration

As Table 4-1 indicates, there are a considerable number of different types of stud wall exterior surface materials. Some have been tried, almost immediately found to be wanting in some way, and abandoned; while others have been used off and on over a number of years. With the exception of brick in the "brick-veneer" system, the four most common siding materials in use in recent years have been wood, aluminum, stucco, and shingles. The brick-veneer wall will be considered separately as almost another generic type of exterior wall. The reason for this distinction is owing in part to how the walls are put together and in part to a structural consideration. Typically, the four siding materials listed above are attached to a wall-sheathing material that in turn is secured to the stud system. This sheathing is a more or less continuous cover on the studs and ideally constitutes the structure of the wall between the studs. For example, up until the mid-1940s, when plywood became a more common residential building material, most houses were sheathed in 1 inch × 6 inch planks applied on the diagonal to the studs. In recent years, sheathing has been plywood or various types of "composition board," that is, panels fabricated from wood chips and cellulose fibers. Thus, the individual elements of an exterior stud wall, specifically the exterior siding (or surface), the sheathing, and the studs, are built together to form a sort of composite structure. On the other hand, brick on a veneered stud wall is only lightly attached to the sheathing at discrete points with small metal clips. The brick exterior surface is very much independent of the stud wall, it can move relatively freely of the stud wall, and the distress patterns that commonly develop are rarely interrelated. That is, the exterior distress tends to be similar to that encountered in masonry, while the interior distress is more typical of stud-wall problems.

Each of the siding materials has its own advantages and disadvantages. Each type ages differently and is subject to uniquely different distress characteristics. These variations in properties can be characterized as follows:

Wood siding is relatively less used today than in the past. The reason, as is so often the case in building-material selection, is economic. The basic raw costs are high, and maintenance is a constant, costly requirement. Nevertheless, if a value judgment had to be made of the relative worth of wood siding versus other materials, wood would still rate very high. The desirability of wood is very much a function of its versatility. It has almost endless aesthetic adaptations, it has many structural advantages, it is the best insulator among the common siding materials, it certainly is a proven material with few surprise characteristics, and finally, repairs and restoration can be almost undetectable.

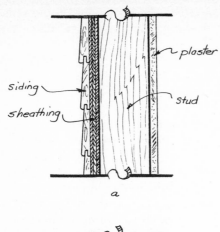

a

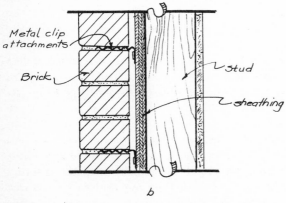

b

Fig. 4-5 (a) Wood-sided stud wall. (b) Brick-veneer wall.

Wood is used as a siding material in three very different ways. The oldest and, until recently, the most common wood-siding method consists of horizontally applied, relatively narrow planks or simply "horizontal siding." The planks range from ⅝ to 1 inch thick, while the widths vary from as little as 2 to 10 or 12 inches. Since most often the planks are overlapping along the lower edge, "lapped siding" provides a good weather seal and allows for the inevitable movement of the wood. There are dozens of ways that the upper and lower plank edges are grooved to fit together, and hundreds of surface contours produce varying patterns. As so often happens with differing building details, every siding shape has been given a name. Since the concept of siding on a house is essentially the same as that of the planking on a ship, we have "shiplapped" siding, which is perhaps the most common. In addition, commonly encountered siding types are German, Boston, beveled, channel, rustic—it would seem that every mill a hundred years ago developed its own siding pattern and gave it a name. "Clapboard" seems to be a generic name used by many to describe all horizontal wood siding and by others to specify the simplest form of tapered siding that overlaps lower boards, without any milled groove along the lower edge. One of the extremely important criteria for the siding contour is how the water runs off, and particularly how water runs off the bottom edge. If the shape is wrong, water will travel back to the joint and create a permanent damp spot at a particularly vulnerable location—that is, on the underside, which is already sheltered from the drying effect of the sun, where there is less air circulation, and hence, where a potential location for dry rot exists. It is for this reason that very rarely did anyone attempt to install a flush surface, horizontal siding. Certainly there are relatively few old examples, because the inherent decay problem was soon evident, and because the repair method was simply to re-side completely with one of the more standard siding patterns.

Another of the common wood-siding methods is "vertical siding," which consists of individual planks running vertically. Vertical siding can be "tongue-and-groove" or shiplap, similar to horizontal siding but with a flush surface (i.e., without a drip, which, of course, is unnecessary). Some space must be left between the joints to allow for the inevitable movement of planks. Obviously, the vertical siding joint is less well protected against water intrusion, and often an additional wood strip or "batten" is added to protect the joint. In less sophisticated siding the joints are simply butted and the batten is added to create what is commonly known as "board-and-batten" siding.

One of the common complaints about vertical siding is that heavy concentrations of paint often get into the joints and simply jam the joints, thus preventing movement. It is probably for this reason that vertical siding is often left unpainted. Another fairly common problem with vertical siding occurs when it is assembled too tightly without the space necessary to move. In extreme cases, the siding will expand, close all the joints, and simply buckle off the building. Of course, the problem is quickly identified, and it is to be hoped that ample space is left between joints during the reinstallation.

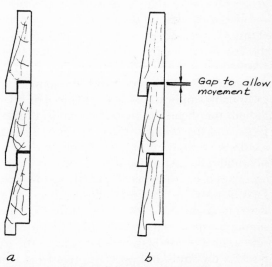

Gap to allow movement

a   b

Fig. 4-6   Sections cut through horizontal siding.

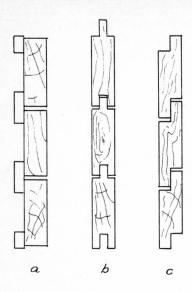

Fig. 4-7 Vertical wood
siding patterns.
(*a*) Board-and-batten.
(*b*) Tongue-and-groove.
(*c*) Shiplap.

a   *b*   *c*

Since the mid-1950s various wood-panel products have been available for use as exterior siding, notably plywood, which is generally patterned or scored to provide an attractive surface. Since these panels are 8 to 12 feet high, the butt-joint detail can often be made at each floor level where the weather protection method can be hidden or at least worked into the building aesthetics. The protection of this butt joint is perhaps the most serious weakness of paneling. All sorts of flashing details have been tried. The ones that are functionally acceptable often have a rather abrupt or ragtag appearance, while the ones that are well hidden, for example by a wide board "belting the house," create a potential area for wood decay. The plywood itself is "exterior-grade plywood," that is, its surface is closed and relatively continuous and the glue used to bond the various layers or "plies" is adequate to continuously withstand the sort of moisture environment to which siding is exposed. In the few examples in which plywood has been used as a siding material for a long time, it seems to have proven itself. Thus, the major weathering problem generally is associated with the joints.

In many applications, a single piece of plywood has been used to function as both the sheathing material, that is, the structure of the wall between the studs, and the siding surface. In many respects this is reasonable, because it would be redundant to have a surface of plywood sheathing overlaid with a plywood siding. Unfortunately, one very fundamental structural requirement often has been overlooked. Sheathing provides two basic structural functions. First, it provides structural closure between the studs in the same way that flooring spans floor joists. In addition, it provides most of the lateral (or sideways) stiffness to a stud wall. Visualize a stud wall without any sheathing, siding, or interior plaster. The nails at the top and bottom are adequate to position the studs and prevent them from being pushed inward or outward, but beyond this they provide little resistance to bending. Thus, without siding,

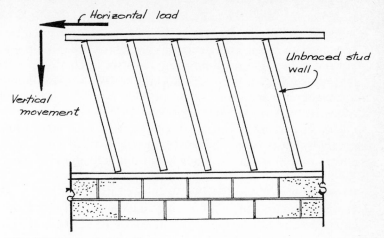

Fig. 4-8   Unbraced stud wall.

a stud wall can "rack" or literally hinge over, as shown in Figure 4-8. To stiffen a building and prevent such racking, diagonal braces are built into the wall, and when plank sheathing of 1 × 6s is used, it is applied on the diagonal, as shown in Figure 4-9, to increase the lateral stiffness. Since plywood cannot be easily deformed out of its rectangular shape, it is an ideal stiffener against the possibility of sideways, or lateral, movement of a stud wall. Only one thing is required to make plywood the ideal lateral bracing material—nails! All the building codes specify the frequency of the nailing pattern of plywood to studs. Nail patterns vary from edge to interior nailing, but an average of one nail every 6 inches is required in order to ensure adequate lateral bracing for a stud wall. This is not an unreasonable requirement, and when plywood is used as a sheathing material, this requirement is generally complied with. The nailing requirements of plywood used only as a siding material are far

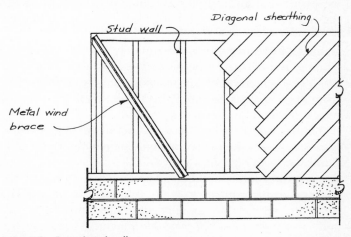

Fig. 4-9   Braced stud wall.

less; moreover, since the nails are exposed to sight, small nails with relatively small heads are used—often only "finish nails." Unfortunately, when plywood is used as both siding and structural sheathing, too often the aesthetics dominate and only a few small finishing nails are applied.

Needless to say, it is a little shocking to feel a house literally sway under a light wind or when someone pushes sideways against the building. Once in a while the inadequacy goes unnoticed until the interior plaster wallboard is applied. The wallboard may actually stiffen a wall against movements from light loads, but plaster wallboard is *not* a structurally adequate material, and in the extremes of lateral loads it will not contribute to the strength of the building.

A whole variety of distress problems can develop from this deficiency. While inadequately braced buildings seldom actually blow over, it is not uncommon to find houses that shake in the wind. Various interior plaster cracks characteristically develop, particularly vertical cracks in corners and near openings. Another distress that is often attributed to the lack of adequate bracing is the so-called plaster wallboard "nail popping." The dry wall is, of course, nailed to the interior of the studs. The nail is driven below the plaster surface and then "spackled" or covered with a plaster patching compound, sanded, and painted. In some houses the silhouette of these nails actually shows through the plaster cover, and in the extreme they may pop out and become exposed. There are various explanations for this popping, but a common one is that the motion induced in the wall from inadequately braced walls works the nails out. No truly orderly research has been done to confirm this contention absolutely, but if a house is poorly braced, sways, *and* has popped dry wall nails, it seems fair to conclude that some causal relation might exist and remedial action should therefore include improving the lateral stiffness.

A fairly recent innovation in residential building technology is to use various foam plastic materials as sheathing. Such materials, particularly when used with aluminum siding, certainly provide far less lateral stiffening than the more conventional methods used in the past. There has been some recognition of this problem, and most builders are increasing the diagonal braces, as shown in Figure 4-9. Unfortunately, there has been neither the required quantity nor elapsed time necessary to establish any pattern of distress as a result of this method of construction; yet it represents such a major departure from previously proven methods that it might be considered a factor in evaluating certain crack patterns.

The remedies for any lack of lateral stiffness are generally self-evident. For example, in the case of inadequate nailing, the nail quantity and size can simply be increased. As a general rule one well-secured panel at each corner (in each direction) should be adequate, but in particularly large houses more nailing may be required to really stiffen the structure. If any increase in nail pattern should be unacceptable, it is fairly simple to remove a complete panel and insert commercially available diagonal steel straps. The only problem with such an operation may involve the water-seal or flashing method at the top and bottom of the panels, and care must be exercised to reestablish the seal integrity.

As part of the consideration of lateral bracing, some of the details of so-called window walls should be reviewed. Starting in the late 1940s, large pieces of glass became easily available for use in residential construction. The first application of these large pieces of glass was the so-called *picture window*— a single window 7 or 8 feet wide. Later, sliding glass doors were introduced, and gradually people found that changing architectural motifs and the low cost of glass as a wall material made it practical to make an entire wall in glass. Sometimes the glass is actually inset in a frame, but often sliding glass door frames are rigidly set in between wall structure. Such extensive use of glass will be limited as various energy-conservation building codes are enforced, but in certain parts of the country window walls may still be used to good advantage on walls facing south. Independent of any energy consideration, however, glass contributes nothing to the structure of a wall. Furthermore, unlike other material combinations that lack lateral stiffening capabilities, it is sometimes impossible to sensibly work any diagonal strap bracing into such a wall. Finally, when sliding glass door panels are lined up one after another to form any extremely long wall, there is often only marginally adequate structure between the various panels. The net result is that walls with unusually large and continuous expanses of glass sometimes lack adequate structural strength. There is no general rule for correcting such an inadequacy since the combinations are so varied, yet if a wall has extensive glass and seems flexible in the sense that light wind can be felt in the wall or a person can easily shake it, then an engineer or architect should be consulted about the adequacy of the wall.

Aluminum siding is the most common modern substitute for wood siding. Aluminum siding is sheet aluminum deformed into the contour of wood siding and applied in bands analogous to wood planks. Some siding is backed up with various types of insulation and composition board, while another is simply a single sheet of aluminum. The original product came in strips 20 feet or so long, and thus there were periodically vertical joints on the side of a house. More recently "seamless" siding, which is formed in a mobile machine from continuous coils of flat aluminum, has become available. Strips of any length can be made that eliminate the vertical joints.

Aluminum, away from a salty environment, deteriorates very little and thus has proven to be an unusually trouble-free building material. The factory-applied surface finishes show relatively little weathering characteristics, and one of the few complaints voiced is the difficulty of changing a house color.

For new construction about the only major problem that has developed with aluminum siding is that some people find it noisy—it makes popping sounds as it shrinks and expands with changes in temperature. The manufacturers have tried to overcome this problem with different types of slotted nail holes and even special nails, but the problem persists and is probably an inherent characteristic of the product about which nothing can be done. Many people claim that the noise decreases with age, but since there is no logical explanation why this should be, it seems more likely that people simply get used to it and learn to ignore the sounds.

A more serious problem can develop with the use of aluminum siding applied to older houses. In a way the problems have more to do with the application of the product, that is, how and where it is used, and not so much with the aluminum product itself. Thus, it seems rather unfair to attribute the problems to aluminum siding per se. Specifically, in earlier chapters the idea of the effects of a change in the environment of a building has been considered. In this chapter the details of moisture movement through walls has been discussed. Now, one common application of aluminum siding is to cover wood and shingle siding on older buildings. The impetus for doing this is that aluminum often costs little more than painting, is more durable, and requires little maintenance for a number of years. Different methods of application are used, but the net effect is (1) to increase the vapor barrier on the outside of the original siding; (2) to increase the heat resistance of the wall, again on the outside of the wood; and (3) to cut off air flow to the surface of the wood. Thus, the three elements required for the existence of rot appear—warmth, moisture, and lack of air flow. The warmth requirement is particularly aggravated in houses with no insulation on the stud wall, because as insulation is added on the outside, more heat is necessarily held in, and the interior wall temperature increases for any given set of conditions. Since the development of rot is a relatively slow process, the consequences of re-siding with aluminum are just beginning to be observed. It should be emphasized, however, that older houses *can* be re-sided without problems developing. Generally the key is to provide some positive means of air circulation against the original wood siding. Also, fungicides and insecticides are available to coat the wood surfaces before application of the aluminum.

For those people who have recently bought or are buying an older wood-sided house that has been re-sided in aluminum, several simple observations should be made. The first is to sense with the nose—in a closed house the telltale odor of rot, a musty smell, may be a sign of rot in the exterior wall siding. If there is any question about the condition of the wood below the siding, a few panels of the siding should be removed and the condition of the wood checked for rot and insect infestation. A good place to remove siding is below windows and at the roofline—in other words, at the top row of the siding. Finally, the two extremes in thermal environment of a house should be checked—namely, the north and the south walls. There seems to be no rule that dictates which side of a house is more likely to develop rot, but on any individual house, a preferential side will exist.

Earlier in this chapter, some of the details of *stucco-on-frame* construction were discussed. A large number of stucco houses were built from the turn of the century to the late 1930s in greatly varying climates. From these examples fairly consistent distress patterns have developed that permit predictions as to when in the history of the buildings and under what conditions distress and deterioration will develop.

Stucco finish on wood structures has been in use during our entire history. The buildings at Jamestown, Virginia, were of a cementitious material plastered over twigs interwoven among vertical structural members that are the equivalent of our modern studs (see Figure 4-10). More common in recent years has been the application of stucco to wood sheathing in such a way that the bond between the wood and stucco is developed by nailing an "expanded metal" or wire-type material to the siding, as shown in Figure 4-11.

In many respects it is surprising how successful this exterior wall surface has been. It does not seem to be as vulnerable to water intrusion and eventual freeze damage as stucco-on-masonry. The reason for this difference is two-fold. First, if water penetrates the surface of stucco-on-frame and works its way between the wood and stucco, there are slight voids that allow the water to run down and dissipate over a large area. In the case of stucco-on-masonry, the stucco is bonded directly to the masonry and water can collect in any void, freeze, and break the stucco off the surface. The second reason the frame system seems to withstand freeze damage is that the stud wall is relatively more flexible than masonry. If water does collect between the stucco and sheathing, freezes, and expands, the wood wall will push in with roughly the same ease as the stucco will push out. Thus, in stucco-on-frame construction it is very rare to find large sections of stucco broken off the surface as a result of trapped water freezing.

The most common crack patterns that develop in this siding material are relatively light cracks radiating from window and door openings. Since these cracks develop in the first year or two after the stucco is applied, they are not at all unexpected. As the concrete stucco dries it shrinks, and it must shrink

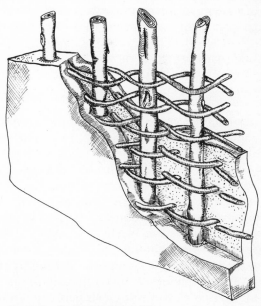

Fig. 4-10 Daub-and-wattle wall.

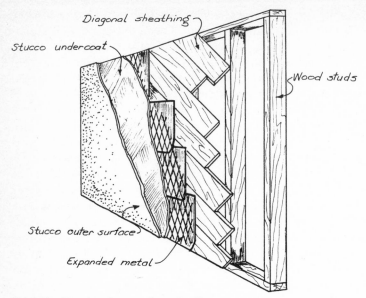

Fig. 4-11 Stucco-on-frame wall construction.

around the relatively rigid window and door openings. The maximum-strain points necessarily develop at the corners, and in extreme cases cracks occur. The average person probably has an intuitive understanding of how a continuous surface, if allowed to shrink, will crack at the sharp corners of a rigid material placed in the middle of the surface.

In evaluating the cause and significance of cracks in stucco surfaces, it is important to differentiate between the initial shrinkage cracks and cracks from any other source, and the best criteria for judgment are age and location of cracks. Shrinkage cracks, if they are going to occur, develop within the first year or so; also, they most often occur at the discontinuities in the wall. Very often such cracks go unnoticed by an owner for a number of years. Cracks are simply not something the average person notices in the normal course of events, but let some unusual event occur that alerts an owner to the possibility of crack damage developing and previously unnoticed cracks become apparent. For example, in neighborhoods close to new construction sites where heavy equipment is operating, some people inevitably examine their houses for cracks, discover old ones, and assume they are new and may be related to the new construction. This is particularly true near sites where there is either pile driving or blasting.

Thus, it often becomes essential to be able to distinguish between old and new cracks in stucco surfaces. Actually, this same problem arises with cracks in many brittle building materials including plaster, concrete, and masonry work. Assuming that a house is roughly ten or more years old, there are several simple observations that can be made to help *date* an exterior wall crack, that is, to distinguish between a ten-year-old or older crack, and a relatively recent one. To begin with, the edges of a recent crack are sharp, whereas only a few years of exposure to weather will round or soften the edges of an older crack. Insects often live in cracks, and they leave telltale signs such as discarded shell and spider balls. Dust and debris will often collect in cracks, particularly at locations that are protected from water. In many cases cracks tend to channel water flow across a wall surface in a slightly different direction, and thus there may be a difference in surface color and weathering from one side of a crack to another. A good example of this may be seen in the photograph of Figure 4-12. Here it is clear that there is some abrupt change in surface characteristics across the crack—a situation that would not exist in a recent crack. Finally, the most exact evidence of crack age is paint! If paint is actually *in* the crack, it is obvious that the crack occurred before painting.

Thus, new cracks have clean, sharp edges and surfaces. From one side of the crack to the other there should be no preferential weather or color changes. Cracks that can conclusively be identified as old and particularly those forming in the first year or two of the existence of the walls should be of little concern. They should be sealed against water intrusion; however, they obviously do not signify some new distress mechanism.

It is the more recent cracks that may be an indicator of trouble. Ground settlement can produce building movements that create cracks in stucco siding, and the key to relating this cause with a particular crack pattern is whether the crack continues into the foundation wall (see Chapter 3).

Another common type of damage that occurs to stucco-on-frame *is* caused by water infiltration but *is not* a result of any freeze phenomenon. Most stucco is secured to wood sheathing by various types of wire, the most common being expanded metal lath. In addition to creating a bond between the two materials, such wire also provides some degree of reinforcing for the stucco

Fig. 4-12 Crack through stucco.

to actually hold it together and minimize crack advancement. If water can penetrate to this, metal corrosion can occur. Sometimes the wire is galvanized and any corrosion that does occur is negligible; however, on plain wire if the corrosion is extensive, the bond surface can be broken. In such situations it is not uncommon to see relatively large chunks, of up to several square feet in area, spalled off the surface. The cause, rusted wire, is left exposed.

Fortunately, repair procedures are relatively simple provided the water source can be identified and cut off, for there is no harm in simply reapplying the stucco over the old, exposed wire, rust and all. If the rust is not heavy, a slight layer does not harm the bonding characteristics.

As described earlier in this chapter, stucco is almost pure portland cement, and, therefore, it is generally exceptionally strong and hard. Once in a while someone will apply a stucco that is simply weak—perhaps because of excessive sand or more commonly owing to too much lime in the mixture. Weak stucco, like weak concrete, does not weather well. The surface is soft, and moisture can penetrate over a large area. Unfortunately, such weak stucco is not something that deteriorates quickly enough to be identified and corrected during the first few years. Instead, it may survive for a number of years. The first signs of deterioration are random "craze" cracks or a crisscross crack pattern leaving little patches 3 or 4 inches across uncracked stucco. For some reason such stucco is more commonly found in houses that have reproduced the English Elizabethan style of "half-timber." Of course, the exposed timbers are not really the primary structure as they were in the prototype sixteenth-century buildings, but the exterior wood-and-stucco detailing is the same. Often accompanying such weak stucco is rotten timber surface, and if not this, water-damaged sheathing below the stucco. If stucco is suspected of being weak and a poor water barrier over the entire surface, any wood in contact with the stucco may be damaged and should be thoroughly inspected. The corrections in such a case can be so extensive and complicated that each individual case must be examined separately.

The typical stucco-on-frame house has a masonry foundation wall that extends several feet out of the grade before meeting the wood construction. In some cases the stucco stops at the bottom of the wood, thus leaving the foundation wall exposed, while in other houses the stucco continues across this wood–masonry intersection and extends below the grade line. Based on the very different properties of wood and masonry, it is not surprising that the stucco, as it crosses this intersection, is subject to differential movements. Rarely does stucco totally survive this transition. Most commonly a crack line develops relatively early in the history of a building, but even when no crack appears a clear line of demarcation develops in the form of a discoloration across the two backing materials. Neither of these distress patterns is particularly serious, yet surprisingly it is not uncommon to see a wall survive thirty or forty years and relatively suddenly have the stucco applied to the masonry spall off. The explanation for such a long delay is that it has taken that long for water to progressively penetrate between the masonry and stucco and destroy the bond. In Northern climates the mechanism of this bond failure

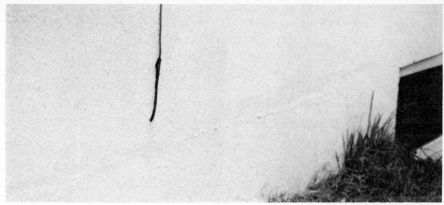

Fig. 4-13   Stucco crack between frame and masonry.

is most often attributed to the expansion of freezing water that has collected between the two surfaces, but similar distress develops in the extreme South, where temperatures never reach the freezing point. In such cases, the explanation revolves around differential thermal- and moisture-induced movements. The truth is that the damage is probably due to a combination of all these causes, but one thing is almost universally true—the distress is always aggravated or accelerated by the presence of excessive moisture. In the photograph (Figure 4-14) the stucco on the lower wall survived for thirty-eight years until a leak in the gutter discharged excessive water against this wall. The stain mark shows the path leading to the spalled stucco at the foundation line.

Fig. 4-14   Failed stucco on masonry wall.

In summary, stucco has proven to be a relatively reliable siding material, modest damage is easily patched, and the most important maintenance consideration is to keep water out of cracks and from around the edges of windows and doors. In evaluating the significance of cracks, the time of occurrence is important, and generally old, nonadvancing cracks have little significance. Unfortunately, when stucco-on-frame is grossly deteriorated, the damage may extend to the sheathing and, in extreme cases, to studs and sill plates. In such cases a complete and detailed inspection is required and obtaining professional advice is sensible.

Shingles, both wood and composition, are in themselves relatively long lasting. Composition shingles fracture if struck by a hard object. Wood shingles, which are most often either cyprus or cedar, last for literally hundreds of years, even in damp environments. The fundamental concept of shingles being individual pieces might best be thought of as a precracked wall—a wall surface that can easily move in response to temperature and moisture variations without producing stress and therefore the potential for cracking. The chief complaint about shingles is that they do not provide a continuous surface, are not a barrier against air and insect infiltration, and thus require a continuous membrane on the sheathing surface.

Repair of Wood-Frame Exterior Walls

In many cases the method of repair for wood structure is immediately evident, and because wood is so easily worked and because craftspeople are available to do the work, there are few obstacles to completely restoring damaged wood. There are, however, a few precautions, special techniques, and materials that should be considered before repairs are made.

If wood in a residential building is rotten and decayed over an extensive area, then almost certainly it must be completely removed, and new wood reinstalled. If the factors contributing to rot, namely, warmth, moisture, and poor air circulation, cannot be eliminated completely, then the repaired wood should be treated against rot and insect damage. Fortunately, today most lumberyards carry lumber that has been chemically treated against rot and moisture decay. Most of these treatments involve soaking or pressure-injecting salts into the wood structure. Unfortunately, after a finite period of time these salts leach out and leave the wood unprotected. Thus, for extremely long-term protection, the only treatment processes available involve petroleum-based chemicals such as tar, asphalt, and most commonly, creosote.

In working with any of the wood-preservative chemicals it should be recognized that some are extremely toxic and special handling precautions should be observed. Creosote is probably the most troublesome product, and it is not uncommon for people to develop rather serious skin disorders from only slight contact. These precautions should apply not only to craftspeople during the installation process but also to the in-service conditions. For example, in crawl spaces under a house it is common to see creosoted lumber used to replace decayed structure. This is a good material selection, provided the crawl space is not accessible to children to play in in future years.

Most preservative products are well labeled, with the constraints for use clearly defined. If there is any question about a given product, organizations such as university extension services, the USDA, and local health departments can generally provide details of possible health hazards.

Just because wood is damaged is not necessarily a sufficient reason to remove it. Certainly, if the basic structural integrity of a building is jeopardized, the equivalent structure must be restored; but this can be done in a variety of ways, many of which do not include actually removing the distressed wood. Central to the decision of removal is the method of temporary support. Several times, earlier in this text, the inherent problems associated with jacking of buildings have been discussed. Specifically, the idea was presented that jacking can induce a new geometry of movements and therefore distress, and that since most sagging and distortion of buildings have taken place over a comparatively long time, rapid return to the original shape may create more problems than it solves. Some of these same arguments are applicable to any shoring operation required during removal and reinstallation of damaged wood. Pragmatically, such methods almost always involve some amount of jacking.

In many cases, particularly when the damage is due to insects, the partially destroyed timbers can be left in place and a new member simply placed alongside. This sounds simple enough and often it is, yet there are several rules that should be followed when "partying" or "sistering" wood structural members. First, such a procedure is only applicable when there is clearance to fit the new member into place. If the damage is so great that the wood has crushed and distorted to the point that a comparable-sized member cannot be fitted alongside, then jacking and complete removal of the wood may be inevitable. The dimensions of standard lumber sizes have decreased over the years, and it is not uncommon to find that a modern 2×10, for example, will loosely fit, with ample clearance, alongside an old, damaged 2×10. Remember that in such cases the modern timber may not be the structural equivalent of the original, but this fact may be still another incentive for sistering damaged members. The argument for this is that the original, damaged member is not structurally worthless and that the two combined members are more than adequate for support.

Probably the biggest problem with sistering joists and other framing members involves the method of blocking the new member tightly enough to receive any load. Understand that once a new member is in place, it certainly contributes to the *ultimate* strength, that is, the strength associated with actual collapse; but any looseness requires that the original member deform sufficiently to take up the clearance before the two members can act together. Often an undue reliance is placed on a few nails. Typically, floor joists carry loads up to several thousand pounds, while individual nails can transfer forces of less than a hundred pounds. Thus, a few nails between sistered joists are of little value.

The proper method of developing load sharing between old and new members is to initially fit them as closely as possible and then drive wood wedges to take up any slack. The only precaution is to remember that a tapered wedge can develop a very high mechanical advantage, that is, a low driving force can result in a much larger force at the face of the wedge; and people sometimes get carried away with the ease with which a wedge can be driven and create a new class of distress by overdriving the wedge.

For several reasons the local areas around the bearing ends of studs and joists are traditional locations of damage both by insects and rot. They are often the dampest region, with poor air circulation; hence, they are vulnerable to rot. In addition, such bearing ends are the first wood in the path between the earth and the rest of the building, and thus the first wood likely to be encountered by termites. Earlier in this chapter some of the mechanical properties of wood were discussed, and it was pointed out that wood is relatively weak in compression for loads applied perpendicular to the grain. Thus, at locations where the wood is relatively weak, namely, the bearing ends, an area of likely insect and decay damage exists. The result of this doubly vulnerable area is a rather unique yet commonly encountered repair dilemma. Specifically, in many older homes a wood sill plate rests on the foundation wall and both joists and studs bear on this plate. All three intersecting elements are sometimes damaged locally around their bearing ends, and the sill plate is often the most obvious and extensively damaged of the three. The tendency is to cut out the sill plate in short sections in such a way that little or no shoring is required, and then to replace the sill plate with treated lumber.

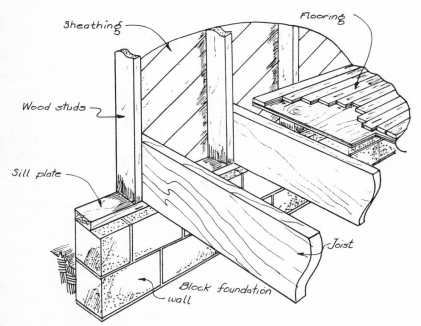

Fig. 4-15 Sill plate, stud, and joist intersection on foundation wall.

Over the years, as the plate gradually became more damaged and deformed, it compressed the fibers and sort of spread or *cushioned* the loads from both the studs and joists. The new plate, being sound wood, lacks this cushioning capability, and shortly after the new sill plate is installed the joist and stud ends, now being the weakest elements in the chain, undergo a new set of deformations. This new movement is not likely to occur immediately after the installation of the sill plate, for wood takes time to deform and the full load may occur later. In any event, it is not uncommon to have to repeat a repair project at such a location several months after a sill plate is replaced. Of course, the answer is to evaluate more carefully the extent of distress in all three elements.

It is appropriate at this point to introduce another repair technique. This technique may be particularly adaptable to those sill plate-bearing locations which, because of the lack of accessibility, are particularly difficult areas to repair. There are on the market today several different *plastic* compounds that can be injected into wood as a fairly thin liquid and later polymerize and harden. Several of these products are sold in a container that is also the pumping device, but when they are not it is easy enough to get a large hypodermic syringe at a farm store and inject the substance by this means. This is a very satisfactory repair method, but obviously it is restricted to relatively small areas measured in a few square inches. Not only is it expensive for large amounts, but it is sometimes questionable how uniform and continuous multiple injections might be.

The final repair to any wood exposed to the weather is, of course, *paint*. The whole subject of wood painting is very complex and unfortunately one about which there is considerable debate. Each paint company espouses the virtues of its own product, and in the case of more conventional oil-base paints some judgment of relative paint quality can be made by simply comparing the proportions of the various constituents printed on the can. For some of the newer paint compounds the significance of the ingredients is obscure to all but a paint chemist, and some other judgment of paint quality is required. Several consumer and government publications report on durability tests, but these are often not appropriate because they rarely include the variable, less than optimum conditions that exist for the average home-owner.

At least equal and perhaps more important than absolute paint quality (there are a number of good-quality paints on the market) is the condition of the surface to be painted. First is a question of compatibility of the old and the new paint; second, the old paint surface; and third, the moisture condition of the wood. A simple set of rules that pertain to the painting surface are:

• Avoid switching generic types of paint. Except in rare situations latex paints should not be applied over old oil-base paints and vice versa. As complicated new paint compounds are developed, paint retailers often lack the exact knowledge to predict the long-term results of applying one type of paint over another. If the issue of compatibility is vital, then require that the paint salesperson give you an example of a house with conditions similar to yours that has had the paint in question applied for at least five years.

• Paint in general and particularly exterior oil-base paints can build up to a considerable thickness after repeated applications. At some point the collection of paint layers is so great that it completely seals the wood against any moisture migration and the wood can no longer "breathe." During the winter excessive moisture will build up behind such a layer and, combined with freeze-thaw cycles, actually cause the paint to peel off the wood. The characteristics of this phenomenon are thick layers of paint and surprisingly clean, almost totally paint-free wood surface where the paint is peeled off. In such cases the rule is to allow only a limited number of layers of paint to build up before taking off all the paint back down to the wood surface. There seems to be no absolute rule, but most painters seem to agree that three or four layers is the limit.

• The other surface-condition rule involves cleanliness of the surface, and this includes not only dirt and foreign particles but also excessive buildup of paint oxides. One of the ways paint maintains a fresh, clean appearance is to allow metallic oxides to build up on the surface. Gradually, these oxides wash away, leaving a fresh-looking surface. In general, such surfaces maintain their qualities of durability, but rarely do they allow a good surface for bonding a new layer of paint. In any event, excessive buildups of paint oxides should be washed or sanded off before repainting.

• New paint should be applied to wood only when the wood has a fairly limited moisture content. There are a number of reasons why this is so, and all the mechanisms are not too clearly understood. Certainly moisture content affects bond, but equally important is the question of moisture-induced expansion and contraction of the wood. If the paint is applied and dries on wood at one extreme of moisture content, it may not maintain its bond when the wood has expanded (or contracted) owing to the other extreme of moisture content.

The moisture content of wood can be easily measured in place with a "moisture meter"—a device that when properly calibrated gives very exact results. Unfortunately, these meters, while not particularly expensive, are not available to many painters and paint retailers. Most government paint specifications require the use of one, and people familiar with such work may be able to direct you to someone with a moisture meter. Certainly anyone familiar with paint around historic-preservation projects will be familiar with such a device. The technical specifications (not necessarily those on the paint can) of most paints will recommend optimum wood-moisture contents for painting surfaces.

Masonry Wall Distress

While exterior masonry walls vary considerably in terms of materials, appearance, and details of construction, the major types of distress are more or less common to all. Walls faced with fired-clay brick are certainly the most common, and with few exceptions such walls suffer most of the generic types of distress. The following discussion will concentrate on this type of wall, and the few significant exceptions will be discussed later.

The distress patterns in walls faced with fired-clay brick (referred to simply as "brick" hereafter) can be characterized as follows:

- Cracks
- Bowing
- Mortar deterioration
- Brick deterioration

Crack Damage

Crack damage in brick walls is certainly the most commonly encountered distress pattern, and while certain patterns do portend further, more extensive and severe problems, many cracks are relatively unimportant; furthermore, other than the sealing of openings against water intrusion, such walls do not require any complicated remedies. Obviously, the trick is to be able to distinguish between the cracks that are important and those that are not. The key to such a judgment is an understanding of the *cause* of any cracking. Many of the causes of masonry cracking have been discussed in Chapter 3; however, some causes and therefore patterns are unique to above-grade exterior walls. The principal causes of masonry wall cracking are as follows:

- Construction and design errors
- Temperature and moisture
- Overload
- Settlement
- Accidents

Construction and Design Errors   In developing an understanding of these causes an extremely useful approach, which has previously been recommended in connection with diagnosis of other distress patterns, is to observe analogous or comparable houses for similar distress. Such observations may not only suggest a cause and the frequency of occurrence, but also a method or even need for correction. For example, before the late nineteenth century lintels over window and door openings in masonry walls were either some form of masonry arch or stone acting as a beam in bending. The proportions of the formal Georgian house had evolved over a period of several hundred years, and through the pragmatism of experience, design, and construction, detailing was such that surprisingly few cracks occurred around the lintels of such houses. As time went on many of the same window details were applied to other types of buildings. Small town houses and larger, loft-type buildings used brick arch lintels; and all went well until two fundamental design changes were made. First, in the 1880s and 1890s in many cities a bay-window detail

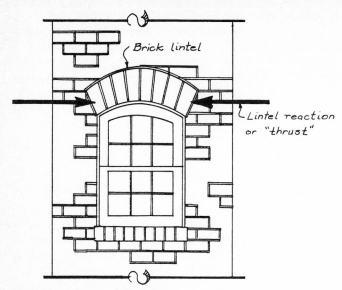

Fig. 4-16 Masonry arch lintel thrust.

Fig. 4-17   Failed masonry lintel.

was introduced along the front fascia of previously straight-walled row houses. Now, to support any type of masonry arch the walls on either side of the opening must withstand the *thrust* or lateral force required to keep the arch from spreading out. When the fronts of row houses were comparatively flat, there was sufficient masonry to withstand this thrust; but when the bay detail was used, the masonry on either side of the opening was narrowed and was not enough to resist the lateral forces. The result was that in literally miles of row houses with this bay-window detail the arch failed.

Analogous failure occurred in the windows of loft buildings—buildings with many rows of arched windows. On the windows toward the center of the building the thrust of adjacent windows was equal and opposite and no problems occurred. The last, end window, lacking both a wide expanse of masonry or another window, was inadequately supported and the typical arch failure developed. In both these examples the mechanism of failure is perhaps a little subtle for the average person to diagnose; however, in both cases if an owner had observed comparable buildings and noticed that time and time again the same distress was associated with the same window and wall relationship, the explanation for the failure would have eventually become evident.

Incidentally, in both these examples, the bow-window row house and the multiwindow loft building, failures began to occur very shortly after the buildings were completed. When builders and designers realized their error, they changed the details. In the case of row houses a switch was made to deep stone lintels, and a dozen or so years later, when cast-iron or steel lintels were readily available, they switched back to the arch detail, but this time without the need for lateral support of the masonry. Figure 4-19 shows this progression in design.

The solution in the loft buildings was not to change the lintel detail, but

Fig. 4-18 Loft-building lintel.

a

b

c

Fig. 4-19 (*a*) Failed lintel.
(*b*) Stone lintel at bay window.
(*c*) Lintel at bay-window arch.

to provide sufficient masonry next to the outside window. This thickened masonry often took the form of a dummy pilaster at the corners. A good demonstration that this was most likely the metamorphosis can be seen by walking down a street of old loft buildings and noting details and how they have changed with time.

In several other chapters the importance of distinguishing among different geometries of masonry wall cracks has been emphasized. Specifically, the difference should be noted between cracks in bricks alone, cracks in the mortar both across the joint and along the intersection between bricks and mortar, and finally cracks that run more or less continuously through both the bricks and mortar. The particular path a crack takes is partially related to the relative strength of the brick compared with mortar. In Chapter 1 rough rules for judging these strength characteristics were given.

A fairly common crack that is restricted to the face of individual bricks can be very disturbing to homeowners when it is discovered. At random locations in a wall a vertical crack will exist across the face of individual bricks. Otherwise, there is no visual difference among any of the bricks, and, very importantly, there are no cracks in the surrounding bond joints between the bricks and mortar. First, consider the possibility of an isolated opening *developing* in the interior of the surface of a composite, brittle material. Certainly, none of the bricks actually were removed. Could a brick wall be strained or loaded in a way that would produce such an isolated and limited rectangular opening? The answer, of course, is no. Such a crack, if it developed after the wall was erected, would have to be accompanied by a continuation of the crack either into other bricks or along mortar bond joints. The fact is that such cracks were in the bricks when they were laid up and have simply gone unnoticed ever since. Often owners will first notice such cracks when something unusual occurs in the neighborhood, something that they believe may produce crack damage. Thus, should an explosion or blasting occur, or should particularly heavy trucks pass by frequently, then many homeowners will start to examine their exterior masonry walls. Under such circumstances it is difficult to be convinced that these brick-face vertical cracks are not new.

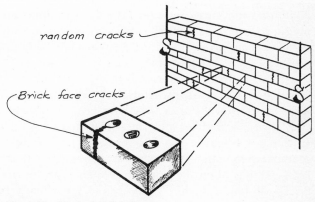

Fig. 4-20   Cracks in brick face.

The origin of these cracks is in the shrinking process that takes place during firing in the brick kiln. Such cracks are almost exclusively found in particularly hard-fired bricks, and even more particularly ones with several circular holes or cavities, as shown in Figure 4-20. The crack generally extends from the face into one of these cavities. In many cases the crack is not really continuous, and the brick may not even split along such a crack if struck with a hammer.

Except for relatively minor water intrusion, such cracks are of little consequence and are most often left alone.

Probably the most common construction error leading to brick distress involves mortar strength and certain details of preparing the bricks for laying. Masonry mortar is a combination of cement, sand, and lime, the lime being added to produce certain characteristics of workability. If either too much sand or lime is used, or if water is repeatedly added to keep the mortar from becoming stiff and unworkable, the mechanical properties of the mortar can be seriously reduced. Not only will the compressive strength of the mortar itself be lowered, but also the bond strength between brick and mortar can be compromised. Fired-clay brick, unlike cement block or brick, should be partially wet before placing to increase bond characteristics and decrease differential shrinkage. As construction procedures deviate from the optimum, more distress will eventually develop in a masonry wall.

The most typical sign of deficient mortar or installation procedures is hairline cracks running randomly in the bond joint. The essential factor in relating this distress pattern to faulty installation is the randomness of the cracks. If they meander along and turn from horizontal to vertical and back again, and particularly if they periodically cross, they are most likely a result of weak mortar-to-brick bonding. Obviously, such a condition is not desirable, but the remedy may be worse than the malady. As in so many similar situations, the best policy is to wait and see how further distress develops. If the mortar strength is sufficient, if the cracks do not advance, if the wall does not allow water leakage, and if the cracks are not too extensive, then it is probably best to ignore these cracks.

Many people feel that under such circumstances something ought to be done, and the most common remedy is to apply some waterproofing compound to seal the masonry surface against water intrusion. The desirability of this repair procedure is subject to many questions; the problem is that sometimes it works and sometimes it does not. If the sealant simply fails to work and yet remains passive, it will probably be considered a totally acceptable repair. Unfortunately, very dramatic problems can develop with some masonry walls after they have been waterproofed.

All bricks will allow some moisture migration into and out of the surface. In this way bricks are said to *breathe*. The best bricks will allow a moisture gradient to exist that is in some way consistent with the strength of the surface layers so that when the bricks freeze and the internal moisture expands, the bricks will hold together. Some bricks, particularly relatively soft bricks with a glazed surface, will permit an excessive moisture buildup right behind the glazed surface. When the moisture freezes it literally blows off chunks of the brick surface. It is very common to see such distress on parapet walls close to the roof surface where splashing water keeps the brick surface excessively wet. Most often in such cases just a few random bricks have their surfaces popped off. Once the impervious surface is removed, the bricks can breathe again, and the deterioration does not advance.

Unfortunately, some bricks do not relieve the problem by spalling off the surface, but continue to keep breaking off in thin layers almost indefinitely.

Just as in the case of hairline cracks in bond joints between mortar and brick, such face spalling often prompts an owner to apply a waterproof compound. Result—the spalling is even worse! Evaluating the desirability of surface waterproofing on brick is grossly complicated by the inconsistency of results: Sometimes it works and sometimes it does not. Rather than accepting a salesperson's judgment based on sincerity or references to successful jobs (the failures are unlikely to be used as examples) a reasonable approach is to experiment. Apply the sealant to a restricted but representative area and see how it works for a minimum one-year test period.

If a brick-masonry wall can be demonstrated positively to be either leaking water or undergoing surface spalling due to freezing, and if for one reason or another surface waterproofing compounds are unacceptable, a satisfactory surface and sealant is cement. Obviously, this would be a dramatic and perhaps intolerable aesthetic change; nevertheless, with one exception, it is almost certain to solve the problems. In brick buildings that are later stuccoed sometimes the problem described in the chapter on foundation walls arises; that is, groundwater is drawn up by a sort of wick action into a masonry wall. Groundwater contains various chemicals in solution that can cause serious brick deterioration. Everything else being equal, the application of a relatively impervious moisture layer to the outside of a wall near the grade line will almost certainly increase the potential for this "damp-rise" phenomonen. Thus, recently stuccoed brick walls often spall the stucco within a foot or two of the grade line and show the signs of deteriorating brick that are symptomatic of this phenomenon. For this reason, it may be wise to stop a stucco coating within a few feet of the ground.

Obviously, this problem was identified a long time ago and was then forgotten. In many cities where there have been a number of adjacent row-type buildings removed over a number of years, it is almost standard procedure to seal an exposed brick wall by stuccoing it. The older stucco almost always stops 2 or 3 feet above the grade, while recent applications run down to grade or sometimes actually below. Fairly regularly the stucco on such walls is spalled and the brick below is hollowed out and crumbling.

Temperature and Moisture   The property of masonry materials to expand and contract with changes in moisture and temperature has already been discussed in some detail; furthermore, the mechanisms whereby such movements can produce strains, which if large enough produce rupture, has been reviewed. Thus, it is not surprising that exterior walls that cycle through the extremes of both moisture and temperature should be significantly affected by these factors. In a number of ways this cyclic motion can be detected. In large structures expansion joints are actually built into walls and floors, and where a flexible material such as caulking is inserted in such a joint, it is often very apparent that it has extruded from the joint. Similarly, cracks in masonry from any source become in effect expansion joints, and the movements of a wall are most evident at these cracks. Even with fairly casual monitoring of such cracks the amount of movement can easily be observed.

In the evaluation of the cause of any specific crack, thermal and moisture movements are given as an explanation almost by default. When all other explanations fail, the movements induced by thermal and moisture changes are blamed. In many respects this is not an altogether unreasonable way to figure out the cause of distress. Somewhat like Sherlock Holmes's synthesis process of excluding the possible and arriving at the improbable, the diagnosis of cracking excludes the obvious, and the more subtle, less understood thermal- and moisture-movement phenomenon becomes the explanation.

Remember, the mechanism that leads to cracking is contingent on some *differential* movements occurring. That is, a continuous wall, no matter what size, that simply uniformly heats up and expands will be unstrained and therefore uncracked providing it is not restrained or stopped from expanding freely. Thus, the key to detecting thermal- and moisture-induced cracking is the identification of nonuniform expansion or contraction. The three variables that allow nonuniform movement to occur are (1) material changes, (2) geometry changes, and (3) environmental changes. If none of these factors is present, do not be ready to accept thermal- and moisture-induced movements as being the explanation of a particular crack pattern.

One of the best examples of distress due to these causes involves parapet walls on buildings. These are exterior walls that continue up above the roofline, generally a few feet or so. Such walls are not too common in residential buildings today, although from the beginning of this century to the late 1930s an architectural style was quite popular that incorporated parapet walls on the gable ends of houses. In recent years parapet walls are used on many flat-roofed buildings, particularly garden-type apartment buildings, which are often brick masonry. Also, the motif is used in the South and Southwest in the so-called mission style of architecture.

Now, consider the environment of the walls around a building with parapet walls and in particular the variable or changing conditions. (1) The parapet wall is exposed to the weather on both sides. (2) The wall immediately below has a protected interior surface. (3) The roof side of a parapet wall receives an excessive amount of water from roof splash. (4) From one side of the building to the other the south or sun-facing wall has a relatively different relation to the wall immediately below it. That is, normally a north wall never sees the sun and therefore receives no heat or drying from the sun. However, the north parapet wall does receive sun on its southern, exposed face above the roofline. (5) The top of a parapet wall is relatively more exposed to rain and sun than are the sides. (6) The parapet wall is essentially unloaded, while the wall immediately below it receives loads from the roof. Actually, the list goes on and on, and each item represents another change condition. The net result is that parapet walls undergo a whole series of thermal- and moisture-induced distress patterns. The most standard is a long, horizontal crack more or less at the roofline. According to the color of brick and roof surface, the roof-flashing details, and parapet height, there seems to be a very slight tendency for this crack to form on the north parapet. This would suggest that it is more related to solar effects and therefore is thermally related.

In south- and sometimes west-facing parapets the crack patterns most often seems to be random vertical cracks near the center of the building that are generally more noticeable on the interior or roof side. It can be inferred that these cracks not only may be thermally related, but also are associated with the excessive dampness on the north-facing (nonsun-dried) side of the parapet. Finally, it is not uncommon to see all four corners of the parapet actually pushed out an inch or so beyond the wall below. The parapet walls, being exposed on both sides, may reach average temperatures of 70 to 80°F (21 to 35°C) above (or below) the walls immediately below. As they expand, they literally push the end wall at right angles off the wall below. This is a classic example of the lack of reversibility of many building deformations. At first it would seem reasonable that if a wall could be pushed *out,* it could also be pushed *back.* To a certain degree this is true, but once any cracks develop, the process becomes exclusively one-way. A wall in motion can first close up a crack and only then exert a force across the crack; but as expansion occurs and the crack opens, no pull force can exist across the crack opening. Furthermore, debris tends to work its way into open joints and to prevent any easy return movement.

The example of the parapet wall has the variables of geometry and environmental changes that allow the moisture and thermal variations to produce movements and cracking. An example of a material change that can lead to cracking involves window sills rather than lintels. In many brick houses sills are often cut stone or concrete. Most stone materials are significantly less water-permeable than brick and are relatively more stable dimensionally ow-

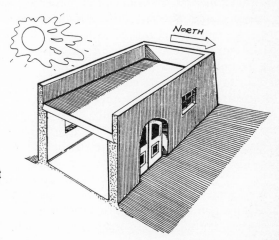

Fig. 4-21 Section of house with parapet wall.

ing to moisture changes. In many brick houses with stone sills a crack develops at the lower window corners. These cracks randomly run off a few feet and gradually disappear. The explanation is that the sills are, of course, set tightly in the masonry opening to prevent water intrusion. As the bricks contract around the sill, the sill does not shrink an equal amount, and eventually the corners are forced open. A case might be made that this is also due to thermally related movement, but this is somewhat unlikely because most stones have very nearly the same coefficient of thermal expansion as do bricks. Furthermore, such cracks at stone sills lack the directional consistency generally associated with thermally induced damage, that is, north versus south walls.

One of the extremely frustrating characteristics of thermal- and moisture-induced crack damage is the unpredictability of it. In the design process there are few concise analytical rules that can be used to predict how and where such cracks will occur. Even more random is the time relation for development of cracks. In a collection of nominally identical houses a particular crack that can be clearly established to be, say, thermally induced, may develop soon after completion in nine out of ten cases. In the tenth house no crack occurs until quite suddenly, after many years, an identical crack appears. While in individual cases explanations are often given for such seeming inconsistencies, still there simply are not completely satisfactory, universally applicable explanations. If any rule is to be adopted, it should be that there are no rules. This may seem to be a superficial explanation, yet in the synthesis process it is important to recognize that there are exceptions and that discovering random inconsistencies does not invalidate all other observations of such an extremely complex mechanism.

Overload   Masonry cracks due to excessive loads are relatively rare, although overload is regularly but inappropriately blamed for many other cracks. When crack distress does result from overstressing, it almost always occurs at a point of load concentration. At the sides of any openings, the loads from above are "collected" on a beam above the opening and transferred to the sides. In this way the loads at the sides of any opening are higher and can be said to be concentrated. Similarly, if the floor or roof structure bears on a beam that transfers a collection of loads to one location, there will, of course, be a concentration of load at the bearing ends of the beam. Thus, overload distress is frequently discovered below steel beams that carry a significant area of floor or roof. Another common location for load-induced cracking is below excessively narrow brick piers between openings or between the end of an opening and an outside wall.

Many observers may argue that in the case of a crack below a beam at the bearing point, it is more related to the movement restraint to the wall provided by the beam than to the load per se. In other words, one of the variables necessary for cracking related to thermal- and moisture-induced movements is a geometry change, and it is obvious that a single steel beam bearing at an isolated point in an otherwise continuous wall certainly represents a geometry change. Perhaps a less controversial explanation is simply to say that it is the presence of the beam that has caused the crack; but when cracks appear at obvious points of load concentration, the magnitude of the applied loads should be checked to determine if a load-induced failure is likely.

Cracks caused by excessive loads must obviously be treated very differently from cracks resulting from any other cause. Simply filling a crack does not solve the problem—the potential for overload may still exist. Every situation is unique, and if there are any indications that a failure has been caused by overload, a professional should be consulted.

Settlement-induced cracks have been discussed in Chapters 2 and 3, and the patterns and details of repair that pertain to foundation walls are applicable to above-grade walls. In the case of damage due to accidents the relation between cause and effect is self-evident and rarely requires any further diagnosis.

Repair of Crack Distress in Masonry Exterior Walls   Three incentives for repairing masonry exterior wall cracks are (1) to assure aesthetic quality, (2) to reestablish structural integrity, and (3) to prevent water intrusion. The third reason, the maintenance of the water resistance of the wall, is, practically speaking, the most important, because additional or excessive water in and around a masonry wall can lead to a whole new set of distress and deterioration problems. Obviously, if water penetrates the interior finish surfaces, it can strain and deteriorate these finishes; furthermore, water reduces the insulating characteristics of all materials. Water within a wall will produce added moisture movements and finally, internal water in masonry can lead to freeze-thaw distress.

Superficially, the answer to masonry wall cracks is simply to fill them, but this approach may not be adequate. The general criterion for determining the details of filling cracks evolves around two issues. First, is the source of the cracking likely to reoccur and produce more cracking, or was the crack a one-time occurrence, as in the case of initial ground settlement? In determining the answer to this question, special care must be taken to determine whether the damaging mechanism is truly complete or just dormant. The second issue to evaluate is whether a crack from any cause has effectively become an expansion joint that will continue to open and close in a cyclic manner. The answer to the first question requires a reasonable understanding of the cause of the crack, while a simple monitoring will determine if there is movement across a crack.

The point is that static, one-time cracking can and should be filled with masonry mortar roughly comparable in properties to the original mortar. On the other hand, cracks that cycle in width may best be filled with a flexible caulking material. Finally, cracks that are actually advancing should be closed on a temporary basis with an extremely elastic caulking material that can be removed eventually when the movement has ceased and final repairs are to be made.

Earlier the procedure for grouting or pointing masonry cracks was discussed, and specifically the need to completely fill crack cavities was addressed. On a weather-exposed exterior wall this is particularly important. A ¼ or ½ inch of mortar across the face of a crack may actually be worse than nothing, because it can trap water in the crack and prevent drying. When cracks are large and follow irregular paths inside the wall, it often becomes extremely difficult to properly ram the mortar back into the void. In such cases "pump-grouting" techniques can be useful. While professionals are available to do this sort of work in many communities, acceptable equipment can be adapted from a number of readily available parts. One of the easiest adaptations is to secure a tube tightly on the end of an old, empty caulking gun, load it with a mortar mix, and pump the crack full. Again, remember to try to estimate the crack and grout volume and thus establish that the crack is being completely filled. If the mortar is to be quickly installed, a sand and cement mixture (3 to 1 parts) is generally adequate, but if the installation time is lengthened to an hour or more, some lime should be added to the mixture to prevent premature setting. If the individual constituents are not easily available, then premixed masonry mortar will suffice.

In the case of known cyclic cracks the best method of repair might require some experimentation. If a good-quality mortar can reestablish the original tension bond across the joint, and if the elimination of the crack does not prevent wall movement in such a way that cracks develop elsewhere, then a mortar closure is definitely preferable. On the other hand, a crack-filling material should not be used that complicates alternate repair procedures if the first repair attempt does not work. For example, sometimes a crack is filled with a soft mortar that fails and crumbles almost to a dust when pressure is applied across the joint. The problem is that such mortar is almost impossible to get out, particularly where it adheres to the original surface; and with the weak mortar in the crack any other joint filler will never function optimally. Thus, if there is a question about what to do at a certain crack, select representative sections of a foot or so in length and actually try several different materials and installation techniques. The trial period should never be less than one year and preferably two full years to assure completion and recycling of any movement pattern.

Bowing of Masonry Walls

The singularly most dramatic distress pattern that can occur to masonry walls is a bowing of the entire surface of a wall. Technically a top-to-bottom warping is called a "bow," while a side-to-side curve is called a "sweep." Such bowing is almost always outward, and thus it is sometimes referred to as "convex-outward." In brick-masonry houses in general, and in solid-brick masonry (i.e., brick as the interior backup material as well as the face material) in particular, this is an extremely common phenomenon. Surprisingly, in many cases it goes unnoticed by owners and casual observers alike. One reason for this is that in many houses it is relatively difficult to observe. Drain downspouts, bushes, and the like make it hard to sight along the face of a building wall. In most cases the bowing takes place slowly enough that the brick can deform without cracking, and thus there are often no other crack patterns to suggest that something is wrong even when the bow (and/or sweep) reaches an inch or more.

Most often the first signs of the problem are on the interior of the house. At the lines of intersecting walls and ceilings, plaster cracks and separations occur that reflect the outward bow of the wall. Specifically, a ceiling–wall-intersection crack starts from nothing at the side wall of the house and widens to a maximum at the middle.

Similarly, cracks between exterior walls and intersecting interior walls reflect this same increase in opening near the center of the outside wall. According to how floors are structured and anchored with respect to the bowed wall, the crack may or may not reduce in width at upper floors and the roofline.

There is a definite preference for south- and west-facing walls that would suggest that the bowing is thermally related. The general consensus is that the phenomenon which produces the bowing is related to both moisture and temperature. It has already been established that owing to thermal variations exterior walls have a tendency to bow outward in the summer and inward in the winter. Several different phenomena are active and must be kept in mind in understanding the consequences of this annual tendency to bow. First, under typical climatic conditions the *average* temperature differences between inside and outside are very nearly the same for both summer and winter (for a 70°F house the average outside temperature may be 50°F during the winter and 90°F during the summer, for a difference of 20°F winter and summer). The extremes, and particularly the regularity and the duration of the extremes, on a sun-facing wall (south) are more severe in summer than in winter. If the wall is hot on the outside and cooler on the inside, the outside expands, the inside surface contracts, and the wall bows convex-outward. Keep in mind that during the summer months there is relatively little vapor-pressure difference across a wall and therefore little moisture migrates through the wall.

During the winter it is true that the colder exterior surface tries to shrink with respect to the warmer interior, which tends to bow the wall the other way, concave-outward. This bowing is partially offset by the moisture gra-

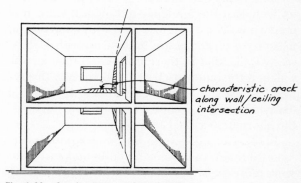

Fig. 4-22 Crack pattern at bowed wall.

dients in the wall during the winter. In most climates there are less drying effects during the winter; moreover, the vapor-pressure differences pump more water through the wall that is concentrated toward the outside. In any event, a moisture gradient exists in the wall that tends to bow the wall convex-outward during the winter in opposition to the thermal effects.

Coupled with these movement characteristics is the lack of reversibility of many building components. This has been referred to before, and it includes such phenomena as the following: (1) It is easier to pull a nailed joint apart than to push it back together; (2) as voids form, as for example where joists fit into a wall, debris falls into the joint as it opens, and such debris cannot necessarily be pushed out as it closes. Thus, every time a wall bows outward, it can be drawn back to its original position a little less; and over a long period of time, the tendency is for it to remain permanently bowed out.

The times required to produce noticeable bowing seem to be a minimum of forty to fifty years and more often much longer.

Like so many other building distress phenomena, masonry wall bowing is relatively random. In what appears to be almost identical situations one wall will bow, while another will not. The explanation of the variability is in part related to the fact that an extremely small *net* bowing occurs each year, perhaps $\frac{1}{50}$ an inch or less. Thus, very slight changes in any of the characteristics may have a profound effect and not allow any bowing to develop. The characteristics of walls that seem most susceptible to bowing are:

- Relatively thin masonry, particularly 8-inch-thick walls
- Uninsulated walls or walls with interior plaster applied to wood battens against the wall
- Sun-facing walls (once in a while a north-facing wall inexplicably develops a healthy bow)
- Walls a minimum of forty to fifty years old
- Walls with a poor interior vapor barrier
- Solid walls as opposed to cavity walls
- Solid brick or brick- and clay-tile walls

Since today walls are rarely built with many of these characteristics, it seems unlikely that the tendency to bow will exist in modern masonry walls. Most modern walls are well insulated with good interior vapor barriers. Also, most masonry walls today are backed up with CMUs, and in addition, many are cavity walls; that is, there is a 1- to 3-inch air space between the inner CMU wall and the outer brick wall. Apparently this type of wall works particularly well because the anchorage between the inner and outer walls (or withes) is not particularly directional and the wall, if it does bow, can fully return during the alternate seasonal changes.

It is extremely rare to find any significant bowing in the brick homes of colonial times. In most eighteenth- and early nineteenth-century houses walls were more massive, and two-withe walls are comparatively rare. As wall thicknesses decreased, the incidence of bowed walls significantly increased.

The exact relation with solar environment may be influenced by such parameters as wind direction and vulnerability to wind. In one Eastern city there is a block of identical row houses on either side of an east–west street. Thus, on one side the houses face south and the fronts are continuously in sunlight during the daylight hours, while the front walls of the north-facing houses have never seen the sun. Not surprisingly the north-facing houses have flat unbowed fronts, while most of the south-facing houses have a sweep in their 18-foot width of 1½ inches or more. The front walls of the last two houses on the north side in this block are, however, flat! These houses are at a comparatively open, windswept corner, and the only difference between these houses and the others seems to be that the walls of these houses might be sufficiently dried by the wind to prevent the development of a permanent sweep.

The solutions to bowed walls are complicated by the facts that since such bowing takes so very long to develop, and since fairly subtle changes can modify the progress of the bowing, it is difficult to be sure whether a particular remedy is working. The first step is to be certain that the structural integrity of the building is maintained, and this can generally be done by anchoring the bowed wall to roof and floor structure in such a way that the wall at least cannot grossly move out. While the details vary slightly according to the way the house floor is structured, a typical correction is to bolt a steel strap to the floor or roof joist and extend this strap through the wall in the form of a bolt. Finally, the load is distributed on the outside of the wall by a washer or steel plate. This exterior washer is frequently fabricated in a star shape, and it is not at all uncommon to see such anchors on the front walls of houses— a signal that wall bowing has been identified and the walls have been anchored to the floors.

A second step in the process of reducing or minimizing the tendency of a wall to bow is to try to modify the environmental factors that most probably contributed to the initial bowing. This remedy presents some difficulties because the parameters that govern the bowing mechanism are not absolutely understood or defined. Certainly insulating the wall and creating a more impermeable vapor barrier can do no harm, but whether this is sufficient correction may take many years to detect.

People have tried to measure the advancement of bowing with, at best,

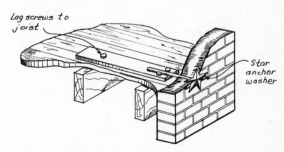

Fig. 4-23 Star bolt wall tie anchor.

marginal success. The problem is that the yearly permanent movement is small on both an absolute basis and in comparison with any given yearly cycle. Thus, yearly net movements seldom exceed $\frac{1}{50}$ inch, while from any given time in the year to another, the movement may differ by only $\frac{1}{20}$ inch. In any event, if any monitoring program is instituted, variations should be recorded so that a continuous record of the yearly movements can be established. This method may provide a clue as to how effective any remedial procedures have been.

Brick Deterioration

Optimally constituted, molded, and clay-fired brick can be an extremely stable building material. It is a form of pottery similar in many respects to earthenware and porcelain ceramic tableware. Thus, under ideal conditions it should not "rust, bust, or collect dust"—in short, it approaches the ideal in building materials.

Unfortunately, the optimum brick is seldom achieved, and the result is that the bricks themselves deteriorate in various ways. Most of the mechanisms of decay have been referred to previously. The deterioration processes fall into two generic categories, mechanical deterioration and chemical decomposition.

It is very easy to distinguish between the two mechanisms. The deterioration process of brick owing to the expansion of water near the surface during freezing occurs necessarily in a planar fashion. Literally, thin layers or wafers of the brick break off the entire surface. These layers are often no more than $\frac{1}{16}$ inch thick and are so uniform that people sometimes suppose that the spalling is related to some defect in the way the brick was molded.

Most commonly, freeze-damaged bricks occur at locations that receive excessive water, such as near the grade, at the bottom of parapet walls, and around leaky roof drains. Seldom are all bricks affected. The more likely

Fig. 4-24 Freeze-damaged brick.

pattern is to find damaged bricks randomly distributed around the damp areas. Once in a great while, a load of bricks is selected that is so grossly vulnerable to freeze damage that all the bricks, regardless of location, have some amount of this damage. This is extremely rare and requires special repair methods. In the more likely situations, that is, randomly deteriorated bricks near uniquely damp locations, the most reasonable corrective step is to try to reduce the excessive water. Often this is merely a matter of unblocking a gutter or regrading to improve drainage and reduce splatter near the wall base.

In dealing with corrective measures for this particular deterioration process, time is on the side of the owner. The progression of freeze damage is relatively slow, and with certain bricks the rate of surface damage actually seems to decrease after the first layer or two break off. There is certainly a rational explanation for some variations in the rate of spalling; as explained earlier, the mechanism is a function of the tensile strength of the surface layers and the moisture gradients existing within these layers. Occasionally a single layer is to blame, and once this has broken off the brick is no longer susceptible to this particular type of failure. In any event, the lack of urgency for making repairs to freeze-damaged bricks permits the luxury of experimenting with various solutions. Rarely do surface sealants prove to be particularly successful, because they tend to worsen the moisture concentration near the surface, and certainly they provide no increase in strength. If they are considered, then a representative area should be selected, the treatment applied, and the results monitored for several years.

If the deteriorating bricks are infrequent enough, it is certainly not unreasonable to consider cutting the damaged bricks out of the wall and installing sound bricks. Many people shy away from replacing individual bricks because of the difficulty of matching the color of bricks and mortar. Bricks are made with such diverse colors and textures that a good match is fairly easy to find. Many brick supply yards will let a customer pick and choose selected bricks for only a modest premium (and a promise to restack the piles). Mortar color can be duplicated by using a nearly white mortar and then painting on dyes. Such dyes are not too permanent, but as they fade the mortar surface generally begins to discolor anyway from dirt and oxidation.

Chemical deterioration of bricks is distinguishable by the surface appearance. Hollow, sort of "scooped out" places develop in the brick surface. Most often the damaged surface is smooth, and while some deteriorating bricks are soft, with a surface that can be dusted off, other bricks remain relatively solid.

With the possible exception of bricks that are deteriorating as a result of chemicals that are drawn up with groundwater, it is rarely necessary to understand much about the chemical process of deterioration. The solution remains more or less the same, that is, to seal the surface from the chemical attack.

In recent years much more chemical deterioration of brick and stone surfaces has developed. The principal sources of the chemicals are the by-prod-

Fig. 4-25   Deteriorated brick masonry.

ucts of burning hydrocarbon fuels. Compounds get into the atmosphere, mix with rain, and in solution attack the brick.

Unfortunately, the remedies for chemically deteriorating brick rarely include cutting off the course of the attacking chemicals. For the present at least, the burning of hydrocarbon fuels is inevitable. If the deteriorating surface is not too large, simply scrubbing it at regular intervals may be a partial solution. Applied surface-sealing compounds have been very successful in some cases, but there are reports that some of these compounds actually diffuse into the brick, change in chemical composition, and cause a new type of chemical decomposition. Obviously, certain sealants can create a freeze-spalling problem that did not exist before.

If absolute prospects for remedies for deteriorating brick seem somewhat gloomy, it is because there are no guaranteed, universally adaptable solutions. When the damage becomes intolerable from either a structural or appearance standpoint, a cement stucco coating always seems to work.

Deteriorating Mortar

Today the constituents of masonry mortar are cements, sand, and lime. Mixed in the proper proportions and applied reasonably quickly, there is very little that can go wrong.

Thus, modern mortar tends to be a stable material that weathers well and is not particularly susceptible to the damaging effects of a freeze-thaw cycle. If too much sand is added to the mix or if the mix is allowed to partially set and additonal water is added (a process called "tempering"), then not only will the strength be reduced but, far more importantly, the durability can be significantly compromised.

Mortars in walls built prior to the 1920s and 1930s may suffer from still another deficiency. For somewhat obscure reasons masons often added all sorts of random materials to mortar, almost as if they were concocting a witches' brew. Generally these additives were another form of lime; for example, ground-up bone and oyster-shell chips were common substitutes and additives. Such materials were not only not in as stable a form as hydrated lime but also often had organic compounds that deteriorated with time. Several modern mortar compounds still have animal bone in addition to the lime, but it is highly processed and controlled in such a way as to enhance the mortar properties, particularly that of workability. Coal chips and dust were common additives along with horse hair, straw, various clays, and even iron filings. The strange thing about these additives to mortar is that there seems to be little or no pragmatic justification for any of them. It may simply have resulted from our fast-moving, transient culture, which never developed craftspeople who had fully observed the results of experimentation. In any event, mortar in many old buildings is decidedly weak, and generally such weak mortar does not resist weathering well.

The weathering mechanism in mortar is somewhat analogous to that of brick. It deteriorates as a result of movements induced by thermal and moisture cycles. Mortar, however, does differ from brick in the way it actually fails. It is not uncommon to find brick walls with mortar that is so soft it can be racked out ¾ inch or more deep with just a pencil, yet this mortar may have remained essentially intact and in place. Exposed edges at corners may be slightly rounded, and any shape to the mortar joint may be vague. Bricks of comparable fragility will almost certainly grossly deteriorate either by the chemical decomposition process or by freeze-thaw cycling of moisture-laden bricks. Weak mortar will absorb substantial quantities of water, but apparently the moisture gradients or changes in the moisture content through the thickness in some way are balanced with the strength and flexibility so that layers of mortar are not spalled off the surface in a fashion comparable to the brick-failure mechanism.

Thus, weak, absorbent mortar does not seem to deteriorate uniformly over the entire surface of a wall. Instead, the damage pattern is extremely preferential, far more so than brick, and is primarily characterized by being in areas of water *flow*. In such areas the mortar is simply undercut and recessed into the wall surface by as much as ½ to 1 inch. Typical locations for such mortar disintegration are:

• Adjacent to broken drainpipes in a geometry that obviously follows the path of water flow down the wall (see Figure 4-26).
• In a unique triangular pattern below windows, particularly ones with slightly extended sills that are flush with the window jambs (see Figure 4-27). The water path in such cases is directed back along the sill and down the wall, and the deteriorated mortar follows this path very closely.
• For the full height of buildings along the corners. This is particularly true on walls at right angles to a windward wall, that is, a wall that faces a dominant wind direction.

Fig. 4-26 Deteriorated mortar at broken drainpipe.

Fig. 4-27 Deteriorated brick and mortar below windowsill.

There seems to be some disagreement as to the exact mechanism of such mortar damage and its relationship to the water flow. One view holds to the theory of the deterioration resulting from excess moisture expansion during freezing. While this may be true in some cases, it is certainly not the dominant mechanism of failure, because the same level of distress can be found in totally different environments, some of which have few or no freezing conditions. Colonial houses in Charleston, South Carolina, and Boston, Massachusetts, can be found with almost exactly the same degree of mortar undermining at comparable locations and under such extremely different winter weather conditions it is difficult to conclude that any freeze-related phenomena would be the same in both cities.

Another theory relating deteriorated mortar to water-flow paths is that either harmful chemicals are washed into the mortar by the water or, conversely, protected surfaces and chemicals are washed away. Finally, some observers argue that it is merely the mechanical scrubbing of the water flowing across the surface that removes soft mortar. Certainly this has some effect but must not be the principal mechanism, simply because both horizontal and vertical joints are typically recessed the same amount at locations where the water flow obviously tends to wash one surface more than another. Thus, almost by default the deterioration must principally be related to harmful chemicals that are supplied to or removed from the mortar.

Beyond the recognition that mortar deterioration is dominantly influenced by water flow, it may not be necessary to understand the exact details of the mechanism of failure and certainly not the chemistry of failure. Remedial work should start with a walk in the rain or, if an owner thinks the neighbors might question his or her wisdom in standing in the rain and looking at a water-soaked wall, a garden hose can be used to simulate water flows. If a unique flow path can be identified corresponding to an area of disintegrating mortar, the first step is to try to alter the water-flow path. In some cases this may be impractical, but in others it may involve inserting a small strip of metal in a mortar joint or extending a joint beyond the surface of the surrounding bricks to channel the water in a more uniform path and away from the affected area.

Actual repair of recessed mortar joints involves "pointing" (also called "tuckpointing") the mortar joints. Select a mortar with strength characteristics as close to the existing mortar as possible and yet one that has sufficient weathering properties. Excessively loose mortar should be racked out. The wall should then be hosed off to clean the surface of loose, dusty materials. Finally, the actual pointing involves ramming or driving the mortar tightly into the joint. One common problem that often arises with pointing of old brick is that the joint line cannot be made clean and precise because the edges of the bricks are chipped and rounded so that there is not a regular surface to use as a guide for finishing the exposed surface. Because of this, mortar joints are often irregular and smear out on the face of the brick. Later attempts to clean the brick surface are not very satisfactory and can actually cause irreparable damage if harsh chemicals or abrasives are used. One solution may be to create a mortar joint that has a differently shaped surface, with edges slightly recessed below the brick. Such a detail may also create different water-flow patterns across the wall surface and thus minimize recurrence of damage.

Brick-Veneer-on-Wood Frame

Brick-veneer-on-wood frame is a hybrid wall—a combination of brick and wood which, it is hoped, will combine some of the best properties of both. Some people refer to any brick-faced wall that is not also backed with brick as being "veneered," and so far as the language is concerned this is an appropriate use of the word. More commonly, however, "brick-veneer wall" refers to the construction, as shown in the cross section of Figure 4-5.

In recent years brick-veneer-on-frame has been widely used with good success. If for no other reason houses will have veneered walls because of the comparative ease of insulating them. Not only can fiber insulation be installed between the studs, but sheathing materials can also be selected that have good temperature resistance. Finally, the air space between the brick and wood serves double duty by adding further insulation to the properties of the wall and allowing some air circulation on the interior of the wall—a good inhibitor of moisture.

Surprisingly, veneer-on-stud walls do not share many of the combined distress patterns of masonry and frame alone. Such walls do not seem particularly subject to any permanent bowing problems. Any temperature gradient that develops in the thickness of the wall is primarily in the insulated, inner section, and thus the brick width is more nearly at a constant temperature in comparison with a solid-masonry wall. Secondly, the moisture that migrates from the interior can be removed partially at the middle air gap. Finally, the inner and outer sections, that is, the wood and brick, are not rigidly tied together, and they can move more or less independently of one another. Thus, the characteristics necessary for bowing either do not exist or are minimized.

Of course, cracks do develop in veneered walls. A crack pattern that is almost unique to such walls is one that initially develops in a block (CMU) basement owing to such mechanisms as shrinkage during curing or to excessive moisture during erection. In a conventional masonry house such cracks rarely extend much above grade into the exterior wall, because the upper wall tends to be of stronger materials and can more easily dry out. These cracks seem to occur most often in houses with 12-inch-thick foundation walls, which is consistent in that the basement wall strength is significantly more than just the single withe of brick in the veneer wall. Thus a crack in the basement can be *forced* up into the upper, veneered wall.

The best method of identifying a veneered wall crack with this mechanism is to examine the basement wall crack. The first requirement is that the crack have all the characteristics associated with shrinkage cracks in CMU foundation walls (see Chapter 3). Next, examine the extension of the crack as it advances into the brick veneer above. If the crack generally diminishes in width and turns sort of randomly toward window and door openings, chances are it is a crack forced into the upper wall by the lower wall crack.

Still another crack pattern that seems to be slightly more prevalent in veneered brick might best be referred to as "control-joint cracking." As described earlier, as any masonry wall becomes longer the *total* movements due to environmental changes necessarily become greater. Therefore, if the wall can only accommodate these movements at one or two locations, the movement across these locations will increase with increased length of wall. If the accommodation is in the form of a crack, then the crack will be wider for a long wall than for a short one. If, on the other hand, a joint can be built into the wall that will allow movement, all the movement may occur at this one location and no crack will develop. Thus, designers purposely locate control joints in long masonry walls. Sometimes these joints involve no more than simply omitting a vertical line of mortar and closing the resulting gap with a flexible caulking material. In other cases relatively complicated metal slots are built into the wall—slots that will allow the differential movement and yet maintain the structural and weathering continuity of the wall. These joints function in exactly the same manner as metal "expansion joints" in a road surface on both ends of a long highway bridge.

In the case of long masonry walls there is simply no absolute criteria for where and when to provide control joints. Generally, walls that exceed 100 feet should have an expansion joint—unless they are extremely uniform with respect to openings that otherwise might be weak planes in which cracks could develop. Houses, of course, are rarely this long, so very few houses have control joints built into them. Furthermore, it is not too common to see crack distress that can be related to this phenomenon in residential buildings. In the relatively rare situations where control-joint cracking is observed in residential buildings, it is most often in brick-veneer walls. The characterization of such cracks is as follows: (1) The wall is long, 60 to 70 feet minimum; (2) the crack is nearly vertical and probably runs through window or door openings; and (3) there is significant movement across the crack during any yearly cycle. Such a crack should never be filled with a hard mortar! Once the building has established a particular plane in which to accommodate any movements, it will always tend to occur at or near this plane. If an active expansion joint is restrained, another crack will develop within a few feet, and incorrectly blocking or restricting a series of expansion joints can lead to a collection of relatively severe cracks.

The most practical repair method is to caulk the joint with a flexible caulking material specifically designed to expand and contract over a specified range. If possible, the caulking should be applied at the mean movement condition, that is, roughly halfway between the most-open and the most-closed conditions.

One of the few serious complaints about brick-veneer walls concerns water leaks. Such walls are certainly no more vulnerable to leaking than other types of masonry; but in the case of a solid-masonry wall exterior, leaks show up on the inside within a few feet of the outside opening. This is not true of veneered walls, because the water can travel far down the middle surface of brick and sheathing before entering into the inner stud wall. Thus, a first-floor interior leak may actually have its origin on the second floor. It can be maddening to try to find the source of such leaks, but by sprinkling the wall with a garden hose in controlled experimentation the water path may sometimes be discernible.

Rarely are any of the distress patterns that develop in the exterior walls of residential buildings a signal of some gross structural deficiency that requires immediate action. Under such circumstances a little thought and observations may lead to an accurate diagnosis of the cause as well as a remedy. Take your time—think, observe, and avoid doing anything that cannot be undone if it does not work.

INTERIOR WALLS AND CEILINGS

5

The diagnosis of distress to interior walls would seem at first glance to be a simple proposition in comparison with that of exterior walls. The environmental conditions are relatively benign; changes or gradients in geometry, load, materials, temperature, and moisture content are generally slight; and, with few exceptions, there is only one material—plaster—with which to contend. There is certainly no lack of damage, because no residential building more than a few years old is free of plaster wall distress, and with very rare exceptions, interior walls become more and more deteriorated. The key to understanding interior wall distress is an understanding of plaster.

Since residential ceilings are even more likely to be of plaster than are walls, and since environmental factors are so similar for both, it is appropriate to consider ceilings along with interior walls. Most plaster distress patterns as well as plaster repair procedures are also common to both.

Plaster

Materials

Plaster is composed of three materials: (1) the cementitious material or binder, (2) an aggregate or filler material that is more or less inert, and (3) water. Small amounts of other materials are sometimes added to control the setting time and workability properties of the plaster. In recent years three cementitious materials have been commonly used: gypsum, lime, and portland cement. In very old homes cements compounded of natural-clay products are sometimes found. All three types of cements are made from naturally occurring (or combined) mineral rock. The rock is mined, ground, and fired or heated in a process called "calcining" in the case of gypsum and lime. Next, the furnace clinkers are ground to a fine powder. It is this powder form that is eventually mixed with aggregate and water to form plaster. Of the three cements, only portland cement is truly hydraulic; that is, it will harden in the presence of water, and once hardened it is not soluble in water.

While it is not absolutely necessary to understand the chemistry of the hardening process to appreciate most of the crack phenomena, some of the chemical interactions that cause deterioration require a very modest appreciation of the mechanism of curing.

Gypsum, an ancient plaster material, was used at least as far back as 4000 B.C. by the Egyptians to plaster parts of the pyramids. Paris, France, is founded on an unusually large bed of calcium sulfate, the mineral of gypsum; hence the name "plaster of paris," another name for gypsum plaster cement. The presence of this mineral also accounts for the difficulties of getting good drinking water in the area of Paris, a situation that may have had the salutory effect of contributing to the development of better French wines. Even though gypsum plaster has been known and used for so long a time, it was not in general use as an interior wall plaster cement until the beginning of the twentieth century. The problem with natural gypsum is that the setting time is not predictable or easily controlled. Since then, better quality control of the constituents, the manufacturing process, and small amounts of admixtures have made gypsum cement an extremely reliable material, with the result that today it is the principal plaster cement. Specially processed gypsum can be used in cements that produce the highest-strength plaster available, even higher than portland cement plaster.

Calcium sulfate deposits are the residues of ancient seas and were created as the water evaporated. In the calcining process the ground rock is heated to at least 300 to 400°F, which drives off a certain amount of water retained in the crystalline structure. In this dried form the gypsum is said to be "hemi-hydrated," and when it is again mixed with water the original crystalline form is reestablished in a hard, rocklike material. Gypsum plaster can be mixed with fillers such as wood fibers that produce an unusually high-strength, hard plaster.

Gypsum plaster, once it starts to harden or set, cannot be retempered, that is, returned to a paste form by remixing with water. The setting process is rather abrupt, for the plaster will change consistency from an easily workable paste to a semirigid, totally unworkable solid in only a few minutes. This characteristic can obviously complicate the application process; but, unlike brick mortar, in which retempering leads to weakened mortar and therefore rapid deterioration, retempered gypsum plaster simply does not work, because the rewatered product is so weak and lumpy that it simply falls apart. Additives, called "retarders," can be included in the original plaster mix to extend setting times; however, it is generally not recommended, because such products almost invariably decrease the desirable properties of the plaster. It was not uncommon for old-time plasterers to include a cup of sugar in a plaster mix—a good retarder for setting and a good method of grossly reducing strength and hardness.

Prior to the twentieth century, gypsum plaster was principally a molding plaster used in the production of figurines and fancy, precast plaster decorations. In eighteenth- and nineteenth-century buildings, many of the complicated plaster decorations of molding and classical revival detailing ornamentation were cast in gypsum plaster.

Lime is obtained from processing limestone, a common mineral consisting of calcium or magnesium carbonate, or combinations of both. Marble and caulk are both natural forms of limestone, but not alabaster, which is a form of gypsum.

The burning or calcining process of lime is very similar to that of gypsum, but the chemical mechanism is completely different. In the case of gypsum, heat is used to force the dissociation of the combined water of crystallization; while in the case of lime, the burning process drives off carbon dioxide and changes the form to calcium or "quicklime," as it is commonly called. The final product is recombined with water and ground to form hydrated lime. In the setting process soaked or "slaked" lime is applied and tends to return to its original rock-like state by absorption of atmospheric carbon dioxide, a process that technically is called "recarbonation," but is generally referred to (incorrectly) as "hydration." If the outer surface of the lime plaster hardens too quickly, it can seal the interior to the penetration of carbon dioxide and the hardening process can never take place. This is probably the chief reason that lime is most often used as a thin, surface coating and not as a thick, massive base coat. This mechanism has not always been understood, and much of the lime-plaster deterioration can be attributed to excessively thick coats.

Today lime plaster is restricted almost exclusively to polished, finish coats, but historically lime plaster was *the* building plaster and dates back to the earliest-known civilizations. Any plaster applied before World War I is almost certainly lime plaster for both finish and base coats. The most important reason for identifying the particular type of plaster cement relates to the compatibility of patch materials. For small areas and for crack patching, serious problems generally do not occur, but many plasterers insist on re-placing large expanses of plaster surface with plaster using the same cement. Lime plaster will soften and disintegrate when soaked in water, while most gypsum plasters will soften but not lose their form. Water has negligible immediate effects on the mechanical properties of portland cement plaster.

Portland cement is a combination of limestone, minerals, and claylike sub-stances. While the exact constituents of modern portland cement are not found in nature, there are natural deposits of minerals which, when properly processed, produce cements very close to the modern product. The manu-facturing process is similar to that of gypsum and lime; specifically, after the various raw materials are crushed and mixed, they are fired at an extremely high temperature, near 2700°F. The ingredients actually combine to form a new substance which, when cooled, form clinkers that are subsequently crushed and ground into the finished portland cement. When combined with water, a complex reaction takes place and eventually the cement sets into a dense, hard mass.

Portland cement is rarely used in the interior of typical residential con-struction, and when it is used, it is almost invariably to take advantage of its resistance to water. Of course, on the exterior it is regularly found in the form of stucco—simply another name for portland cement plaster. Once in a while, a builder will go to the effort of applying cement plaster in a bathroom, but more commonly ceramic tiles are used to waterproof bathroom walls. Until very recently, many bathrooms in Northern Europe were equipped with a drain in the middle of the floor, with the expectation that water could flow anyplace throughout the room. Such bathrooms often had portland cement plaster or specially processed gypsum plaster walls with little or no tiling.

The *aggregates* of modern plaster fall into two categories: lightweight and standard. Sand is the most common "standard" (weight) plaster aggregate. Once in a great while for very specialized applications stone chips or "dust" will replace part of the sand, but generally this is not recommended because of the difficulty in sizing the particles and the fact that slight impurities are more difficult to control. In clean, well-graded (for size and shape) sand, dissolved chemicals and organic impurities can sometimes exist. Even small amounts of such materials can have a significant effect on all plaster properties, particularly setting time and strength; and as a practical matter variations in the sand aggregate are the greatest contributor to inconsistent-quality plaster.

The two lightweight aggregates that are relatively common in modern plaster are vermiculite and perlite. Both are "expanded" mineral or glasslike substances, which are literally exploded by heating to create a lightweight, inert filler material. These aggregates not only decrease the strength of the plaster but also tend to produce a plaster somewhat more sensitive to moisture and thermal expansion. On the other hand, the resulting plaster is significantly lighter in weight (50 pounds per cubic foot versus 120 pounds per cubic foot for average sand-aggregate plaster), generally has more precise properties because of relative freedom from extraneous foreign products, and has better sound-absorption characteristics.

Methods of Application

Most people are familiar with what is alternately called "dry wall," "Sheetrock," or "wallboard," a gypsum plasterboard that is wrapped in paper to contain and strengthen the plaster and that eventually constitutes the exposed wall surface. Dry-wall board comes in thicknesses from ⅜ to ¾ inch and in sheet sizes of 4 feet × 8 feet and 4 feet × 12 feet. The sheets are nailed and sometimes glued to the interior wall structure. Along the edges of each sheet is a depression to receive a piece of paper tape that is cemented in place with a plasterlike product known as "spackle." Any irregularities are sanded off, nail holes are spackled, and eventually the paper-and-spackle surface is painted. The dry-wall process has been in use since the late 1930s, and the vast majority of houses built in the last twenty-five years have gypsum dry-wall board on the interior walls. In general, it has proven to be an extremely satisfactory material if for no other reason than its excellent fireproofing characteristics.

With minor exceptions plasters are incombustible, and when they are properly applied they act as a fire retarder to protect structure. The biggest lim-

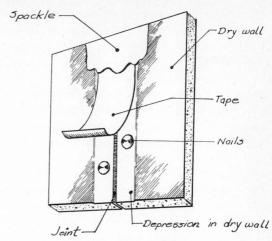

Fig. 5-1   Tape and spackle on dry wall.

itation to this fire-retardant capability seems to be the method of mechanical attachment to the backup structure. Plasterboard, like any other material, will tend to bow and warp as a temperature gradient develops through the thickness. Eventually, the forces associated with the warping can overcome the resistance of the nails, the panel will separate from the structure, and the fire barrier will be lost. Too often builders tend to secure the panel to any structure with an absolute minimum number of nails to avoid the surface irregularities caused by spackling over the nail heads. From an aesthetic point of view this is reasonable, but it lessens the fire integrity of the wall.

Nailing patterns in accordance with code requirements should be used to secure any dry wall to structure. More or less the same attachment problem exists with any plaster product, but with plaster-on-lath there is a tendency to secure the laths sufficiently so that the attachment method is not the weak link in the fire-barrier system.

Dry-wall systems offer several other advantages over conventionally applied plaster, the principal one being that the quality control and therefore the consistency of the plaster (but not necessarily the installation) is excellent and likely to be one of the most repetitious items among houses. For this reason, the various crack distress patterns encountered in plaster-on-lath that are attributed to variations in the mechanical properties of the plaster, per se, simply do not occur with dry wall.

In any plaster system there seem to be some very time-dependent deterioration characteristics. Ignoring the distress patterns that develop in the first few months after installation, certain types of cracking seem to occur after a time period of forty to sixty years. Thus, plaster-on-lath systems installed between forty and sixty years ago that have been generally crack-free suddenly begin to crack and sag. Very little dry wall has been in service that long, and the critical time for dry wall may be different than that for plaster-on-lath. Still, the complete life cycle of dry wall has not yet been fully established. There are modest examples to suggest that some of the first dry-wall applications are deteriorating in ways analogous to conventional plaster.

Plaster-on-lath wall systems have progressed through a number of details over the years, but the basic system remains fairly constant. A material spans the structure, and the wet plaster is applied to this material, called "lath." Twigs interwoven between sticks, as in the daub-and-wattle system (see Figure 4-10, were the earliest form of lath. Next came thin wood strips roughly ⅜ inch thick by 1½ inch wide spanning between wall studs or floor joists. This system was used almost exclusively until the second quarter of the twentieth century. Wood laths were nailed to each stud, and then a rough coat of plaster was applied. No name for this first coat seems to be universally accepted. "Base coat" is the most common term, but sometimes it also is called "scratch coat," "brown coat," or "key coat." Technically, *base coat* refers to any plaster coat other than the final, finish coat, and scratch and brown are the first two coats in a three-coat plaster system. In any event, the first coat was intended to be forced in the spaces between laths and thus actually lock or "key" the plaster to the wall. Additional applications of plaster were made, most commonly two, until finally a finish coat was applied. This finish coat could be smooth or patterned depending on the aesthetics desired, but generally there was an effort made to select a plaster composition that would cure to a particular hard surface.

Over the years, builders have changed their minds as to how many coats of plaster are desirable. Until very recently the norms have been two or three coats. In any repair process it is important to understand why plaster is applied in individual coats and what properties each coat should have. The logic for the application of multiple coats is generally as follows:

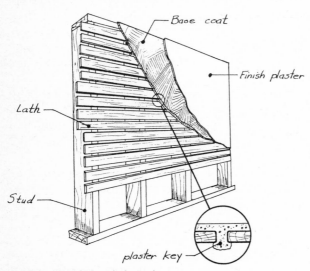

Fig. 5-2 Wood lath and plaster key.

1   *Stiffen the base structure.* Most lath systems are relatively flexible and must be made more rigid before the application of the final coats of material that will dry eventually to a hard, brittle consistency. Several modern plaster systems that are applied to rigid gypsum board work satisfactorily with only one coat. Also, plaster is not applied gently like a very thick coat of paint; rather, it must be forced against the surface to assure a bond between coats and to densify the plastic material in the case of lime plaster. Any base coat and lath must be rigid and strong to withstand these application forces.

2   *Allow cracking in base courses.* Necessarily, as layers of plaster are applied to wood structures, considerable movements occur. Lathing radically changes moisture content, considerable weight is added, and often other construction operations that occur simultaneously with plastering could produce movement in walls. Thus, as subsequent coats are applied, fewer and fewer cracks develop in the surface until, it is to be hoped, *no* cracks occur in the final coat. Based on this information, a homeowner may logically decide to wait as long as possible to allow the maximum movement and attendant cracking to occur before applying the finish coat. With certain combinations of plaster courses this is an admissible sequence, but more often the best bond strengths are developed when successive applications do not exceed a week or two at most.

3   *Optimization of mechanical properties.* The many functions that plaster is required to accommodate would suggest that different coats should have different mechanical properties. For example, the first, scratch coat should be strong and workable enough to permit a key to be forced out around any lathing. On the other hand, a final coat should be able to be finished with the regularity and texture desired. Such variations in properties are rarely consistent and found in a single plaster material. Thus, it is almost inevitable that at least two coats over lath will be required.

4   *Dimensional control.* The ability of plaster to be worked into a smooth, level surface makes it very appealing. The eye can detect extremely subtle variations in surface contours, and when they are obviously unintentional they can be very objectionable. Large expanses of plaster can be applied to within hundredths-of-an-inch tolerance, and such regularity alone becomes part of the appeal of plaster as a surfacing material. Alternatively, in modern dry-wall systems, a major criticism of it is the relatively minute surface-contour imperfections at spackled nail holes. As each coat is applied it can be brought more nearly to the desired surface contour until the thin, final coat can be finished and smoothed to very exact tolerances. Generally, the thinner the coat, the closer the contour tolerance can be controlled; and thus in a finish coat of ¼ inch or less, more precise flatnesses can be achieved than in a 1-inch-thick brown (or middle) coat. Finally, the finish coat does not require any roughening as base coats do to assure bond strength. The resulting surface can be sighted along and the surface work can be achieved to the desired flatness.

5 *Densification and bond.* Lime plaster in particular can actually be made more dense by compressing it in the plastic state. The thinner the coat, the more pressure can be applied without deforming the coat and simply squeezing it out of the way. Similarly, the forces required to press the surface together and create cohesive bonds between coats can best be achieved with relatively thin individual coats. Both these requirements imply that multiple coats are desirable.

6 *Curing.* With gypsum and portland cement, the access to air has nothing to do with the curing or hardening process; however, since lime hardens by absorbing carbon dioxide, the more material that can be exposed to air (and therefore the carbon dioxide gases), the more extensive the chemical change and the harder the plaster. Since lime is almost never used today for base coats, this is not a substantial argument for modern plasterwork; however, it does in part explain what was done in pretwentieth-century houses and therefore may affect repair procedures. Specifically, lime plaster hardens from the outside in, and since little if any carbon dioxide can diffuse through the hard outer surface, the interior only dries out, never changes its chemical composition, and simply remains lime. In many old houses the surface of lime plaster is so hard that a sharp steel tool is needed to scratch it, yet if this hard outer surface is broken away, the interior plaster is soft and spongy. The solution to this problem has been to apply many thin coats, all of which would harden for their full thickness. Ancient Roman and Greek ruins have walls with ten or more thin lime-plaster layers. Such walls have actually been assumed to be marble, which, of course, is chemically and structurally precisely what they are.

7 *Thickness limitations.* Thin coats of materials can be either too thick or too thin. Portland cement plasters tend to crack excessively if the thickness is much below ¼ inch, and ½-inch minimums are most often recommended. On the other hand, if a single coat much exceeds 1 inch, the weight is too great and the coat may simply fall off. Nothing is more frustrating, particularly to a plasterer, than to have an entire wall of wet, overthick plaster simply peel off. On a ceiling the maximum thickness of an individual coat is best kept below ½ inch.

Thus, plaster must almost always be applied in multiple layers. Each of these layers is required to perform a specific function and each should have properties and application procedures consistent with these functions.

Wood lath, while almost never used today, exists in so many older houses requiring remodeling that certain characteristics are worth considering. First is a rather odd controversy concerning the properties of wood lath. Plasterers old enough to remember the general use of wood lath say that it had to be "green" or unseasoned wood. The argument goes that dry, seasoned wood will draw or suck the water out of the plaster in the neighborhood of the key and produce a weaker mortar. In some respects this seems reasonable, but it is not completely consistent with the curing mechanism of lime mortar. Still, these same plasterers refuse to apply gypsum plaster to old, dry wood lath, and for this, there is ample technical justification. In any event, if plaster is to be patched over old wooden lath, modern expanded metal (wire) lath should be nailed to the old lath surface to receive the scratch coat.

One of the oddities of the wood-lath issue is that lathing can still be bought at many lumberyards, and there is no effort whatever made to have green, wet lumber. In special cases where the material is not ordinarily stocked, most yards will be happy to cut a supply of lath from modern framing lumber. This violates another requirement of old-timers who maintain that poplar and pine are the only proper lath materials, but there are many examples of two-hundred-year-old plaster-on-oak, -fir, and even -walnut lathing, implying that the wood species is more a question of availability than any specific physical properties of the wood.

Details of the plaster key in wood lath have an extremely important effect on a particular failure mechanism that occurs principally in ceilings. The cyclic movement of any structure, and particularly of a wood-frame structure, has been reviewed extensively. Consider what happens in plastered ceilings when there is differential movement between the plaster and the wood structure above. A force develops at the junction between the plaster and the wood as a consequence of any such differential movement, and the plaster keys, of course, are the jointing element. Eventually, after repeated cycles of strain, perhaps over a number of years, a plaster key fractures. Once one location in a ceiling has been established as *the* weak place, then successive cycles will tend to continually advance this first rupture in an ever-widening pattern. Eventually, so much of the key bond in a particular area is broken that the adjacent keys can no longer support the ceiling below the area of the broken ones, and the ceiling plaster abruptly collapses. According to the stiffness and surface characteristics of the plaster, areas of broken keys are often extremely difficult to detect visually. Sections of ceiling without any key support can span 4 or 5 feet without any noticeable sag. Generally, however, it is slightly more flexible than securely keyed plaster, and the damage done can be felt by gently pushing up on the plaster. More commonly, damaged plaster, called "fatigued plaster" by some, sags noticeably and thus gives ample warning of an impending disaster.

Such sagging plaster should not be casually disregarded. Just because it has been sagging for a long time is not justification for neglect, because collapse can be abrupt, totally unpredictable, and quite dangerous. A relatively small area of plaster, say, 5 feet × 5 feet, can easily weigh several hundred pounds, enough to do substantial damage to furniture and heads. People often report that a section of ceiling collapsed just as they closed a door; at some point the slightest jar will initiate collapse. It is not uncommon to see ceilings which, perhaps owing to irregularities of cracks and sagging, have been wallpapered. As the keys fail and more and more ceiling area is left unsupported, the wallpaper actually provides some support, and thus more keys can fail before collapse. Then, when the collapse actually takes place, the paper can pull marginally supported plaster down. For this reason, entirely papered ceilings sometimes fall.

Obviously, the remedy for ceilings damaged in this way is to remove the damaged area and replace the plasterwork. Inevitably, the very act of removing key-damaged plaster extends the region of failure, and most people conclude it is best to remove an entire ceiling once this mechanism of failure has begun.

Modern lathing typically takes two generically different forms. One is metal lath, most often the "expanded steel" type. Such lath is formed by simply pulling apart, or expanding, a sheet of steel that has been punch-cut in a staggered pattern. In residential building applications, expanded metal lathing is most often used in forming complicated plaster shapes and is wired to lightweight metal channel sections. More common for flat plasterwork is metal rib lath, similar to expanded metal, but which comes in long sheets that are made more rigid by solid strips of deformed steel.

The other type of modern lath consists of sheets of gypsum plaster sandwiched between two sheets of paper. Actually, dry-wall systems evolved from these materials, but initially they were introduced to replace wood lath. Basically, this lath works like a prefabricated first coat, for the sheets are nailed to wood studs and joists, or screwed in the case of metal studs, and one or two coats of conventional plaster are applied to the surface. Some gypsum lath is perforated with holes at regular intervals, which allows a mechanical key bond to develop, but most builders rely on the plaster simply bonding to the paper surface. People commonly refer to gypsum lath by regional names or trade names such as "Sheetrock," "rock lath," or "plasterboard."

So far, the discussion has been restricted more or less to lath and plaster systems applied to wood or metal walls and ceilings. There is nothing intrinsically wrong with applying plaster to masonry. After all, stucco is an arbitrary designation given to exterior plaster and is regularly applied to masonry. However, there are a number of problems with applying interior plaster to masonry walls and particularly to exterior masonry walls.

An exterior masonry wall with just plaster applied to the interior surface has so little heat resistance that it would have been rarely tolerated even before modern conservation requirements prohibited it. In addition, since

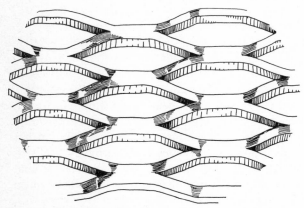

Fig. 5-3   Expanded metal.

few masonry walls are completely impervious to water, any water that penetrates the full wall thickness will certainly discolor and possibly deteriorate the plaster applied directly to the inner surface. Between certain plasters and brick masonry there are chemical interactions that tend to cause deterioration in one or the other of the components. Finally, if plaster is applied directly to the masonry, any crack in the masonry will be completely mirrored in the interior plaster surface. For these reasons, plaster is seldom applied directly to masonry walls.

The typical approach to applying plaster to masonry walls is to "fir" the wall in some fashion. This process involves attaching to the wall strips of wood or metal called "firring strips" and then building the plaster walls on these strips just as if they were studs. Until recently such firring strips were 1 to 2 inches thick and therefore created an air gap between the masonry and plaster that acted as an insulator, a crack stopper, a place for water to flow away from the plaster, and finally a separation between brick and plaster that prevented any chemical interaction. By this means all the problems of applying plaster to masonry were solved. In the last few years, the use of much wider firring strips has been encouraged, so that the resulting cavity can be insulated. Eventually, the firring becomes so deep that it is like building a complete stud wall on the interior of a masonry wall. Such considerations have been responsible in part for the extensive use of brick veneer on wood-stud systems (see Chapter 4).

Most modern firring is simply nailed to the masonry wall with a masonry or hard nail. Mastic materials have also been used. In older homes, particularly those built before the widespread use of nails that could easily penetrate brick, the problem of attaching the firring strip to the masonry was solved by placing wood plugs or strips in the masonry when it was initially layed up. These inserts were at regular intervals, and the firring strips could be easily nailed to this wood with conventional nails. Wood and brick are such grossly divergent materials that it should not be surprising that this procedure of building a wood and brick masonry wall did not always work. The amazing thing is that it *did* work in 99 out of a 100 cases. Unfortunately, when it did not work, repairs were extremely complex. The most common problems involved rot or insect damage. In some cases, the wood strips alternatively became wet and dry with a corresponding expansion and contraction, which had the net effect of cyclically "jacking" the wall from the inner face. In rare cases, this repeated movement has created discontinuities on the exterior wall in the form of cracks or color changes reflecting the interior wood strips.

Since the early 1960s, several new systems of plaster application have been introduced. Obviously, none has yet withstood the test of time to prove its relative durability with respect to other plaster systems; one, however, has been used enough to deserve comment. Several rigid foam plastic insulation board materials were introduced in the early 1960s. Polystyrene (Styrofoam) planks, 1 inch thick and 16 to 24 inches wide, were glued to masonry walls with a special adhesive. On the interior face dry wall was attached, again with adhesive, or conventional plaster was applied to the surface. A reasonably

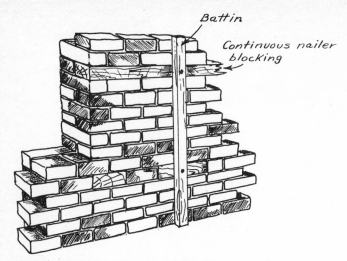

Fig. 5-4 Wood nailer blocking in brick wall.

good insulation barrier was thus created, and yet the interior wall could move more or less independently of the exterior masonry. After fifteen to twenty years of service, most applications have been trouble-free, and the only serious complaints revolve around the difficulty of hanging heavy pictures or mirrors on these walls. There is no stud to nail into, and the masonry is several inches from the surface—too far for conventional picture hangers to penetrate.

Plaster Properties

Mechanical and physical properties of plaster as they relate to distress and deterioration of plaster walls and ceilings are difficult to define precisely because they are so incredibly variable. For example, tensile strengths, or the strengths that are a measure of the resistance to being pulled apart, are reported to vary by as much as 10 to 1 (50 pounds per square inch to 500 pounds per square inch). Furthermore, these values are only applicable to completely dry samples—a condition that rarely exists in the average home. Plaster strength is relatively more affected by moisture than are most other building materials; an addition of 2 percent moisture to completely dry plaster can reduce the strength by one-half or more. On the other hand, plaster can be one of the highest-strength materials in a house; specially prepared and applied plaster can achieve strengths several times greater than typical concrete.

Somewhat the same story is true with respect to other physical properties. All plasters, but particularly old plasters, are variably formulated and applied with the result that it is almost impossible to predict with certainty exactly how a plaster wall will perform. While all plaster is incombustible, some will resist dramatic fires while others will spall and fracture under the application of heat and allow the fire to pass. These variations are restricted to field-applied plaster and particularly old plaster and do not apply to gypsum lath or dry wall—materials that, because of their factory fabrication, are well controlled and have extremely uniform properties.

In the context of understanding plaster distress mechanisms, particularly cracking phenomena, it is better to have a general understanding of how the various properties are related to cracking than to know specific values of any of the properties. Thus, consider the crack mechanism in plaster. The plaster cracks when it is strained (deformed) beyond a certain value, but like so many other building materials, the time involved in application of the strain is critical. Every designer knows that if a plaster ceiling deflects beyond a certain limit, some cracks will develop. For average-sized rooms, ceiling deflections due to the live or "people" loads are limited to roughly ⅓ to ½ inch. When these limits are exceeded, cracks invariably develop, *provided* the deflection occurs relatively rapidly, that is, in a time span measured in months or at the very most one or two years. If the movement is slow, gross deformations can exist without any cracking. Often ceilings are supported by wood joists that have creep deformed over many years and produced deflections of 4 and 5 inches in a 15-foot span. No cracks exist! Similar crack-free ceilings exist with sagged ceilings owing to plaster key failures. The explanation is that plaster, like so many other building materials such as wood, concrete, and masonry, is a relatively ductile material under long-term loading; whereas short-term loads cause the material to act brittlely, that is, to fracture under load before deforming.

Exactly what is meant by "long term" and "short term" in the context of plaster cracking? Unfortunately, there is no reliable data to say that if a wall is strained for a certain period, it will or will not crack. Clearly, periods of one year and less must be classified in the short-term period, because cracks do develop at locations that are cyclically strained owing to annual moisture and thermal changes. A more exact definition is of marginal value for plaster in general, because it is quite clear that variations in plaster quality account for differences over shorter time spans. In adjacent row houses that have been built at the same time and generally by the same mechanics, cracks will occur in one house and not in another until perhaps a year or two later. The only rational explanation to account for this difference is the variation in plaster mechanical properties.

Ideally, then, what mechanical properties would be most desirable? It would be desirable to have a hard, wear-resistant outer surface. Unfortunately, hardness is consistent with brittleness. Thus, the interior of the plaster should have properties that might compensate for a brittle outer layer. Such a property would require a relatively more flexible, that is, less stiff, plaster. Decreased stiffness is generally consistent with lower strength. Furthermore, another desirable property of the interior plaster coats would be one of dimensional stability—specifically dimensional changes related to moisture variations both during curing and after. Since the aggregate is inert, it does not change dimensions with moisture variations. Thus, in general the middle (or brown) coat should be a slightly weaker mix in terms of sand-to-cement ratios. Finally, the first coat should have high bond strength to whatever lath system is used.

This ideal plaster system is rarely achieved, but deviations from the model can be used to account for many variations in crack formation. Unfortunately, some of these properties conflict slightly, and an imbalance can lead to certain distress patterns. For example, there are two somewhat standard crack phenomena that occur on plaster surfaces and that complicate the use of the ideal plaster system. One is a random cracking often called "map cracking," where enclosed areas perhaps 1 foot or more across are surrounded by a crack. There are no particular directional characteristics to the cracks in that they do not run from a discontinuity or otherwise defined location to another. Most often map cracking is not extensive through a house, but rather occurs in restricted areas of a few walls or ceilings. The explanation for this crack phenomenon is the lack of *uniformity* of bond somewhere in the system, either between laminates of plaster or at the backup material. Note that this is *not* an absolute-strength argument, but rather the requirement for uniformity or continuity. If, for example, there is one area in the middle of a wall where the finish coat has not bonded to the brown coat as well as at other places in the wall, map cracking may exist. As the wall undergoes dimensional movements in the plane of the wall, relatively more load will be induced in the area of the poorly bonded finish coat, and at some point cracking will occur. Map cracking does not necessarily show early in the life of a wall, but most often appears during the first twenty or thirty years. The best proof that a particular pattern is due to this mechanism is to carefully break through the plaster at a crack. If the crack does not extend full depth, and particularly if it is obviously restricted to the finish coat, it is most likely the map-cracking phenomenon. Once in a while the finish coat will chip off exactly surrounding the area of the crack, and in such cases it is not uncommon to find an excessively smooth plaster coat below.

This same crack phenomenon often occurs with repaired plaster. Owners

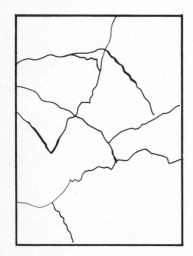

Fig. 5-5 Map cracking.

of an old house with worn, cracking plaster will sometimes have a "skim coat" of finish plaster applied as a renewed finish coat. This is not at all an unreasonable solution, but special care must be taken to prepare the old wall so that a bond can be developed between the old and new plaster. Various bonding agents are available, but these do not always assure the necessary uniformity of bond required to prevent map cracking.

Another cracking phenomenon is called "craze cracking" and has the geometry of map cracking, but the areas surrounded by the cracks are much smaller, most often 1 inch or less across. Furthermore, the cracks are much finer and often a magnifying glass is required to see the extent of the cracking. This pattern is related to improper application techniques that involve both the materials and how they are worked during the final stage of finishing. Like map cracking, these cracks are restricted to the finish surface and most often occur over only a few square feet. If the cracks are fine enough, they can be neglected initially and covered by paint, but they may become visible again as the paint wears and deteriorates. The solution often involves chipping off the affected area and reapplying a finish coat.

Both map and craze cracking are associated with bond of the finish coat, a requirement that is somewhat complicated by the variations in mechanical properties between the two top plaster coats. If the requirement for surface hardness and generally polished smoothness does not exist for the top coat, a thick second coat can be applied to a mechanically roughened scratch-coat surface, and map and craze cracking will never occur.

The final physical property that has a significant effect on plaster cracking are the thermal- and moisture-expansion characteristics of plaster. Recall the earlier discussions of the requirement for *differential* movements in order to produce cracks. If a ceiling or a wall uniformly expands or contracts completely unrestrained, it is not strained and therefore does not crack. Most commonly in ceilings and walls any restraint comes from the wood support, and thus the critical parameter in thermal- and moisture-induced movements is not the absolute values of any changes, but rather the difference with respect to the corresponding properties of wood. Fortunately, the coefficient of thermal expansion of plaster is very close to that of most woods. Since the interior temperature of houses is not only nearly constant but also very uniform from place to place, there is very little plaster crack distress that can be attributed rationally to temperature effects.

The same situation does not hold true for moisture changes in wood and plaster. Not only do wood and plaster absorb moisture at different rates, but expansion and contraction coefficients are in general different. As explained earlier, the expansion of wood is relatively uniform for each increment of added moisture, but plasters tend to expand abruptly with the first addition of moisture and then change dimensionally very little with added moisture. Finally, like so many properties of plaster, the coefficients of moisture expansion are grossly variable for the range of different plaster compounds encountered. Therefore, moisture-induced movements account for a number of different plaster crack phenomena.

Plaster Crack Patterns

Many cracking patterns on interior walls are common to both conventional plaster-on-lath and the modern dry-wall system; however, for several reasons crack distress is relatively more common in plaster walls. The most obvious explanation for this increased occurrence is that plaster walls, on the average, are much older than those with the dry-wall system, which rarely predate the later 1940s. Many of the crack mechanisms are dependent on time. Simply put, everything else being equal, the older the wall, the more likely it is to be cracked. Once in a while a homeowner is very dissatisfied to be told that age is a rational explanation for some cracks. Perhaps it is a reminder of his or her own aging. Sometimes owners are irrationally nostalgic about the quality of materials and work in old homes, but the fact is that gypsum dry-wall board is fabricated with a great deal more quality control than field-applied plaster was in the past and is thus more likely to be of the quality to remain crack-free. Many crack phenomena have nothing to do with the wall-surface material other than the fact that it is a continuous, brittle material that will crack. Certainly a grossly cracked and rapidly settled wall will crack totally independently of the quality of the plaster. On the other hand, certain crack phenomena show a decided tendency toward one or the other system.

The paper surface on dry wall is not brittle, of course, and some light hairline cracks that actually exist in the plaster never show through to the surface. The easiest demonstration that this is the case can be had by quickly bending a small section of dry wall. With care the cracking can be heard, but the paper strains across the crack without tearing and no surface flaw is detectable. It is almost impossible to tear the paper off the plaster surface without breaking off chunks of plaster, but with care the paper and some plaster can be chiseled away to expose the crack. The use of paper to hide plaster crack distress is regularly found in older homes in which an unusual amount of plaster distress has occurred, particularly early in the life of the building. The solution has been to wallpaper any patch and prevent hairline cracks showing through to the surface. If a light is shone flat across the wall surface, shadow patterns reflecting both the patch and new-crack extent can easily be seen. Plaster cracks hidden below wallpaper have been a source of considerable disappointment to people trying to remodel old homes. A relatively regular, paper-covered wall often looks like the scene of a major battle when the paper is removed and a maze of cracks is exposed.

Finally, the continuity of dry wall can minimize certain crack pattern development. Dry-wall boards are 4 to 12 feet long, and such panels can literally bridge potential cracks. For example, perhaps the singularly most common plaster crack is one that occurs above windows and runs from the corner more or less diagonally up to the ceiling line. There are several causes for this crack, some of which have already been considered (see Figure 4-4). The most standard explanation for this cracking is the discontinuity created at corners and exacerbated by the shrinkage and expansion of the wood lintel above the window. Often this crack pattern can be found at every window of a house. In any event, if dry wall is carefully installed with the dry-wall joint (the taped and spackled joint) well removed from the vertical intersection of the lintel and stud (see Figure 4-2), the wall can move below the dry wall without introducing any strain on it. In such cases, no crack will develop.

A somewhat similar situation occurs in row houses. For a number of aesthetic and pragmatic reasons, designers find it desirable to stagger the front plans of row houses. Thus, the fronts of adjacent row houses often vary by a few feet with the result that the party, or separating, wall between two units changes from an interior to an exterior wall at the intersection points. In the majority of such houses having plastered walls, a crack develops more or less at the transition. The mechanism of the crack varies with the exact detailing of the wall and plaster. Sometimes there is a material change, often an improperly bonded wall, while in other cases the crack can be attributed not to a material change, but to the abrupt environmental change between the interior and exterior wall. In recent applications, with everything else the same except that dry wall is substituted for plaster, properly installed panels bridge a modest movement, without a gross crack developing. In such cases, the crack is actually transferred to the corner joint, where it is often not as noticeable. A recognition of this mechanism actually suggests a repair technique that has been proven very satisfactory. Specifically, the plaster is cut away in a straight line 4 feet from the corner and a piece of dry wall installed on the existing firring strips. Purposely the panel is not secured rigidly on one side of the crack, generally toward the corner, which forces all the movements to occur in the corner. Either the resulting straight-line crack is tolerated, or a closure mold is added to hide the opening. In adjacent houses, where one has been repaired with this method and the other with conventional plaster patching techniques, the dry-wall system has completely obscured the crack (remember the wall crack may still exist), while the plastered wall has simply cracked again and looks exactly as it did before the repairs were made.

Some generic crack phenomena have already been discussed, for example, the common crack above window and door openings. It is not always clear whether this can be attributed more to differential movement of the lintel or

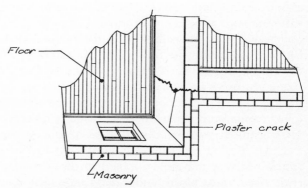

Fig. 5-6 Looking down at wall step in row house.

to a "stress concentration" brought on by the discontinuity of the window opening. Often, but not always, the lintel-expansion-related crack runs vertically for a short distance and almost exactly mirrors the shape of the lintel. In some cases it may even turn back and run toward the center of the window rather than diagonally away. The concept of a *change*, any change—environmental, material, geometric—being a cause of distress has been introduced in earlier chapters. A window represents a change in all these three factors, and it is not surprising that a brittle material that cannot yield to accommodate movements created by these changes would fracture. Thus, wall cracks can most likely be anticipated to occur at discontinuities of any sort—at stair openings, in ceilings, at the intersections of walls and walls and ceilings, and at material changes, for example, around fireplaces where walls often switch from stud to masonry and back again.

Cracks along the *intersection of walls and ceilings* are found in every type of construction, but the basic mechanism producing such cracks is quite variable. To understand this class of distress it is generally necessary to know a little of the details of the framing of the construction and how the wall has been built and finished. Several questions must first be answered in the diagnosis of these cracks:

1. Is the crack restricted to either the interior or the exterior wall?
2. Does the crack maintain a particular orientation with respect to the direction of framing or with respect to the compass?
3. Does it occur at both floor and roof ceiling lines?
4. Is it cyclic in nature and is there evidence of old patchwork surrounding the crack?
5. Is the crack right at the intersection line or is it slightly below in the wall or back along the ceiling?

The importance of answering each of these questions can be appreciated by considering the following examples: Perhaps the most common wall–ceiling-intersection crack occurs in exterior nonload-bearing walls, that is, walls running parallel to the direction of floor or ceiling joists and more particularly at the second-floor ceiling line. Historically, there have been a number of different ways in which stud walls were joined at the butt joints of the studs and also at floor and ceiling lines. In one early method of stud wall framing, the studs were run the full height of the house from the foundation line to the roof bearings. Such framing, called "balloon framing," is seldom used today because it is often difficult to get the long studs required and because, without special precautions, it allows fire to spread more easily between floors. The bearing walls at each floor are rigidly braced by the floor joists that rest on a beam let into the studs, called a "ribbon beam." Unfortunately, on a nonload-bearing wall the studs simply bypass the floor construction and are sometimes very marginally nailed to the closest joist or to the flooring. In such cases cracks at the wall–ceiling intersection eventually develop. This is a particularly frustrating crack to repair, because it is invariably cyclic and

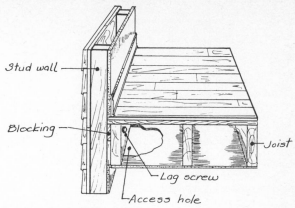

Fig. 5-7   Joist screwed to stud.

impossible to close permanently. One acceptable remedy is to install a piece of wood molding around the room at the ceiling line and simply hide the crack. If "out of sight, out of mind" is not an appealing structural repair philosophy for you, the only permanment fix is to break into the ceiling, expose the last joist, and rigidly connect it to the stud wall. In doing this special care must be taken to assure that the joist is tight against the stud, for otherwise it may temporarily deform against the stud and only later spring back and create a whole new set of distress. Lag screws are particularly good for this job because they can be installed without the pounding required for spiking, through fairly small access holes in the ceiling.

Most modern houses are "plateformed framed." In this case, the studs run floor to ceiling and the joists bear over the top of the studs. The nature of this framing detail makes it easy to run the subflooring, that is, the structural floor deck, out on top of the stud wall and thus brace and anchor the wall and floor together. Cracks are rare in this construction in ceilings below floor lines, for example, at the first-floor ceilings in a two-story house. Unfortunately, on the gable end of plateformed framed houses carpenters often have reverted to a sort of balloon-framing detail (see Figure 5-8*b*) and run the stud uninterrupted up to the roofline. In such cases, particularly where there is no attic floor or no roof trusses used, the ceiling structure is not adequately anchored to the wall and the standard wall–ceiling-intersection crack appears.

Wall–ceiling-intersection cracks are not at all restricted to nonload-bearing walls. Row houses seem to develop extremely predictable crack patterns, and one is a wall–ceiling-intersection crack. Many row houses, particularly those built in this century, have been built an entire row at a time, and while the houses may look like individual units, they actually are a single, block-long building—sometimes as long as 800 feet. Rarely was there a satisfactory expansion joint provided, and even in the rare cases when a perfunctory attempt has been made to accommodate the inevitable movements, it perhaps has led to more problems than it has alleviated. Predictably in such buildings crack

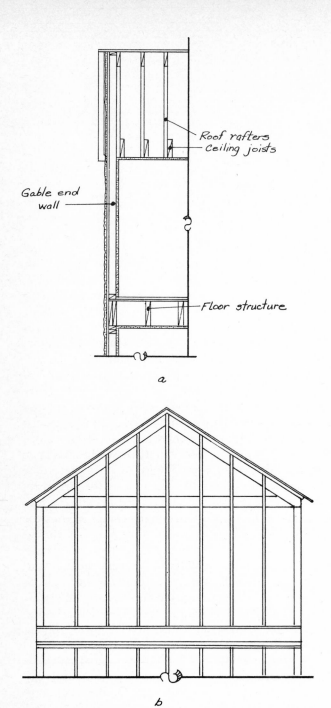

Fig. 5-8 (*a*) Balloon frame at attic floor. (*b*) Gable-end framing.

patterns have developed which, in effect, have become the omitted expansion joints.

Many continuously built row houses have masonry party walls. Such a party wall was generally a fire-separation requirement, and in many jurisdictions the joists were not allowed to bear into these fire walls. The theory was, and still is for that matter, that if one unit burns, the collapsing floor joist will not pull the party wall down. Instead of bearing into the wall, the joist rested on steel hangers, called "stirrups," that were set in the wall. There was no other anchor between the wall and the floor, and these hangers, while completely rigid owing to vertical loads, act somewhat like a hinge to horizontal movements. Thus, no structure anchors the ceiling and walls together, and the only connection is at the brittle plaster corner. In many cases *all* the movement and therefore all the cracking will be restricted to one wall only; furthermore, the cracks in any intersecting walls perceptibly decrease as they move down from the ceiling. It should be evident that a shear-type crack will occur in such cases at the front and rear exterior wall–ceiling-intersection lines; but often the interior partitions remain with the floor, do not move with the ceiling, and thus remain uncracked.

Even in continuous row houses where the floor and roof construction bears on the front and rear walls (leaving the party walls nonload-bearing), wall–ceiling-intersection cracks are not uncommon. Again, the explanation is that in a several-hundred-foot-long building, some accommodation for longitudinal movement must be provided, either intentionally at a control joint, or unintentionally at a location where cracks develop. The junction of the wall and ceiling is the weakest link in the structure, since elsewhere floor framing, flooring, and ceiling combine to form a relatively strong system.

One rather unusual wall–ceiling-intersection crack pattern that, while not necessarily restricted to continuous row houses, is regularly found in them is illustrated in the sketch of Figure 5-10. In this case the actual crack occurs several inches below the ceiling line. In many cases, repetitive patches have formed a section of plaster, above the crack, that slopes inward slightly; yet

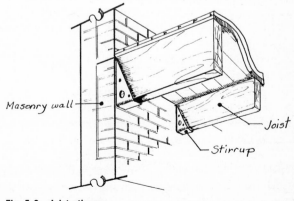

Fig. 5-9 Joist stirrups.

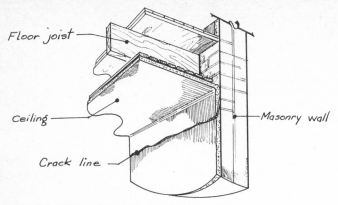

Floor joist

Ceiling

Masonry wall

Crack line

Fig. 5-10 Wall–ceiling-intersection crack.

in the few cases where this crack has never been repaired, it still develops
below the corner. At first glance there is not a ready explanation of why the
crack tends to occur away from the corner, but when such walls are actually
demolished and examined closely, the reason for this particular pattern becomes clear. For some reason, perhaps simply to accommodate a production
schedule, the walls are plastered before the ceiling, and the wall surface is
run off at an angle several inches below the ceiling. Later, when the ceiling
is completed, the plaster is brought down the wall to create a true right angle.
This is a detail common in houses of the 1920s through the 1940s, and the
few craftspeople remaining from this period disagree slightly over the reason
for this detail. The most typical explanation is that a three-coat system was
applied to the ceiling, while two coats were used on the walls; and scheduling
these operations resulted in the detail and eventually the crack pattern. Unfortunately, the crack exists with different plaster combinations, and thus
some other rationale may be correct. In any event, such a crack is particularly
difficult to fix. Universally, there is cyclic movement across a crack opening,
and any timing of a fix will result in recracking. Short of replastering almost
the entire wall and ceiling, it seems most practical to repair the crack by
installing a properly designed and detailed corner molding strip.

In Chapter 4, bow and sweep distortions of masonry walls were discussed,
and in Figure 4-24, the resulting interior crack pattern was illustrated. Wood-
frame walls do sometimes develop a bow in the vertical plan, for example,
in balloon-framed houses; but most commonly this distress is restricted to
masonry and particularly to brick masonry. In general, such bowing and
therefore cracking is very directional in the sense that it is related to a sun-
exposed wall (south) or to one exposed to a unique wind condition. Such
cracks do not tend to be excessively cyclic, and plaster patches will often hold
for several years or until the progressive movement overstrains the patch.

There are two wall–ceiling-intersection crack patterns that are a result of
fairly recent changes in framing systems and details. Beginning in the late
1950s, metal-plate-connected roof trusses (also referred to as "trussed raf-

ters") were introduced as an alternative to the previous standard of lumber rafter and ceiling members. Clear attic spaces were sacrificed for a less expensive, long-span roof structural system. In terms of actual cost of construction to enclose usable space, this may have been a false economy, but if unfinished attic space were not considered in cost comparisons, these trusses were a very cost-appealing system. Structurally, the trusses were certainly reasonable, and because clear spans of 35 and 40 feet were relatively easy to achieve, their use allowed considerably more flexibility in plans and room layouts than existed before.

In many sections of the country, a fairly standard one-story house has evolved for the mass-production market. It is two rooms deep, with the roof spanned 25 to 30 feet with lightweight trussed rafters. The ceiling, generally composed of gypsum dry wall, is attached directly to the bottom member (or chord) of these trusses. Now, to actually carry any roof load, such a truss must deflect. In addition, in the yearly cycle of temperature and moisture the top and bottom truss members are subjected to dramatically different environments. These differences are accentuated when a thick blanket of insulation is installed on top of the ceiling and above the truss members. In such cases, temperature differences between the upper and lower truss members can easily vary plus or minus 70°F or from a norm of 70°F for the lower, insulated and protected chord member, to the extremes of exterior roof temperatures for the upper or top chord member. Under such circumstances it is not in the least surprising that the truss should move up and down in the course of a year; and in extreme cases, movements of several inches have been recorded. Since the truss ends bear on the exterior walls, any upward movement of the truss will simply allow the ceiling, which is, of course, attached to the lower chord, to move away from any interior partitions. The resulting wall–ceiling-intersection crack can vary from a hairline to an actual opening of an inch or more in the course of a yearly cycle. As a remedy homeowners have tried to screw or bolt the top of the partition to the truss lower chord. This *may* be reasonable provided the partition occurs at a truss "panel point," that is, at a point of intersection of the truss diagonal members. On the other hand, if the partition happens to fall below an unbraced point on the truss, as shown in Figure 5-11, this modification may create problems. As the truss deflects it may begin to bear on the partition and actually fail the unbraced lower chord. In some cases this can occur in any event, with or without added attachments; but without an evaluation of each specific case it is best not to meddle with the roof truss but to try to accommodate the movement in some other way. This crack phenomenon is very often incorrectly diagnosed as being the result of slab settlement. Of course, downward movement of the slab on which the walls are founded would produce such a crack, but such movement is unlikely to be cyclic. Furthermore, slab settlement automatically produces wall corner cracks someplace in the building.

Somewhat analogous movements and therefore cracks occur in older town houses. In many cities individual row-type houses were built with rooflines sloping 1 or 2 inches per foot. Since the ceiling line was flat and the sloping

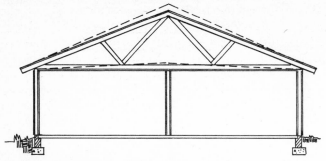

Fig. 5-11   Truss-deflection-induced ceiling crack.

roof only a few feet above, any connection between the roof and ceiling joists created in effect a truss system subject to many of the same problems encountered in modern tract houses with truss rafter roofs. Ceilings actually lifted off interior partitions, and a predictable wall–ceiling-intersection crack developed. The ceiling crack in Figure 5-12 regularly opens ¼ inch in midwinter and politely closes again by late spring. In frustration the homeowners have periodically tried to fill the void and rework the plaster molding detail in the corner. Such effort are, of course, fruitless, and the only result is a very strange, variable mold line. Unlike the previous example where the truss structure was not only intended but necessary for roof support, the attachment of roof rafters to ceiling joists in the row houses was often unintentional. If this can be established and the two elements separated, the crack problem may be eliminated.

Another wall–ceiling-intersection crack pattern that in general is of recent origin is a result of using excessively green, that is, uncured and undried, framing lumber. Because of a combination of economic factors, code changes, and production techniques, relatively wetter framing lumber was used regularly in many buildings from the 1960s through the early 1970s. The consequence of framing floors with such lumber was that the lumber shrank rather grossly within the first six months or so of being in a heated, drying environment. For example, floor joists that were 9¾ inches deep at installation shrank to 8⅞ inches. If everything in the house shortened uniformly, no distress was induced; but if one location shrank and another did not, cracks were inevitable. According to framing details with respect to partitions supported by the floor, cracks appeared at different locations. Frequently, interior, nonload-bearing partitions moved down with respect to ceilings and created wall–ceiling-intersection cracks. There is no hard-and-fast rule for predicting such crack patterns, but they almost always developed within the first year of enclosure, and they represent one-time movement; thus they are comparatively simple to repair permanently. The exceptions to this involve the same basic phenomena but a different sequence of crack development. In some cases, as the floor shrank away from a partition, the partition actually stayed up and remained attached at the ceiling. At least, at first, a separation developed at the floor line. Gaps of ½ inch were not uncommon between the

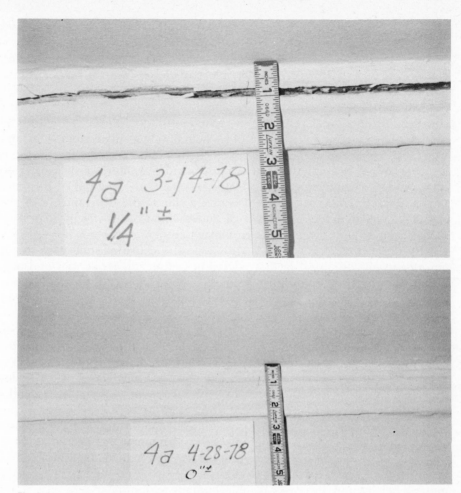

Fig. 5-12 Crack moving at wall–ceiling-intersection line.

floor and base molding. The explanation is not so much that the wall was hanging from the floor above, although in part this did happen, but rather that the dry-wall partition was in effect an 8-foot-deep beam that could actually span between supports to carry its own relatively modest weight. If such walls were left alone, sometimes the plaster deformed gradually, allowed the wall to lower, and left a wall—ceiling-intersection crack with negligible wall cracking. Other times, the wall came down rather abruptly and fairly substantial diagonal cracks (sometimes called "shear cracks") developed near the corners of the partitions. In the cases where the separation first appears at the floor line, simply blocking with wood strips between the wall and floor will probably prevent any advancement of movement.

Distress in general and plaster cracking in particular as a consequence of wood shrinkage is certainly not a new phenomenon. At various times, the practice of the building and lumber industries has been to use alternately better and less-well-cured framing lumber, and thus the incidence of houses with initial shrinkage-related crack damage is variable.

A separation between the floor and a wall above is not at all uncommon and occurs in a variety of different types of houses for different reasons. Particularly if the house is relatively old and it can be established positively that the gap has existed for a long time, there is no particular need for concern. Often simply resetting the base molding will hide the gap. The process of determining the history of such an opening between the floor and a wall involves a close examination to see whether paint patterns are consistent with new or old movement. Most often if paintbrush marks are clearly into the opening, old movement is to blame. Likewise, the amount of dust and debris in the opening can sometimes give a clue to the development of the crack. A generic defect in lumber or construction often will be shared by similar houses; and, if the house is similar to others in the neighborhood, a visit to these houses may give a clue as to the cause of such gaps. Such movements are discussed in more detail in Chapter 6. While new and particularly abrupt movement must always be taken seriously, old deformations causing such openings are rarely of consequence so far as wall distress and damage are concerned.

A crack pattern common to both plaster and dry wall, which is difficult to diagnose, occurs randomly in walls at locations well removed from any discontinuities and irregularities. It has a somewhat unique geometry in that it is generally along a straight, vertical line and "goes no place." Most cracks provide a clue to the probable source of movement or strain by the paths they take. For example, the standard lintel crack of Figure 4-4 patterns the lintel so clearly that the geometry provides the clue to the origin. Likewise, settlement-related cracks generally vary in width along their path in such a way that the geometry of movement is clearly defined. In the middle of an uninterrupted wall a crack that begins a foot or so from the floor, widens at midwall height, and decreases again, eventually to disappear before reaching the ceiling is unusual because it cannot be said to actually run between or along any apparent discontinuities as most cracks do. Such cracks are often caused by "stud warping." According to such parameters as wood species, growth patterns, and how the lumber is milled and cured, all lumber can warp and twist. Partially because of the quality of typical stud lumber and also because of its dimensions, studs appear to be considerably more likely to warp and twist than other framing lumber. Most small planar warps, that is, simply a bow to the side, do not take a great deal of lateral force to restrain, because the stud is relatively weak in this direction, and generally a plaster system can provide enough resistance to bowing without being strained to the fracture point. On the other hand, some lumber has a tendency to twist into a helical shape in its length and look much like a propellar blade. As with larger warps, such twisting can cause plaster cracking. As a matter of fact, one of the criteria for grading lumber takes into account this tendency to twist. If the longitudinal grain pattern of a piece of lumber is not straight but runs in a twisted pattern, even though the lumber is initially straight, there will be a marked tendency to twist and literally straighten out the grain. Lumber with this twisted grain arrangement will be downgraded and, unfortunately, sometimes winds up as stud grade for wall construction.

Rationally, it would be supposed that stud twisting, if it is to occur, will take place in the first year or so following installation, and that any crack will appear early in the life of the building. This is most often true, yet, perhaps following the law of perversity of inanimate objects, studs sometimes twist long after a house has been completed; thus, warp- or twist-related plaster cracks regularly show up in houses ten and fifteen years old. Absolute proof that the crack pattern corresponds to stud twisting shown in Figure 5-13 is obviously difficult to establish, and in the final analysis it is actually required that the wall be disassembled and the faulty stud be exposed. Once in a while, to satisfy various needs, this is done; and over the years the pattern has been pretty well established and identified. Some builders will locate blocking between studs at midheight to minimize this problem, and when "fire stops" (that is, blocking between studs to prevent the spread of fire within wall cavities) were mandatory, stud-warping cracks seldom occurred. Many people also attribute an isolated vertical line of dry-wall nails that work their way out of the surface (nail popping) to this same phenomenon.

One of the final requirements to establish that such a crack is related to wood distortions is that it is *not* cyclic. For this reason such cracks are easily repaired by conventional techniques.

Residential building construction techniques obviously vary widely, if for no other reason than the gross variability in home designs. Still, there are standards and a certain pragmatism by which commonly encountered problems are solved and not perpetuated. If a new material lacks durability requirements, its use is eventually abandoned. It seems surprising, therefore, that an almost universally standard defect has been built into almost every two-story house. Wait long enough and a crack pattern will develop somewhere around the stair opening, either at the wall–ceiling-intersection lines or in the walls. Somewhat superficially, the explanation of such cracks is that a stairwell is the most significant geometric and structural discontinuity in a

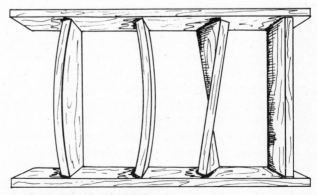

Fig. 5-13 Warped and twisted studs.

house; but with this clearly recognized it would seem reasonable that once and for all the problem would have been solved. More realistically, the problem involves our demand for open stairways. If the average homeowner were willing to follow Thomas Jefferson's approach to stair design and hide the stairway in a closetlike space with walls on all sides, there would be few problems. Instead, we require that stairs be located independently of framing systems and generally as openly as possible. The results are cracks. Heavier structural framing around the openings may minimize any crack development, but there is no indication that it will eliminate cracks absolutely. The only way to permanently avoid plaster cracks around a stairwell is to detail the plaster in some unique way that creates a series of control joints at the corners and intersections. This approach may beg the issue, for in effect it is akin to "precracking" the plaster. Much more to the point is the correction or minimization of plaster cracks at stairwells after they have developed. It is futile to use plaster to close cracks that cycle in the course of a year.

Some of the movement can be minimized by supplementing the framing. In many houses the opening in the first floor (leading to the basement) is framed exactly the same way as that leading to the second floor. While a column or support exposed to the second floor may not be tolerated, it may be admissible in the basement. Presumably such a column is not needed for absolute support, so it can bear on the basement floor without any special foundation. On the other hand, it may be just enough to alter the cyclic movement and thus allow any cracks to be closed with conventional patching plaster. Still another incentive for some form of additional vertical support between the first-floor framing and the basement slab is that such a support can eliminate a potential long-term deformation problem that occurs in many residences. The opening around the stairs is said to be "headered off," with the header beam transferring load to both ends of the opening (see Figure 5-14). In most house designs, the stairs are partially surrounded by an interior wall that is essentially two stories tall, and this wall is often resting on the header beam. Thus, the framing around a stair is required to carry not only any live load but also a relatively heavy dead load consisting of the floor structure weight plus this relatively high wall. How wood tolerates long- and short-term loading has already been discussed. Specifically, in comparison to many other structural materials, wood is usually strong and rigid when subjected to relatively short-term loads, that is, loads applied for months, at most. Conversely, wood will deform rather grossly under modest loads if they are maintained for a number of years. This is *not* to say that the framing is necessarily inadequate to support the applied loads without collapse. This wood characteristic, combined with the relatively heavy interior partition that so often accompanies stair design, accounts for a standard deformation pattern and therefore standard crack patterns around stair openings. The header beam and the joists at either end gradually deform during the years, and wall cracks develop corresponding to the deformation. For example, a standard crack often appears along the line of intersection between a wall at the head of the stairs and an outside wall. Similarly, doors in partitions resting more

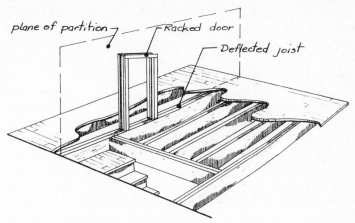

Fig. 5-14 Deflected joists at stair headers.

or less on the end support joist of the header beam may rack or deform out of square by several inches sometimes. Since this takes so long to occur, small cracks progressively develop, are patched, reopen, and are filled again. Thus, it is not uncommon to see grossly racked and deformed doors without any surrounding plaster crack pattern that is in the least consistent with the movements. Of course, any heavy partition bearing on just a few floor joists can deform in this manner, but the phenomenon is particularly common around stair openings.

New owners who are not used to "that funny old door to the rear bedroom that never closes" are apt to discover the cause and try to rectify a situation that has taken fifty years to create. The most common remedy is to install a commercial house screw jack in the basement between the slab and the first

Fig. 5-15 Racked door and wall.

floor, and start jacking. Before doing this, remember that a door deformed by 1 or 2 inches will be accompanied by plaster cracks on the same order of magnitude. It is just that the cracks have been filled progressively over the years, and jacking will only recrack the wall in the reverse direction. If leveling of the floors and walls is a requirement, then almost certainly all the plaster on interior walls bearing on the floor structure affected by the jacking should be removed. If these walls are covered with conventional plaster, an added reward to removing such plaster and replacing it with modern dry-wall panels is the potential for significant weight reduction. Old plaster-on-lath systems regularly weigh twice as much as ⅝-inch-thick dry-wall partitions; and the weight reduction may be enough to prevent a recurrence of the long-term deformation process.

It should be clear that a permanently deformed joist cannot be straightened out simply by jacking. The only really practical way to relevel floors in such situations is to attach new, straight lumber along the top edge of the old, deformed members. Inevitably this requires taking up the floor. The process is similar to sistering of joists, discussed in Chapter 4, except that, since the additional members are not added for any strength requirement but rather to level the top surface only, they need only be a few inches deep—enough to make the connection. Finally, it should be clear that the bottom of a joist is still deformed and that any ceiling attached to this surface will appear sagged. This entire process can get rather complicated and costly, and generally when owners are faced with the complete remedy, they suddenly discover some appealing quality to slightly sagging floors.

While there are often advantages to removing plastered partitions, particularly with regard to decreasing dead weight on supporting structure, there also can be some serious liabilities. One inch or more of high-strength plaster applied to both sides of a wall partition can create a very strong structure—literally a beam 8 or 9 feet deep. If there are no significant openings in such a wall, particularly near midspan, such a beam can easily carry its own weight

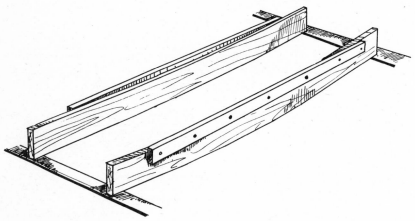

Fig. 5-16 Leveled joists.

and that of other attached structure. Removing such a partition can thus actually weaken floor structure.

Inner-city town houses built in the first quarter of this century tend to have a standard floor plan, in which the front door leads directly to a hall and stairway running along one side of the house. The hall is separated from the adjoining rooms by a partition that runs front to rear. Almost on a random basis this partition is load-bearing or nonload-bearing—there seems to be no set rule by which to judge. Even when the second-floor joists span continuously over the top of this partition to the stairwell header beam (see Figure 5-14), the partition may actually have been providing some support. Remodeling plans sometimes require removing this partition to create a more open floor plan. In surprisingly many cases an experimental approach is taken; that is, a part of the wall is removed, and if the floor does not collapse, it is assumed that a complete structure exists at the second-floor level. The amazing thing is that in some cases the second-floor plastered partitions have actually functioned as giant beams spanning between walls or above the removed sections of partition on the first floor. In subsequent redecoration, the plaster only has been removed from one of these beam-like partitions and unexpectedly the floor collapses. The moral is, of course, do not assume that just because a partition is not obviously load-bearing in the conventional sense, it contributes nothing to the structural integrity of the building. This applies not only to vertical-load support requirements, but perhaps even more appropriately to lateral-load requirements such as resistance to wind. Many older houses have had their interior, presumably nonload-bearing partitions removed only to find that the resulting shell does not create the freedom of open space but instead creates the freedom to be a wobbly mess that vibrates in the wind. Fortunately, any real deficiency is almost immediately recognized in such cases and necessary bracing can be added to the structure.

Plaster and dry-wall ceilings share certain crack patterns. Long cracks running perpendicular to the joist direction and near the center of a ceiling are often attributable to excessive deflection of the ceiling support joists. Just when ceiling plaster will crack is difficult to predict, because it involves a number of variables. For example, the general rule of thumb used by most designers is to provide a floor stiff enough to limit the deflection to a value equal to the narrow room dimension divided by 360. This is a reasonable criterion if the deformation is due to the application of live load and can be expected to be applied fairly quickly and remain for only a short period, several weeks at most, before being removed. The problem is that in most situations wood will more readily deform plastically than will plaster. If this were to occur, the wood would deform excessively before the plaster could deform plastically and cracks could develop. Another assumption made when arriving at deflection limits that will not allow plaster ceiling cracks is that the deformed ceiling is a uniform, smooth surface and does not have any abrupt change in direction. Such a deflected shape corresponds to that produced by a uniform load—a not altogether unreasonable assumption of the likely load distribution. If a very local or concentrated load is applied to ceiling joists, cracks can develop at much lower deflections. The two most common sources of concentrated floor loads are partitions and bathrooms. In one case, a house that had been occupied by the same family for its thirty-year life suddenly developed deflection-like ceiling cracks. One member of the family had become ill and was required to soak in a nearly full bathtub several times a day. The tub was near the center of the living room ceiling, but had only been used rarely and perhaps never had been filled to the brim. The floor was framed to support the load and there was no possibility of collapse; still, the abrupt, concentrated load created a deflection pattern that eventually produced plaster cracks.

An adequate proof that excessive magnitude or an abruptly changing deflection shape is responsible for ceiling cracks is simply to sight along the ceiling and estimate the deformation. Another estimate of the deformation may be made by holding a flashlight tight to the ceiling and shining the light along the surface. Of course, on a perfectly flat ceiling the light will fall all the way up the wall, but on a bowed ceiling a shadow line will pattern the shape of the deflected surface.

Two other construction deficiencies that often account for ceiling plaster cracks are (1) inadequate framing below a partition, and (2) lack of adequate "bridging," or structural blocking, between joists, which helps distribute load from one joist to another.

A ceiling distress pattern found on plaster applied to narrow gypsum lath is a series of cracks running at right angles that define the joints of the lath. The identification that the cracks are along the lath joints can be absolute by simply measuring the spacing of the cracks. If the cracks occur at a regular spacing, particularly at multiples of 8 or 12 inches, the cracks are almost certainly along the lath joints. Dimensions for gypsum lath are somewhat variable, the most standard being 16 inches wide × 48 inches long, although 24-inch widths are not uncommon, and in some sections of the country 8-

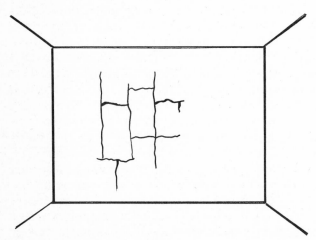

Fig. 5-17 Ceiling lath joint cracks.

inch-wide boards are sometimes used. This particular crack pattern seems to occur randomly, and this very randomness contradicts most of the standard explanations. Simply attributing the cracks to "weak plaster" is somewhat superficial, because, as explained earlier, low-strength plaster tends to be relatively more flexible and may even be less vulnerable to cracking under these conditions. Moreoever, the most likely source producing the joint strains, namely, wood cyclic movements, involves forces so much greater than a ½-inch thickness of plaster can continuously withstand, that for practical purposes a plaster of almost any strength will eventually succumb and fracture. It is not true that this crack phenomenon necessarily occurs in the early life of a building. Houses thirty years old have suddenly developed ceiling cracks of this pattern. Finally, in areas of repetitiously detailed houses, where the plastering techniques reasonably can be expected to have been very consistent, lath joint cracks are randomly encountered. What then is a good explanation and why the variability? Recognizing that the eventual fracture pattern is a result of cyclically strained plaster at the joints, and that moisture-content variations account for the largest strain cycles in the average house, the best explanation is one that has often been repeated. The moisture content of wood can vary considerably from one house to another, and more importantly, the yearly variations in moisture can vary even more. Sometimes the variations involve some property intrinsic to the house—something to do with the way it is constructed, detailed, or insulated. More likely these moisture variations are a result of the way the house is lived in—the habits of the occupants. People who prefer New England boiled dinners, long showers, and high inside temperatures during the winter will simply produce more moisture than can eventually be absorbed by the wood. If this seems unreasonable, consider the houseplant-watering schedule of different people. Some claim to water a robust plant once in two weeks, while a neighbor must water the same variety (potted the same way) twice a week.

The remedy for ceiling lath joint cracks is difficult because of the extent of the cracking. First, very few plasterers will ever recommend skim coating a large area of plaster over paint, although it is regularly done over small areas as part of local crack patching. Second, the added weight of a few pounds per square foot may be more than old bonds can take and thus may lead to other types of failure. A fairly standard approach is to use one of the texture materials intended to be skim-coat applied and then worked into some regular, overlapping, fan-shaped pattern. The idea is that the heavy texture of the surface will hide slight irregularities at the lath joint. Sometimes this works satisfactorily and sometimes it simply peels off like an extremely thick wallpaper. There has been a bond or adhesion failure at one of the many contact surfaces. The problem of the bond integrity is obviously not simply a matter of the most recent coat of paint but the type and sequencing of all the paint layers on a ceiling. Actually, many coats of enamel paint alone, applied to a ceiling over many years, will often fail at one of the first contact surfaces. The result is that sections of paint, often several square feet in area, will simply peel or chip off. Many painters attribute this failure to the effects of the combined weight of the multiple layers. This explanation seems improbable. More likely, the paint peeling is a result of some bond failure due to chemical reactions at the paint–plaster interface or a mechanism very similar to that which produces map cracking in plaster. In any event, it dramatically illustrates the potential weakness of old paint-to-plaster bonds and therefore the inappropriateness of skim coating large areas of old, painted plaster.

In a few restoration projects owners wanting to preserve as much of the old plaster as possible have tried sanding and even grinding off the old paint and perhaps part of the plaster finish coat in order to create a suitable bondable surface for a new skim coat. This is not only an incredibly dusty process, but it also has sometimes precipitated plaster failures at the lath key. Thus, the best policy is to avoid, if at all possible, skim coating extensive areas of old, painted plaster. The alternatives, of course, are to knock down the entire ceiling plaster and then to either replaster or apply dry wall. One very strong incentive in favor of dry wall is the added fire security. To repeat, most plasters are incombustible, the notable exceptions being wood-fiber-filled gypsum plaster and some of the acoustic plasters. On the other hand, not all plaster systems by any means provide the same amount of fire protection. Variations in constituent materials and bond characteristics between coats account for some of these differences, but the methods of attachment to the base structure probably account for the most differences in fire-retarding characteristics between plaster systems. Dry wall with the "Fire Code" rating, installed according to code requirements, offers a substantially better fire barrier than typical old-plaster-on-wood lath.

The installation procedure for dry wall requires that the nails be driven slightly below the surface. The resulting depression and the nail head are then covered with a spackle compound, which is later sanded and eventually painted to create a smooth surface. In some instances the nail head works partway out, cracks the spackle, and creates a bump in the dry-wall surface. Such nail popping is found on both ceilings and walls and can occur almost anytime in the history of a building. There seem to be several valid reasons for this phenomenon, but in any given situation it may be difficult to pinpoint the specific reasons. Dry wall is best secured with a nail that has a roughened shank surface with good withdrawal resistance. Many people argue that nail popping occurs when smooth-shank nails are used, but this is not an adequate explanation, because in the same wall both smooth and serrated nails have been known to back out or pop.

Particularly flexible framing seems to correlate rather closely with this phenomenon, but since all wall studs are nearly equally stiff, this cannot be a completely adequate theory. A more precise explanation is that walls and ceilings that are subjected to movement, particularly in a plane perpendicular to the plaster surface, are significantly more likely to experience nail popping. Thus, ceilings attached to lightly framed floors and flexible bottom chord truss members often develop this imperfection. Similarly, minimally sheathed walls are relatively more flexible to movements due to wind forces and thus share the problem of nail popping.

Carpenters suggest other possible mechanisms that can account for dry-wall nail popping. Floor joists can be installed with blocking, or bridging, between alternate joists. The purpose of this bridging is to help distribute load between several joists so that when one joist is stepped on, several adjacent ones will deflect. Recently, codes have not required as much bridging as was generally used in the past, and in houses built without bridging there are reports of more nail popping.

Certainly no one has carefully surveyed enough houses to be able to establish an absolute judgment of the cause of nail popping; instead, the generalized observations of individual builders and mechanics are the only sources of the incidence of occurrence. Unfortunately, there are so many exceptions to the explanations that a dogmatic position is simply not valid. For example, some people argue that nail popping is associated with either wood species or wood condition (principally moisture content) at the time of installation of dry wall. Examples can be found of dry-wall nail popping in houses with any of the half-dozen or so major framing-lumber species. Furthermore, the very fact that nail popping can develop so many years after construction is not consistent with the theory of wood-moisture condition at the time of installation.

The repair method for nail popping is simply to redrive the nail and respackle the hammerhead depression. This seems to work in most cases, but occasionally an owner reports that repeated repairs, even with different nail types, has not prevented recurrent nail popping. In such cases the structure has been found to be flexible or subject to abnormal deflections, and the only solution has been to stiffen the structure in some way. Like the correction methods for many other problems in residences, repair techniques for dry-wall nail popping should be approached on an almost experimental basis. Try one technique in a restricted area and see if it works. Conversely, avoid using any questionable repair method at too many locations; and above all, try not to use an irrevocable method of repair.

Plaster and Dry-Wall Repair Techniques

Plaster repair work, perhaps more than any other type of repair in a residential building, is an art-skill combination that the average owner cannot readily duplicate or fully appreciate. For this reason an owner is more subject to the opinions of the particular mechanic doing the work, and any specialized knowledge or judgment the owner may have counts for very little. Carpenters seems to be more passive than plasterers; you can argue with carpenters and they may even change their minds about how to repair something. Plasterers, however, will do things pretty much their way, and the average homeowner can do little to influence the method or details of repair. Another problem with plaster repairs is that there are so many different opinions on the subject, some of which are matters of real controversy. For example, a common repair technique involves cutting out a line of plaster several inches on both sides of the crack, inserting a layer of glass cloth in the space, and replastering the gap. The glass cloth, of course, is meant to reinforce the new plaster. Glass is recognized as being an extremely inert material, and rarely are there any interactions between glass and other materials. Nevertheless, several researchers have found that glass filaments in cements and plasters have adverse effects after a long period of time. In recent years, several new glass compounds have been developed specifically for use in certain cementitious materials, but the general use as well as the durability is still a matter of considerable debate. Certainly in terms of a few years such a repair method has proven to be satisfactory, but if an owner is interested in a permanent repair, other methods should be considered. Expanded metal lath gives the same or better reinforcement characteristics, has a three-dimensional surface for a better bond, and has a time-proven history.

One of the principal issues that should govern any judgment regarding plaster repairs is whether the crack is static. If a crack opens and closes in the course of a year, it should not be repaired with the same materials and methods used to repair a static, one-time-open crack. While the latter type most commonly occurs during the first few years following construction, it also develops in older homes. It is not always simple to measure a crack with a ruler and to determine whether it is moving. To begin with, the same ruler should be used for all subsequent measurements. Not only are printed scales on rulers subject to some variations, but more importantly, variable graphics between scales make it difficult to be consistent. Since movements are likely to be no greater than a few sixty-fourths of an inch, the width of a scale division can be important. If a "screw-set" divider from a drawing-instrument set is available, it can be used to determine the movement across the crack. With the divider set at any arbitrary opening, simply press it gently into the plaster surface just enough to be able to see the pen holes. Maintain the setting and periodically compare the set opening with the gauge marks on the wall. Ideally such a comparison should be done for a full year, for remember that there are three possibilities: a static crack; a cyclic crack, that is, one which opens and closes; or a continuously opening crack.

The *static crack* is obviously the simple one to repair. There are many plaster patching compounds on the market. The cheapest is simply called "patching plaster" or plaster of paris and is a fine-ground, fast-setting, low-shrinkage gypsum plaster. Several premixed compounds are available, but since they are necessarily air setting (they harden by simply drying out), they tend not to be as good for deep cracks as a true plaster, which hardens by hydration. The only real technique involved is to pressure the patch material deep into the cavity. If the plaster is smooth and untextured, two coats are best, with the final coat lightly sanded to assure a flat surface across the crack. For some reason many people insist on using a very wide putty knife and spreading a thin layer of plaster for several inches on either side of the crack. This method

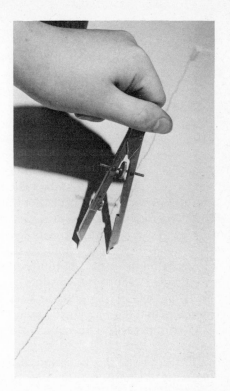

Fig. 5-18   Dividers to monitor crack.

looks fine at first, but after painting, it leaves an unnecessarily wide swath that can create a noticeable silhouette below the paint. One or two such areas situated randomly in a room may not be objectionable, but a lot of patches of this type can be very distracting.

Before selecting a patch technique, hold a flashlight against various wall surfaces and shine the light along the wall. Any imperfections will be amplified and the wide type of path will be noticeable.

Textured or "stippled" finished plaster poses special repair problems. It is difficult to match the randomness of the original rough surfaces, and any order and smoothness become very apparent. A small, dry paint roller can often be run across the patch to recreate the continuity of the original surface texture. Unfortunately, such plaster patching is one of those skills which, though the technique may be perfected and the job complete, by the next repair time is forgotten.

Cyclic cracks simply cannot be easily and permanently repaired. If the crack-producing mechanism can be identified and corrected, then the problem simply resolves itself into the repair of a static crack; but since most cyclic cracks involve yearly moisture and temperature changes in wood structures, they are almost impossible to stop. If filler materials seem to be the only expedient, then certainly the crack should be filled when it is at its widest open position, *and* the filler material, it is to be hoped, should be as flexible as practicable. Some of the premixed materials are relatively flexible, but it is not uncommon to see a noticeable bulge where a patch material has actually extruded from a crack as it closes.

As discussed earlier in this chapter, there are often ways of either hiding a crack or at least minimizing its effects by redetailing the surrounding plaster and incorporating straight-line control or expansion joints. In colonial times the craftspeople must have clearly recognized that in many buildings they could not eliminate plaster cracking from certain particularly vulnerable locations. These houses, therefore, were often detailed with such devices as crown molding along the line of the ceiling–wall intersection, wood-mold details at both inside and outside corners, and wood panels above windows. Similar methods are still adaptable today, but since an entire room must be consistently detailed, it often becomes prohibitively expensive to change over to such a method of obscuring cracks.

One of the best ways to handle a cyclic crack is to apply a panel of plaster lath (or board) centered along the cut-out crack. Sometimes the board is strong enough to distribute the movement over the entire surface and the crack never reappears. In other situations, the crack can be transferred to one edge, where it appears as a straight-line opening, which is generally less objectionable than a jagged crack. If the board is secured on one particular side of the crack or the other, the crack can be made to exist at a certain location.

The most standard method of major crack repair is to cut out a swath of plaster and simply reapply new plaster in a band several inches wide. As a repair method for cyclic cracks this is rarely permanent. Surprisingly, such a system will hold for several years, but eventually the old crack reappears. If the patch band is reinforced, the crack may take a new path, but this just adds to the problem by widening the area of distress.

Continuously increasing cracks, unless they are moving extremely slowly as in the case of cracks caused by bowed masonry walls, are simply a waste of time to repair. Once in a while, new owners of an old house, who lack the perspective of knowing the history of crack development, will suppose their house is literally falling apart when they see cracks almost continually open. Of course, what has happened is that the previous owner dutifully patched all cracks—static, cyclic, and increasing ones. When suddenly, therefore, within a period of a few months a number of cracks open, new owners sometimes conclude that the house is uniquely damaged. For buyers of used houses who find freshly painted, crack-free walls, the flashlight-along-the-wall-surface method of inspection may provide an indication of previous plaster cracking.

In the past the methods and extent of plaster repairs have been governed largely by such parameters as aesthetics, cost, available skills, and of course, extent and type of distress. In recent years a very substantial additional ingredient has been added—the need for improved wall, floor, and ceiling insulation. Thus, based strictly on the economics of future fuel savings, more-extensive plaster repairs can be justified if they can also include adding insulation. With plaster removed, insulation batts can be installed between studs.

For the really determined energy saver, wall cavities can be widened by nailing additional studs on existing ones and 6- or 8-inch insulated walls can be created. In such situations vapor barriers can be located at the ideal position with respect to the insulation, without the possibility of creating serious water-condensation problems within the wall system. In evaluating such a repair, remember that not all walls have to be insulated to make it worthwhile. North-facing walls and walls facing the principal winter winds are most in need of insulation, and in some special cases insulating walls with southern exposures may be of marginal value at best.

Conclusion

Interior wall distress, while it may be a signal of significant structural damage requiring immediate attention, rarely requires urgent repairs; instead, a time to explore and think about the options is available. The great error is to make repairs that are both unnecessary and irrevocable. When plastering is involved, the final repair success revolves around the skill of a craftsperson, and his or her opinion should be consulted and past work examined.

The explanations of interior crack distress are almost as numerous as the opinions solicited, but the criterion of *reasonableness* should still govern—the reasons for distress are not a part of witchcraft; and while there is a little formal research to define the problems, rational explanations do exist.

FLOOR STRUCTURE

6

Floor structures in residential buildings are, from a practical standpoint, restricted to concrete for on-grade construction and combinations of wood for framed construction. It is true that in some specialized cases framed floors of concrete have been used in residential construction, and some on-grade floors are brick or stone masonry. Similarly, floor joists of either steel or aluminum have been used in limited amounts, although wood is still the dominant floor-framing material for homes.

Clearly, all the inherent wood-related defects such as rot, decay, insect infestation, shrinkage, and load-time-related deformations potentially exist, and an understanding of how these mechanisms relate to wood-framed floor distress and deterioration is a simple extension of ideas that have been discussed already. As always, a knowledge of the various types and details of wood-frame construction will simplify the diagnosis of the distress process. There is, however, an additional incentive for understanding floor-framing details. Extensive remodeling or additions to homes often involve modifications to the basic structure. Such structural elements as walls can very often be rather grossly altered with almost negligible overall effect on the rest of the building. For example, one of the simplest modifications is to change a window opening into a doorway by simply cutting out the wall between the sill and the floor. Obviously, this has no structural significance. Similarly, nonload-bearing partitions can be removed completely with little or no regard for the surrounding structure. The same is not true of floor construction, and both in relation to previous remodeling and in planning future work, the details of the floor construction and how it is modified have a profound impact on distress patterns. The details of such seemingly innocuous enterprises as eliminating a stairway may create distress and damage in the future. A good example of the problems created by such repairs occurs in the case of many nineteenth- and early-twentieth-century houses. It was not in the least uncommon, particularly in larger, more rambling houses, to have two or even three stairways between the first and second floors—most often a front stair and a rear stair leading to the kitchen. For a variety of reasons related both to how we use houses and to changes in such facilities as toilets and heating equipment, many people now prefer to have only one stairway leading to the upper floor. More usable floor space is created on both floor levels, and it certainly seems simple enough just to remove a stair and to install a new floor in the opening. The problems, of course, are that the floor above may not have been structured to carry the additional load, the stair may have actually provided some vertical support on the enclosing walls, or the added floor structure simply may have been installed poorly. In any event, a surprisingly common defect in old houses is an odd, rectangular crack or deformation in the ceiling of the kitchen, for example. When the source of this irregularity is finally diagnosed, it turns out to be the reframing at an old stair opening. There are many other examples of how floor modifications, done without an adequate understanding of the structure and detailing of the floor system, have led to significant distress and deterioration problems.

Wood-Framed Floor Structural Systems

The basic method of how floors are structured in wood is almost universal and independent of time, geography, and culture. The details, however, vary considerably, with some of the most significant modifications occurring since the early 1960s. In the simplest situation the traditional method has been to space small beams at regular intervals varying from 1 to 4 feet apart. On top of these beams, or joists, structural wood deck is placed, consisting of planks spanning at right angles to the joists.

In the houses built before lumber mill equipment was developed, or in sections of the country before such equipment was available, each mill cut was costly and time-consuming. Thus, there was an incentive to have either as few beams as possible or, if the number was to be necessarily large, to have many small ones with the minimum milled surfaces possible. This constraint resulted in a beam-framing system in which a number of relatively small, short beams framed into one or more large beams. These main beams, called "summer beams," were often well beyond available milling capacity and were simply hewn by hand from a single tree trunk. There seems to be some controversy over how the name *summer* became applied to these primary beams. Some say it comes from "sum" (the Latin, *summa*), as in summing up the load, or from the season of summer, referring to when the tree was cut. Since it was generally recognized to be bad practice to cut trees in the summer when wood-sugar content was high, the former explanation seems most likely.

The limitation on the spacing of the small beams or joists was and still is a function of the floor deck planks, which, for various reasons, are optimized in the ¾- to 1¾-inch range. Within this range the criterion is not so much one of strength as of flexibility—if the deck is too thin it feels weak, even though it may easily carry any applied load. There seems to have been no rule or standard of spacing or sizing beams, joists, and deck thickness, but as modern mill practices became more widespread in the midnineteenth century, the dimensions of floor structure became more standardized. Several other imputs also have influenced our modern standards.

Fig. 6-1   Summer beam system.

If flooring plank is simply laid and secured to the joists, gaps will eventually form between the planks as the wood shrinks. Inevitably dirt will filter on down through these cracks from the shoes of people on the second floor to the heads and tables of first-floor occupants. Needless to say, this could lead to a messy situation; and while it might have been tolerated in a rough farmhouse, it was certainly not acceptable in finer houses. There were several alternatives. For one, the floor deck could be made of a "tongue-and-groove"-type planking, and as the shrinkage occurred, the tongue would simply pull partway out of the groove and still block the dirt from filtering through. Another alternative was to apply another layer of wood on top of the structural deck. This top layer generally was a wood of better appearance, and as time went by it became tongue-and-grooved, not only to minimize the dirt-filter problem, but also to help hold adjacent planks aligned to provide a continuous smooth surface. Out of this combination evolved our modern practice of a structural floor deck or "subflooring" topped with finished "flooring." Until the late 1940s, subflooring was 1×4 or 1×6 plank, sometimes laid on the (45°) diagonal with respect to the joists, and other times simply at right angles to them. Whether the plank should be perpendicular to the joists or on the diagonal is another matter of some controversy. The practice seems to be quite variable; and in adjacent houses built more or less simultaneously one will have diagonally laid subflooring, while the other will have perpendicular subflooring. Since diagonal plank has to span further, it is more flexible than plank at right angles to the joists; but a modest argument can be made that the diagonal plank creates a sort of truss network in the floor plane, which helps to stiffen the house against side or lateral forces. Today, subflooring is composed of some form of wood panel, either plywood or various types of manufactured wood-chip and -fiber products. Many new houses have no flooring whatever; wall-to-wall carpet simply covers the plywood subfloor deck.

Another alternative to eliminating the filter of dirt from one floor to another is, of course, to plaster the ceiling. Originally, plaster was applied only in recesses between the joists, and now many designers try to simulate this effect by such devices as placing dummy beams of wood or even plastic against conventional dry-wall ceilings. The details of this plaster system vary somewhat, but the most common arrangement is as shown in Figure 6-2. Several inches below the flooring wood lath was set between the joists and plastered. Not only did this detail prevent dirt from filtering down from the floor above, but it also created a substantially better sound barrier. In adjacent rooms of buildings being remodeled, one with the inset plaster intact and the other with it removed, the sound-transmission differences are dramatic. Soundproofing was probably not the initial incentive for incorporating this detail into residential buildings, but it may have been a significant factor in such buildings as taverns and small shops, where it was desirable to separate acoustically the various floors. This may account for the fact that in old architectural references such ceilings are called "tavern ceilings."

The modern practice, of course, is to secure the ceiling covering directly to the bottom of the floor joist. The significant exception to this practice occurs in houses with air-conditioning systems requiring that air be ducted to individual outlets. Often the ducts are attached to the ceiling, a light wood frame is built around the duct, and plaster is applied to this frame (see Figure 6-3). These duct enclosures are one of the most common areas of dry-wall and plaster crack distress. Not only do corner cracks and separations occur at the vertical and horizontal intersection lines, but cracks in the narrow

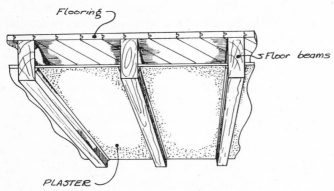

Fig. 6-2 Tavern ceiling.

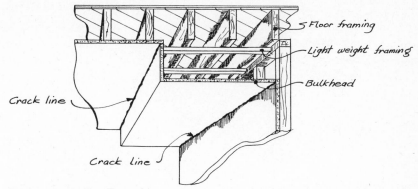

Fig. 6-3 Bulkhead air duct.

vertical side band are common. There are several reasons why these "bulk-heads" are so uniquely vulnerable to cracks. First, on the reentry corners it is perhaps a little more difficult to "tape and spackle" with optimum care, and very often a separation occurs where the taped joint is inadequate. More often the source of the cracking can be attributed simply to inadequate framing of the enclosure. Elsewhere in the ceiling the dry wall is secured to floor joists that are inevitably stiff members. The general practice is to frame the ducts in very lightweight members that are not only relatively more flexible than the joists but also not big enough to adequately hold a conventional nail. If such cracks develop and continuously increase, the only alternative is to remove and rebuild the frame around the duct with adequate, stiff materials.

Sometimes the argument is presented that such cracks are due to unusual drying conditions related to the duct. Duct enclosures are often warmer than the surrounding ceiling, and therefore greater drying of the wood frame could occur. Since this cracking phenomenon occurs with well-insulated ducts as well as uninsulated ones, however, it would seem that any drying mechanism is not the dominant cause of the cracks.

Since the mid-1950s several manufactured floor-joist systems have been introduced and widely used. One type involves building up a wood beam by gluing small wood strips together, while the other is a flat truss connected at various intersection points by a metal plate device. Either nails are driven through the plate, or sharp spikes are punched out of the plate and driven into the wood. Many of the products typically are referred to by one of several trade names, but generally the glued-up beams are called "glue-lams" (short for glued and laminated), while the trusses are generically called "metal-plate-connected trusses."

There are many incentives for fabricating wood members by gluing smaller pieces together. First, the individual pieces can be of more selective quality, and pieces with knots and areas of irregular grain simply can be discarded. Second, in the laminating process the direction and continuity of the grain can be varied randomly in such a way as to actually create a stronger material than the sum of the individual members. Lumber in which the grain runs

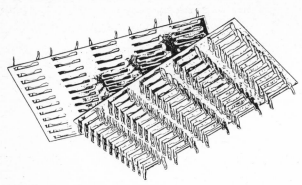

Fig. 6-4 Metal plate connectors.

straight from one end to the other is significantly stronger than lumber of comparable species in which the grain curves and twists in the length. In effect, a series of short pieces can be glued together to form a straight-grained timber. All the increased benefits of glue-laminated lumber are, of course, predicated on the assumption that the glue is as strong as the wood *and* that precise, smooth, well-fitting joints can be machined. In recent years glue technology has created some glues that, properly applied, are significantly stronger than the surrounding wood. Furthermore, modern machining and material-handling equipment has made it economically feasible to produce competitively priced lumber. The final incentive for using such products is one of conservation—the smaller the usable wood part, the less waste.

Glue-laminated beams for house construction take several forms. One is a conventional beam of rectangular cross section, with either horizontal or vertical glue joints. Another is a method of fabricating an efficient beam not only from a materials standpoint, but also in terms of improving the geometry over the conventional rectangular beam. Bulbous ends or "flanges" are fabricated from horizontal glue-laminates and a center diaphragm (see Figure 6-5c) of plywood joints these ends together.

The application of glue-lams in residential construction represents an almost classic case of an undeniably better product not necessarily offering any added benefit in service. The reason is that while the strength of such beams is for most practical purposes substantially greater than that of conventional

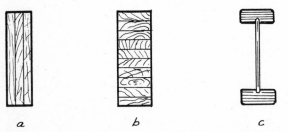

a   b   c

Fig. 6-5 Fabricated wood beams. (*a*) Vertical laminated beam. (*b*) Horizontal laminated beam. (*c*) Laminated flanges and plywood web.

rectangular timbers of the same size, many joist applications are not strength-limited but rather stiffness- or deflection-limited. Later in this chapter the importance of floor stiffness will be discussed, but for the present it is sufficient to understand that simply having a beam of greater strength without a corresponding increase in stiffness is of benefit in only a limited range of floor spans.

Metal-plate-connected flat trusses for framing residential floors can be fabricated from a variety of lumber sizes, but most commonly they are built up from 2×4s placed with the wide dimension in the horizontal plane, as shown in Figure 6-6. Such trusses are relatively more efficient when they are used in place of deeper lumber members and therefore in longer-span applications. Thus, when spans are much less than 14 or 15 feet, conventional framing lumber is more appropriate.

One of the most desirable features of trussed joists is that electrical wiring and plumbing lines can be run between the "wed" or diagonal members. In some applications a rectangular opening can be made to allow the passage of air-conditioning ducts. By definition a truss is a continuously connected structure whose members enclose alternate triangular spaces, and the introduction of a rectangular "panel" or enclosed space actually violates the truss structure. Near the midspan of a joist this can sometimes be tolerated, and in such applications the added freedom of locating air-distribution ducts can be worthwhile.

Of all the acts of poor practice in residential building construction, perhaps none is so common and eventually causes so much distress as the cutting of joists to allow the passage of wiring and pipes. Traditionally the various building trades have operated pretty much independently of one another. Carpenters place the floor joists and deck; electricians drill holes in joists to run their wires, with little regard for the structural requirements; and finally, plumbers cut out anything that stands in the path of their pipes. Unfortunately, the structural problems caused by these practices may not develop for

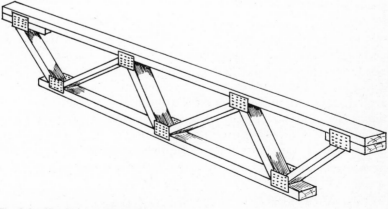

Fig. 6-6 Metal-plate-connected truss.

a number of years. When plumbing lines leak, the water can sometimes drain along the outside of a pipe for several feet. If the pipe penetrates a joist, the water inevitably drips off around the hole. Then the conditions for rot, that is, damp wood and poor air circulation, are ideal. The result is that in a significant number of older houses rotten joists below bathrooms and kitchens accompany deterioration of the plumbing. In some situations cutting through joists to install plumbing lines seems almost inevitable, but when the trades really look at one another's needs it often turns out that such simple devices as varying the joist spacing below a bathroom or heading a few joists at complicated intersections eliminate any need to cut joists.

For a period spanning roughly the first half of the twentieth century, a detail of installing bathroom floors also eventually contributed to framing deterioration. The exact metamorphosis of this detail is somewhat unclear, and both old books and mechanics differ as to the reasons and development of the method. Specifically, ceramic-tile floors for bathrooms became popular, and it is known that tile laid directly on wood deck did not survive either the shrinkage of wood or the periodic wetting of the bathroom. In Europe the practice had been to lay a sheet of lead on the floor and turn it up at the wall edges. A mortar setting bed was spread on this lead "tub" and the tile set in the mortar. A few bathrooms in this country were built this way near the turn of the century; but either because of the price of lead or because builders actually thought they were making an improvement, a different detail was introduced. "Centering" or form work for a concrete slab was placed several inches below the top of the wood joist of a bathroom floor. The tops of the joists were cut off and a concrete slab was installed. Finally, the tile was set in a bed of mortar on top of the concrete slab. As time went on, the joist tops were often trimmed to a rough point, as shown in Figure 6-7, rather than squared off. Some insist this was intentional, while others claim that the carpenter was directed to hack off the top of the joist and the pointed ends were the result of a halfhearted attempt. Whatever the original intent, the pointed ends eventually become accepted as standard form. Turn-of-the-century manuals show slabs placed between headed-off joists, with shallower joists below the slab. This certainly makes sense, whereas the rationale for the eventual standard practice is certainly obscure. The eventual consequences of this detail have been greatly less than satisfactory. Obviously a bathroom is heavy. Typically the room is small, often with heavy, tiled walls. Finally, the concrete slab and floor tiles are unusually heavy. The net result is that at the location of maximum weight in the average house, the joists are actually cut down and weakened. To add to the problems is the potential for floor-joist rot in the typically wetter-than-normal environment. Finally, above the joist points the slab is thinnest, and cracks often appear in the tile directly above these pointed joists. In most applications at least part of the plumbing lines were run in the concrete slab. This is a reasonable detail until a leak occurs, and then the only recourse is to break out the concrete slab, make the repair, and then replace the concrete.

The most common ailment resulting from this concrete-on-trimmed-joists

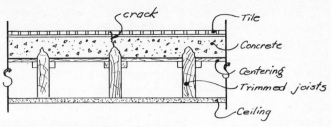

Fig. 6-7 Bathroom floor construction.

detail is a sagged, deformed floor in the vicinity of the bathroom. The extent of the deformation is very much a function of details and geometry of framing, and the location of partitions below. Such lower-level partitions, even though they may not originally have been intended to be load bearing, can transfer loads to a lower floor level and allow a load-sharing mechanism to exist between alternate floors. The most dramatic deformations occur when heavy bathrooms are located above large rooms with long floor spans. A standard house plan places the stairs to the second floor in one side of the living room, with the bathroom on the second floor located almost above the middle of the living room. By standing on the stairs and sighting along the living room ceiling, you can spot any deformation easily. Sometimes it is a little confusing to try to measure the amount of this sag by stretching a string from side to side. An easier means of at least estimating the deflection is to shine a flashlight along the ceiling surface, as described in Chapter 5. Sags of 1 to 1½ inches are not uncommon and generally can be tolerated if it can be definitely established that the movement is a long-term phenomenon and occurred neither abruptly nor recently. If the deformity is much greater than this, probably a professional should be consulted, and certainly the joists should be visually inspected.

Repairs for any joist deformation due to long-term overloading (e.g., joists that are "plastic-creep-deformed") obviously are a major undertaking. Ceiling and floor lines can be leveled in various ways, but inevitably correcting such problems requires actually adding more structure. Creep deformation is a "bending-stress"-related phenomenon; that is, it is related to the stresses toward the midspan of the joist and is independent of the end-bearing conditions. For this reason any added structure can be limited to strengthening the portion of the joists away from the ends. Often simply screwing or bolting new lumber sections in the middle two-thirds (length) of the deformed joist will provide the needed additional strength. Another common stiffening technique is to attach a section of steel plate to the joist.

In addition to glue-lam and metal-plate-connected trusses, another recent modification to the traditional floor-framing methods has been the use of glues to secure plywood structural floor deck to the joists. The two most commonly used glues are the caseins, sometimes called "white glue," and a product generically called "construction adhesive." The later comes in a tube cartridge and can be dispensed with a conventional caulking gun. Both glues fix the plywood to the joist to create a "T-beam," a much more efficient beam shape. The mechanism is analogous to the difference in stiffness between a telephone book and a single piece of cardboard of the same thickness. The telephone book is pliable because the individual pages slip by one another, but if they were all joined together, they would be like a single piece of cardboard and therefore extremely stiff. The difference between the two glue types is that the casein is in a thin layer that dries relatively hard, while the adhesive types are thick and remain soft enough to be permanently deformed if a load is applied for a long time. Because of this the adhesive can be credited with increasing the stiffness of the floor only when subjected to short-duration loads and does not add to total strength. On the other hand, casein glue, if properly applied, increases both stiffness and strength. In such a system the joint between plywood panels becomes the limiting element; but with tightly fitted tongue-and-groove edges, floor-strength increases of four and five times the conventional, unglued methods can be achieved. At first this seems like an extremely desirable property, but as a practical matter the advantages might not be worth the added expense. By taking full advantage of the strength increases, you might change the floor weight and stiffness in such a way as to produce a very uncomfortable floor to live on. These effects will be discussed later in this chapter, in connection with floor stiffness.

Even when glue is not used in the initial design it may sometimes be used to solve certain difficult repair and alteration problems. Several examples have been given of the complications of strengthening existing floor structures. One very satisfactory method is to glue plywood to old joists. In extreme cases the addition of closely spaced wood screws in conjunction with gluing can create a substantial increase in both strength and stiffness.

One floor application, while not structurally different from the conventional systems, is in such a grossly different environment that it deserves to be considered separately. Many floors are built, not over enclosed spaces, but directly above the ground surface. Sometimes these "crawl spaces" are well enclosed, but oftentimes, particularly in the Southern states, they are only shielded from the outside by latticework or screens. Such floors are subjected to a unique environment of moisture, insects, temperatures, and sound. Over the years many combinations of detailing have been tried, but none seems universally successful. The basic problems center around how to insulate the floor, protect it from excessive moisture, prevent insects from nesting in the enclosed space, circulate some air around the structure to minimize rot and ground odors, and allow some plumbing and electrical services within the structure. Many of these constants are conflicting, and solving one problem worsens another. Finally, between the extremes of climate, almost completely opposite solutions are required; but it is in the Middle Western states, which have both cold winters requiring insulation and hot, humid summers with associated ground-moisture conditions, that the solutions become most complex. In these zones the first inclination is simply to block off the crawl space so that no cold air can enter, then with a conventional joist and wood-deck floor structure several feet above the ground, assume that the crawl space will stabilize at a reasonable temperature partway between the ground and room temperatures. In some cases a modest effort is made to actively supply heat to the crawl space. The first problem is that the floor stays much closer to the ground temperatures because the warm room air rises and there is generally not a lot of air circulation near the floor level. Living on a floor with temperatures in the mid-50°F range is decidely uncomfortable, particularly in bathroom areas. The completely enclosed crawl space becomes an optimum winter home for insects and small animals, which are almost completely impossible to seal out. Finally, many soils, particularly those with organic materials, have an unpleasant smell, and their odors can easily seep through conventional floor structures. In the summer, if any moisture is in the soil, it will evaporate into the crawl space, and since there is no positive ventilation, the floor structure literally can become saturated. Thus, it is almost universally accepted that completely sealing off the crawl space is not a reasonable solution; however, this example does suggest that a partial solution may be to place a thin layer of concrete (2 to 3 inches thick) on the ground surface to help cut off moisture and ground odors. There is one problem with this approach. Any large trees whose drip lines cover part of a house built over a crawl space will almost certainly have part of their root systems below the house. While young trees can adapt to changes in surface conditions above their roots, old, well-established trees can rarely tolerate having the surface above their roots significantly altered.

The other general approach to solving the problems of a floor built over a crawl space involves various combinations of insulating and sealing the volume of the floor structure. The source of moisture and method of ventilation are the critical areas of concern. In many situations the direction of the vapor-pressure gradient changes between the winter and summer temperatures, which requires that a complete water-vapor barrier exist at both the top and bottom of the joists. Since such barriers are never 100 percent complete, air somehow must be circulated through the joists. Finally, the lower barrier must be bugproof as well as waterproof. Some materials combinations that have been tried include transite panels as the lower vapor barrier, and plastic film or aluminum foil insulation backing as the upper vapor barrier. Ventilation is provided by using 2 × 2 wood batten strips nailed at right angles to the floor joist below the flooring. The air is vented either through screened holes on the outside walls or up the walls into an attic space. This is a fairly expensive floor system, and it is difficult to get plumbing in and out of it.

The inescapable conclusion is that in designing a new house, floors over crawl spaces should generally be avoided; and in modifying an existing house over a crawl space, all the rather unusual constraints should be examined before deciding on a particular method of insulating and enclosing the floor-structure volume.

A somewhat analogous condition to the crawl-space problem exists in certain types of new homes. Split-level houses have become very popular, and one of their appealing features is that an owner can leave an unfinished, below-grade area as a basement or convert it to conventional living space. Below-grade concrete-slab floor spaces are fine for recreation rooms, but many people object to having bedrooms and bathrooms on cold, damp concrete. Owners have tried to solve this problem by laying wood strips or "sleepers" on the floor and building a plywood floor deck above. Sometimes they even insulate the void between sleepers. First, the wood must be treated to resist both rot and insects; but even with this precaution excessive moisture can build up below the floor if there is no positive ventilation. Remember that just because there has never been standing water on an exposed basement slab, it does *not* prove that there is no moisture coming from the ground through the slab. In the average basement there is enough air circulation to evaporate any moisture that does come through the slab. A crude test to see if a basement slab is transmitting moisture is simply to set a tight-fitting, impervious container on the slab, such as a metal bucket. After a few days look under the bucket to see if the floor has a damp, discolored spot. if so, moisture is coming through the slab and is being evaporated normally at the surface. Try this test at several locations, and preferably both in summer and in winter. When a sleeper on slab floor is applied, a gap between the flooring and wall should be left along the edges to allow air to circulate. If new stud walls are to be installed on the basement walls as an insulation device or to create a finished surface, then the ventilation air can simply flow up between the studs to the ceiling line.

Floor Stiffness

As discussed in Chapter 5 in connection with plaster ceiling distress, floor structures are seldom inadequate with respect to the absolute strength of the wood framing members. Occasionally an individual floor joist may crack under some unique load condition, but one almost never hears of a mass fracture causing collapse of a residential floor. In the relatively rare cases of floor collapse, the causes are generally related either to inadequate support conditions or attachment methods. The most common structural deficiency in residential floor construction framing involves stiffness. Stiffness inadequacies are of two generic types—long-term, permanent deformation (creep deformation); and short-term flexibility, which can be sensed in the "springiness" of a floor. Both types involve deflection of the floor joist, but they are not necessarily related; and there is no guarantee that a flexible floor will plastically deform in the future or, conversely, that a sagged, deformed floor is necessarily springy.

The principal sensation of flexibility in a floor is a human physiological response to the dynamic characteristics of the structure, that is, a relation involving displacement, time, and weight (mass) of the floor assembly. People respond in different ways to different combinations of these three variables. In one case a two-hundred-year-old house was originally built as an extremely humble farm residence. Local, primitive materials were used. The floor joists were hewn from small trees, and even though the spans were short, the resulting 6 × 6 beams were extremely flexible and could rather grossly deform under any static load. Today the building is an esoteric suburban dwelling and is the result of numerous modifications and additions. New flooring was simply applied on top of the old at least three times, and plaster was installed between the joists. The result is that this initially extremely flexible floor is very massive. The floor is permanently deformed several inches, and when someone stands in the middle, the initial deflection is actually visible in the ceiling below. The amazing thing is that it does not feel particularly flexible to walk on, the reason being that the extreme mass produces a dynamic response that is not particularly noticeable or objectional physiologically. On the other hand, modern floors can be extremely stiff and yet of a relatively lightweight structure. In recent years the practice of gluing plywood subfloor-ing to floor joists has become quite standard. This substantially stiffens the floor without necessarily making it any stronger. Dry-wall ceiling finish is lighter in weight than plaster, and finished flooring is often thin and light. The result is a stiff, low-mass floor that people often complain about as being flimsy and flexible. The fact is that such a floor may be nearly optimum for wood construction and meets or exceeds every code requirement for both strength and stiffness.

One builder of housing projects constructs sample panels of different floor framing systems as part of the design process of a new housing type. People are asked to walk and jump on the floors and describe which they sense as being the most comfortable. There is no absolutely clear consensus, but generally people prefer floors with low vibratory frequencies, and in general they are unaware of the absolute deformation of the floor structure.

In furnished rooms the dynamics and sense of flexibility can be even more confusing. Weight and arrangement of furniture can have a profound effect on the response of a floor. Delicate glassware and china in slight contact will vibrate in some rooms and produce the sensation of a flexible floor when in reality the reverse is true. The whole issue is that it is difficult to make any concise judgment of the quality of a floor structure based solely on how the senses respond to walking and jumping on a floor. Furthermore, what to some people may feel like a floor that could permanently deform may, in fact, be uniquely resistant to this problem.

The problem of long-term, permanent deformation of floor structures is a function of the particular wood species and the level to which it is per-manently stressed. Unfortunately, little research has been done on the long-term deformation characteristics of various types of wood, but it is clear that there is considerable difference among species. Some woods will become permanently deformed under their own weight. A very graphic example is in shelving. Some rather nondescript, visually irregular-looking boards will remain true and straight for many years, while other boards that look sound will sag in a few months. Both temperature and moisture can affect wood bowing, but in the range of variations in the average house these are probably not significant factors.

The dominant parameter affecting long-term deformation and the one that can be most easily controlled is the stress level. As discussed earlier, wood is a material that can easily sustain a relatively high stress for short periods but that will seriously deform under a permanently applied stress of grossly lower magnitude. In most residences the most significant sustained load on wood floor joists comes from partitions and concentrated loads from stairs. The practice has always been to provide two floor joists below a partition and on both sides of a headered stair (see Chapter 5). Analytically and practically this procedure has been justified on the basis that the joists are not over-stressed to the point of fracture, nor will they deform noticeably in the first few years following construction. The troubles begin after twenty or thirty years, when floors sag and plaster cracks. Modern partitions often weigh one-third to one-half as much as conventionally plastered ones, and it is to be hoped that relatively less distortion will eventually occur than has been the case in the past. Unfortunately, the tendency toward larger rooms and there-fore longer joist spans may have absorbed any margins, and some houses built in the late 1940s with lightweight dry-wall partitions are already showing signs of significant wood-joist plastic deformation.

The remedy for this problem during the construction phase is, of course, simple—overdesign by conventional standards and provide perhaps three joists at stair headers and below partitions. After-the-fact remedies are rel-atively more complicated and costly, and since very few people live in one house long enough to actually witness the progression of such deformation, it is not the sort of repair an owner is likely to make as a preventive measure. On the other hand, during extensive remodeling, adding stiffness to the floor structure below partitions may be a reasonable operation to consider. In such situations it may be extremely difficult to work additional joists in the floor structure below partitions, but remember there are two other reasonable alternatives. One is to lighten the partition by removing heavy plaster and reinstalling a thinner, lighter dry wall. The other is to locate additional joist members not in the plane of the floor below the partition, but above the floor within the thickness of the wall. This solution is necessarily restricted to walls that do not have door openings in them.

The secret of minimizing long-term plastic deformation in wood framing members is to avoid higher than average stresses that will be more or less continuously applied. If permanent, heavy loads are inevitable, such as a tall bookcase or a piano, then try to locate them on the floor where the load is distributed between the most members and also near the bearing ends.

The details of how the newer factory-fabricated joist members will sustain permanent loading have not yet been fully established. The estimates of allowable loads designed for metal-plate-connected floor trusses may have been somewhat overly optimistic in the early days of use; and there are some reports of deformation that might be attributable to either the connectors working loose with time, or creep deformation of the truss wood members. Similarly, glue joints of any sort are relatively new in wood structural elements of residences. Not all the materials or methods have stood the test of time required to prove their durability. Recognizing this, most manufacturers and designers have been relatively conservative in their performance estimates of glue-joined floor members.

Wood-Framed Floor Attachments

Owners can generally learn to live with building sags and modest distortion phenomena, providing these occurrences develop rather slowly. A much more legitimate concern is the possibility of collapse. As explained earlier, wood rarely fractures to cause collapse. On the other hand, when actual or potential collapse occurs, it is often related to some failure of an attachment detail. Nails, screws, bolts, glue, and various fabricated sheet-metal fittings are the standard wood-attachment methods, but nails are by far the most common.

People who have little interest in things mechanical, or who generally have a poor intuitive understanding of building structures still might have a vague appreciation for the support requirements for a floor joist in a house. Perhaps it is merely a matter of applying some sense of proportions—a piece of wood "so big" should reasonably bear on a piece of wood of a certain size. In light of this, it is surprising how shockingly deficient are many connector details that are made presumably by experienced professionals. For example, floor joist end reactions are typically in the range of 400 to 800 pounds. A single nail, optimally installed, may carry close to 100 pounds for short-term loading, whereas nail loads range from 40 to 80 pounds (varying with the wood species and nail location) for sustained loading. Yet, floor joists are regularly found to be "toenailed" into an abutting wood member, with three or four nails. Toenailing involves driving a nail near the end of a plank on an angle so that the nail can engage two intersecting timbers. Thus, it not only penetrates part of the thickness of one member, but it is so near the end that the wood can easily split out in the neighborhood of the nail. At best such a connection device can provide only a fraction of the required capacity. Why then is it so common? The standard answer seems to be tradition—it has always been

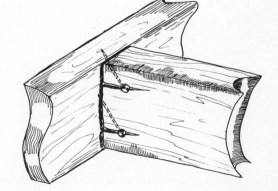

Fig. 6-8   Toenailed wood joint.

done that way! One contractor, trying to impress a young apprentice carpenter with the inadequacies of toenailing floor joists, told the novice to build a ladder out of 2×4 lumber, which would then be climbed. Every rung was nailed through carefully with two nails plus a wood block between adjacent rungs. This was a design perfectly consistent with supporting a single person and on an order of magnitude stronger than the young carpenter's normal practice.

The problem of inadequate connections is further complicated (and perpetuated) by the fact that houses are built with marginal connections and survive for hundreds of years, without ill effects. Some argue that this clearly demonstrates that the connection is adequate, but the simple reality is that the joint never has been subjected to a full live-load condition. Next, the hypothesis is suggested that no floor *ever* receives the conventionally specified live loads of 30 to 50 pounds per square foot, and for this reason connections of low capacity can be tolerated. General Custer used the same logic when he told his troops to surround the Indians at Little Bighorn. Rarely is every square foot of a floor fully loaded; but regularly, substantial portions of floors receive the design live load or even more. Several people grouped around a piano can easily exceed 50 pounds per square foot distributed weight. The important issue is that inadequate connections can and *do* allow floors to collapse; and of all the marginal connections, those in which nails alone carry loads, and specifically toenails, are the most troublesome.

The framing around stairways is a likely location for finding abutting lumber and therefore a likely place for toenailed connections. In basements without ceilings the details of the carpentry can be seen easily; furthermore, details that are used in the first-floor framing are likely to be repeated in upper floors. In a sloping stairway ceiling where it meets the main-floor ceiling, a characteristic bump in the plaster occasionally develops. This distortion is unique in that it is restricted to the outside corner of the stair opening and extends for a foot at most. If at the comparable location in the basement, a toenailed, stair-header joist exists, the chances are good that such a distortion in upper levels is a result of a toenailed header joist that has begun to deform.

The solution for inadequate nailing and particularly for toenailing is *not* to drive more nails. Too many nails near the end of a timber will eventually cause the entire end to split apart; moreover, there are some readily available, easily installed connection devices that can be used to correct such problem connection points. These are sheet-metal clips formed in different ways to fit a variety of combinations of framed joints. In some cases they are nailed across the joint with special short nails, while in other cases they actually hook over one timber and hang down to create a ledge or stirrup for an intersection joist. Generically they are called "sheet-metal framing anchors," but they often go by the name of one of the early manufacturers and are just called "TECO clips." Any lumberyard will have a variety of different types of clips for different applications, and easy-to-follow instruction sheets are generally available. One important requirement when installing framing anchors is to

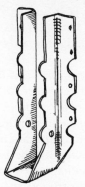

Fig. 6-9   Sheet-metal framing anchors.

use the special nails designed for the purpose, and to use them in the recommended quantity. Some carpenters seem intent on perpetuating the tradition of poor-quality nailed timber joints. Even when they use proper framing connections, they use the wrong number and type of nails.

Another nail-dependent attachment detail that is commonly found in both
old and new houses is referred to by some as a "ledger board support."
Specifically, where joists bear into a beam, a narrow piece of wood, often 1½
inches square, is nailed along the bottom of the beam (see Figure 6-10a). The
intersecting joists, if they are the same depth as the beam, often are notched
at the bottom to fit over the ledger board and thus provide a uniform depth
of structure so that a smooth ceiling line can be attached below. The basic
idea, at first glance, seems reasonable; and perhaps it is particularly appealing
because it looks so neat and orderly. Unfortunately, there are two serious
limitations to this method of construction. One of the limitations on wood-
joist loading is related to the area of the joist cross section near the bearing
end, that is, the "shear" strength. If the joist and ledger board are the same
thickness (which they typically are), then a measure of the relative shear
strength of these two members can be made by simply comparing their re-

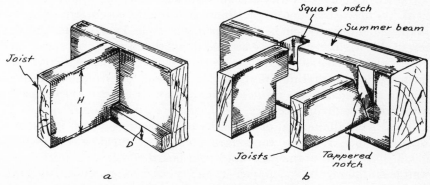

Fig. 6-10   (a) Joist bearing on ledger plate. (b) Beam notch details.

spective depths, H compared to D in Figure 6-10*a*. Thus, joists 8 to 10 inches deep are regularly resting on a ledger board 1½ inches deep, and it should comes as no surprise that such ledger boards often fail in the shear mode of wood failure.

The second common deficiency with this detail is the nailing. The nail is not only driven through a relatively narrow board but also penetrates into the beam very near the bottom, often within ¾ inch or so. Both these nailing conditions are extremely vulnerable to splitting, either of the ledger or of the beam bottom. Finally, to further complicate matters, rarely are enough nails provided; and if anything, they tend to be fewer in number than in typical toenailing. For example, four toenails are fairly standard (even though they may be totally inadequate) in joists spaced 16 inches apart, or comparably one nail for each 4 inches. Often ledger boards are installed with one nail per joist or, at the least, 16 inches on center.

Following World War II, mass-production techniques were applied to building construction. One such project involved preassembling sections of floors that were trucked to the job site and set on the foundation walls. To keep the individual floor panel sizes relatively small, the joists were set on a 1½-inch-deep ledger board, which in turn was nailed to the beam at 16 inches on centers—literally optimizing all the possible deficiencies of such a detail. Predictably, failure occurred. Wood split from being nailed too close to the edge, nails bent from being overloaded, and the ledger board failed in shear. The result is that hundreds of houses have almost exactly the same sagged floor and deformed bearing partitions above.

It is interesting to examine how individual owners of these houses have dealt with the problem over the past thirty years. In some cases the failure occurred very shortly after the houses were originally occupied. If the problem was correctly diagnosed, it was relatively easy to repair by any of a number of reasonable modifications, and in many cases the deformed floors were jacked back into their original positions. Other owners saw the deformation and associated it with plaster cracking, patched the cracks, and sold the houses, assuming that it was some generic, irreparable defect. The second owners, of course, eventually noticed the sagging, but without the benefit of having witnessed any corresponding cracking, guessed it was simply a result of sloppy work. As the years went on and more deformation occurred, owners often perpetuated the problem by the "repair-sell" cycle. Finally, after thirty years, few of the original owners are around to tell the history, and new owners of grossly deformed but plaster-patched houses cannot easily identify the sequence of events and the fundamental problem. They most often conclude that the deformation is a result of a foundation settlement—a conclusion that can lead to totally unnecessary, costly, and even damaging repairs.

Aside from the appeal of simplicity of this ledger board, it is somewhat surprising that, in light of the failure rate, it has survived as a fairly common detail. The origins of the idea of a ledger board may be in a detail associated with joist framing into a summer beam system. Two standard joints for this type of construction are shown in Figure 6-10*b*. In one case the joist ends were tapered in a fashion similar to what is today called a "fire cut," and the beam was chiseled out to form a pocket of the same shape. The alternative method of joining was to notch the bottom of the joist and set the joist into a corresponding hole in the beam. Naturally this substantially decreased the end shear capacity of the joists, and many failed by splitting out horizontally from the notch. Almost exactly the same detailing is found in the deck construction of wooden ships, and the house detail may actually be a carry-over from ship carpenters who settled on land and switched to house carpentry.

Not all ledger boards are inadequate by any means. On short spans, particularly common around stair framing, it is a reasonable attachment method; but if either long-span joists are involved or bearing partitions must transmit their loads through such joints, then remedial measures should certainly be continued. The most satisfactory corrections generally involve installation of one of the metal joist hanger devices, although framing anchors may be acceptable.

Bolts and screws are not often used in the initial construction of houses, because they are relatively expensive to purchase and install. Bolts and screws, however, are a common repair connector. As a general rule the load capacities of nails, bolts, and screws are limited by the failure of the wood and not of the connector. According to the direction of loading, grain pattern, and wood species, the wood failure mode can be in compression around the connector, in splitting out the wood along the grain, or in the so-called tear-out mode, where the wood symmetrically breaks out toward the end of the plank. Thus, the load capacity of any connector device tends to increase with increased diameter and thickness of engagement.

One of the great fairy tales of the house-building industry concerns the use of plywood as a connector or supplementary framing stiffener. In a number of ways plywood is an outstanding construction material, but it is still simply wood, and in particular wood with its grain pattern laminated in such a way that roughly half the grain runs in one direction and half in the other. In the general discussion of wood properties it was pointed out that wood is grossly stronger in the direction parallel to the grain than at right angles to it. Thus, if plywood were loaded in the plane of the wood, (as opposed to perpendicular to the plane, as it would be in the normal floor-deck situation), it is reasonable to suppose that it would be weaker than a piece of conventional lumber of the same general quality if it were loaded parallel to the grain. Possibly because plywood comes in sheets and a large piece of any shape can be cut out, people must have made an analogy between plywood and other continuous sheet materials such as steel plate. In any event, plywood is often used to make timber connections as if it has properties similar to metal, which, of course, it does not. For example, once in a while someone will propose that a lumber beam, say, a 2 × 10, be spliced with pieces of plywood screwed to both sides across the joint. Plywood ½ inch thick is suggested. The total of 1 inch of plywood only has half its grain running in the direction of the original timber, and thus may have much less than one-half the strength of the original 1½-inch-thick timber.

Another common use of plywood is in what is called a "flitch beam." This is a beam composed of a thin piece of steel plate sandwiched between two wood timbers. The incentive for the creation and use of such a beam was that the combined strengths of the wood and steel could be used; that the wood stiffened the thin, flexible steel plate against buckling; that it was relatively narrow; and that the exposed faces were wood and could receive conventional nails. With steel rolled sections, familiarly called "I-beams," readily available, the use of a flitch beam is hardly justifiable today. Still, a holdover from such beams is a "plywood flitch beam" [sic]. When a lintel or beam is required, some carpenters will sandwich a ½- or ⅝-inch-thick piece of plywood between two standard lumber pieces and suppose that the additional plywood actually adds significant strength. This practice should not be confused with that of adding a piece of ½-inch plywood between two lumber lintels as a filler piece to bring the combined width to 3½ inches (1½ plus 1½ plus ½), the width of a conventional stud wall.

Where plywood is applicable as a connection piece in lumber construction, its limitations should be clearly recognized; and as a general rule when it is used to join floor framing lumber, the combined thickness of any plywood should be at least as thick if not thicker than the piece to be joined.

Standard Floor Framing Distress Patterns

In the process of describing floor framing types and generic problems, many common problems that may eventually develop into a distress pattern have been discussed. There are several other situations that may lead to damage and distress.

In the discussion of interior walls the details of wood-stud partition construction were described, specifically, how a 2×4 plate is laid flat on the subflooring and the 2×4 studs are rested on this plate. In the average house the stud loads are relatively uniform, and there is no effort made to make every stud bear directly above a joist. In many cases this is impossible, because the joists and studs are spaced differently. The rationale for load transfer from the studs to the joists is that the plate plus the subflooring can carry the stud loads in bending between the joists. In general, this is a satisfactory system, but at a door opening not only are the loads in the (jack) studs typically higher than average, but the 2×4 base plate stops at the edge of the door and certainly cannot distribute the load between two adjacent joists (see Figure 6-11).

Again, few problems arise with the average door, but for a wide opening in a bearing wall, this lack of continuity of the base plate can lead to serious problems. The correct detail is either an extra joist inserted under the edge of the base plate, or wood blocking inserted below the floor and between the joists.

Of course, the eventual consequence of the incorrectly supported jack studs is that the studs literally punch through the flooring and drop the partition

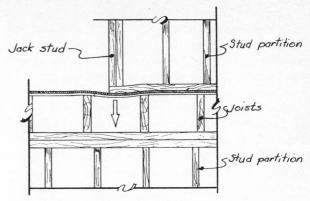

Fig. 6-11   Deformed floor at jack stud.

and any floor above. In recent years this problem has been aggravated because many houses are built with only a plywood subfloor, and the floor covering has been wall-to-wall carpet rather than wood tongue-and-groove flooring. As spacing between joists becomes greater and plywood deck thinner, the potential for damage increases. Sometimes a distortion at the edge of a wide opening caused by this framing error can actually be felt before it can be clearly seen. By running a hand along the floor, you can feel the telltale depression that is a sign of this problem. The solution for such a situation is to insert solid-wood blocking below the partition to either transfer the load to a bearing partition below, if one exists, or to span between joists. For this repair there is a tendency to want to jack up the partition and return everything to its original, undeflected position. If, over a number of years, cracks have developed as a result of this stud settlement and have been patched progressively, then jacking will only produce "reverse" cracks. Also, remember that wood attachments, particularly nailed joints, do not always allow exactly the same movement in both directions; and whereas a nailed joint may have pulled opened, it may not easily be pushed closed. In short, if jacking is essential, advance the jack as slowly as possible at rates of no more than inches per week, and expect some additional cracks to develop.

Bundles of framing lumber appear to be extremely uniform in size and grain characteristics, and it would be reasonable to assume that this uniformity would continue after installation in a house. Unfortunately, this is not now, and never has been, true. The only consistency of lumber has been its dimension at the time of finish milling. Growth history that affects grain characteristics, and eventually such properties as strength and warping, are obviously variable between any two pieces of lumber, but perhaps even more critical are the variations in moisture content. The most critical moisture conditions occur at the time of milling, and later when the lumber is actually installed in a house. Since extremes in moisture can produce almost a 10 percent variation in lumber dimensions; that is, perpendicular to the grain, floor joists that typically range from 8 to 12 inches deep can vary, in the extreme, by almost 1 full inch as a result of moisture changes. Consider some of the possible consequences of this phenomenon. Suppose two pieces of rough-sawn lumber differ in moisture content by 20 or 25 percent at the time of finish milling, are packaged together, and dry to the same moisture content by the time of installation. The carpenter is faced with adjusting two side-by-side joists that vary in depth by perhaps ⅝ inch. Years ago when ceilings were of conventional field-applied plaster, it was necessary only to align the tops of the joists so that the floor deck would be flat. The plasterer could vary the plaster thickness and create a level ceiling surface regardless of the joist variation. Thus, in old houses it is not uncommon to find the bearing ends of joists variably notched to adjust for a constant top elevation.

Unfortunately, with dry-wall ceilings the floor structural thickness must be uniform so that both the top floor surface and the bottom ceiling level will be flat, continuous surfaces. Thus, the carpenter must pick and choose among joists to get all constant-depth members. Not only is this time-consuming, but also it invariably means that a few joists are discarded.

Simply culling joists for uniform depth is by no means the only problem. If the joists are the same dimension at the time of installation and yet have significantly different moisture contents, they will naturally shrink differently. Supposedly if all the joists come from the same mill-packaged bundle, this variable shrinkage is unlikely to happen, because similar amounts of moisture should correspond to similar dimensions from the same mill lot. Bundles, however, do get mixed, and sometimes there are sufficient differences in the physical properties of lumber within any grading class to permit such variations. Variations in depth between adjacent joists are rarely noticeable in the ceiling, simply because the joists are resting on their bottom edges and therefore naturally shrink from the top down. Particularly in kitchen floors with composition tile set on thin plywood, the effects of variable shrinkage between adjacent joists can be detected.

Another lumber characteristic that can cause very significant distress is joist bowing and warping. Variables such as grain geometry, species, moisture content, and curing history, often cause floor joists to bow an inch or more. Thick subfloors and tongue-and-groove flooring are generally enough to minimize a noticeable, abrupt variation between alternate joists. In houses that are built with wall-to-wall carpeting applied directly on what is normally plywood subflooring, the bow cannot be confined or perhaps distributed among several adjacent joists, with the result that the ceiling becomes wavy as the joists dry and warp. Any repair technique for this problem is expensive and requires messy and extensive demolition. Some people have actually preferred to pull the dry-wall nails out of a warped joist and allow the ceiling to simply span past the warped member without any support. Obviously, cutting out and replacing the warped member is admissible, but it is also the most complicated solution; and, incidentally, it supposes that a stable joist will be reinstalled. In a few cases owners actually have tried to install a much thicker plywood floor in hopes that the increase in stiffness would hold down the errant, bowing joist. This is hardly a reasonable solution for an entire floor, because doors must be cut down and stairs readjusted; but it does often work on limited-area, confined spaces with few doors.

Such wood bowing and shrinkage-related problems are confined to the first few years, and even more particularly to the first few months after being enclosed. New owners often are so dazzled by the newness or overwhelmed by the responsibilities of ownership that they fail to notice the development of such distortions. Several years later, when they begin to repaint, the irregularities are observed and the diagnosis becomes complicated by the lack of an accurate history. In such cases a careful examination of the complete geometry of the distortion, that is, at both floor and ceiling lines, is the key to correct identification.

Rarely does this class of distress have any structural significance in terms of decreased floor load capacity. It can, therefore, be considered cosmetic in nature, and really nothing *needs* to be done to correct the problem. If new homeowners do, for one reason or another, elect to disregard such distortions, they should try to get a written statement from the builder, identifying the phenomenon and the lack of any structural implications. The purpose of this is to be able to assure the next owner, who may not be as knowledgeable and understanding, that there is not some generic structural defect in the house.

Residential floor structural members are typically sized to support from between 30- to 50-pounds-per-square-foot uniformly distributed load in addition to the weight of the floor itself. This live-load criterion is generally sufficient to support almost any reasonable load condition that is likely to be encountered in the average residence. Typically, bookcases and pianos are the heaviest furniture. A bookcase, fortunately, generally stands along a wall, and if it runs at right angles to the floor joist and thus engages several near their bearing ends, its load is of little consequence. Occasionally, a full-room-height bookcase set parallel to joists will very locally deform the flooring; and bookcases used as room dividers and located near the center of joist spans may, with time, permanently deform the floor joist. As explained earlier, approaching failure is accompanied in such cases by relatively severe deformations that are noticeable and that serve as a warning that something is wrong. Similarly, pianos are really not excessively heavy on a square-foot basis; but the concentrated forces at the legs can be enough to easily deform flooring between joists and, in some cases, the joists themselves. Old upright pianos actually produce more concentrated loads than the average house-size grand pianos, and owners, recognizing this, often prudently have their floor capacity checked. If this is to be done, do not neglect the "moving" condition, which occurs when the piano must be rolled along the center of the floor. If this condition governs, then wide planks can often be laid on the floor to distribute the load during the move.

One of the few load conditions that has led to serious trouble in residential buildings is the presence of water beds. Not only is the dead load significant—remember, water 12 inches deep weighs 62 pounds per square foot—but there can be a dynamic effect as the water sloshes around in the container and frame. One problem with loads of this kind is that they can produce failures, not in the bending mode, in which case the deformation signals potential problems, but rather in shear, which can be relatively abrupt and occur with very little warning.

ROOFS AND ROOF STRUCTURES

7

Most people lump everything above the eaves line into what they generically call the "roof." This can lead to some confusion, because to others the word *roof* refers to the top water-repellent surface exposed to the weather. Actually, the parts of the roof should be separated into (1) the *roof structure,* consisting of the primary support members; (2) the *roof deck,* which is most often planking or plywood spanning between the structural members; (3) the *roofing,* which is the water-repellent surface; and finally (4) the *thermal insulation barrier.*

Peaked Roof Structures

Like floors, residential roof structures are most commonly of wood; however, metal and concrete are used in some specialized houses. The dominant criteria that define exactly which one of the many possible structural systems is to be used are whether the roof is flat or sloped, and whether any part of the structure or deck is to be exposed. The traditional house design, with its more or less symmetric, sloped roof is typically structured either with metal-plate-connected roof trusses (see Figure 7-1*a*) or according to the so-called conventional method, which entails the installation of framing lumber at both the roof and ceiling lines. The name for the sloped framing members (see Figure 7-1*b*) is not at all universally agreed upon. *Roof rafters, joists, beams, purlins,* and even *top chord* are used almost interchangeably, while the words for horizontal members are alternately *ties, tie beams, ceiling rafters,* and *ceiling* (or *attic*) *joists.*

This is one of those situations in which it is probably not valid to quote some recognized authority and say that the correct term is . . . because there

191

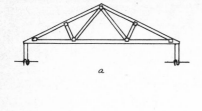

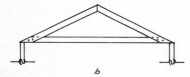

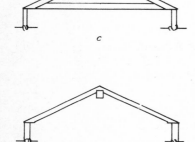

Fig. 7-1 Peaked roof framing systems. (*a*) Conventional truss with intermediate diagonal members. (*b*) Trussed roof without diagonals. (*c*) Tied rafters with central beam. (*d*) Rafters framing from wall to central beam.

are simply so many people that have made another name a part of standard usage. Even in standard references there is a certain lack of consistency; for example, when the sloping member is called a rafter, it seems most often to be restricted to the situation, as shown in Figure 7-1*b* and *c*, where there is also a horizontal member or tie or ceiling joist. On the other hand, in a system without any horizontal ties, the same sloping members are simply called roof beams, as in Figure 7-1*d*. The important issue is that you should not get too dogmatic about names, and in dealing with any written contractual matters or specifications, special care should be taken to define the particular member in some way other than by name alone. This is probably a classic case where a picture is worth at least several hundred words.

For simplicity's sake we will refer to the sloped members in Figures 7-1*b* and *c* as rafters, and the horizontal members as joists. The sloped members in the truss (see Figure 7-1*a*) will be referred to as the top chord, while the bottom horizontal truss element is called the bottom chord.

To appreciate peaked roof structures in general, and the details of one of the most common roof distresses in particular, some of the mechanics of trusses must be understood. If two rafter beams are set freely on a wall, leaned against one another at the center as in Figure 7-2*a,* and pushed down upon from above as a snow load might do, the rafters will simply slide off the top of the wall and collapse. This is true because the rafters require a horizontal force or *thrust* load applied at the lower edge to keep them stable, in much the same way as a ladder leaning against a wall at the top must be restrained at the bottom from sliding away from the wall. If the rafters are secured to the tops of conventional stud walls that cannot provide the necessary thrust restraint, then the walls will simply be pushed out, as in Figure 7-2*b,* and the walls and roof will collapse. There are several ways to stabilize the rafters so that they can withstand a vertical force. One method is to "tie" the lower ends together with a rope or cable or any member that can transmit the thrust force from one rafter end to another. The addition of this tie actually creates a roof truss system in which the rafters form the top chord, and the tie the bottom or "tension" chord. Now the inconsistency in the names of the parts becomes even more apparent.

A second method of stabilizing a rafter system is to make the walls so rigid that they can resist the thrust without collapsing. This is most often done by "buttressing" the walls, and in fact the flying buttresses on the walls of Gothic cathedrals performed just this function (see Figure 7-2*d*). The buttressed walls actually transmit the thrust force to the ground, which transmits the tension from one side to the other. A good demonstration that this is the case can be had by visualizing buttressed walls resting on two floating barges. Obviously, the water cannot transmit the thrust or tension, and the barges would just drift apart if a vertical force were applied to the roof.

Still another way to create a peaked roof with sloping rafters would be to attach the members together at the top or peak so that this top joint would be rigid and would, therefore, not hinge or bend. Actually, this is really a matter of making a continuous beam, albeit an oddly shaped one, that can span from one wall to another (see Figure 7-2*e*). In some respects this sounds like the easiest solution, but as a practical matter it is perhaps the most difficult. For one reason, it means that a single beam must span between walls, while in the buttressed case (see Figure 7-1*d*) the rafters can be thought of as just spanning half the distance between walls. Trusses are simply more efficient than beams for such an application. Another practical problem with this solution is that it is relatively complicated to create a rigid (moment) connection in wood—generally such fittings as bolted steel plates are required.

The final means of stabilizing a rafter system is to rest the top ends as well as the bottom ones on a beam that can transmit a load at right angles to the plane of the rafters. This is analogous to hooking a leaning ladder over the top of a wall. Such a beam at the peak is called a "ridge beam" and is the source of some confusion that on occasions leads to a serious roof problem. Often rafters, rather than just being butted against one another at the peak, are rested against a narrow piece of lumber, perhaps a 1×8, which is sometimes called a "ridge plate." It is not altogether clear why this plate detail is used, but some argue that it simplifies erection, while others say that it makes nailing easier. In any event, it is not a ridge *beam,* that is, a member sufficiently

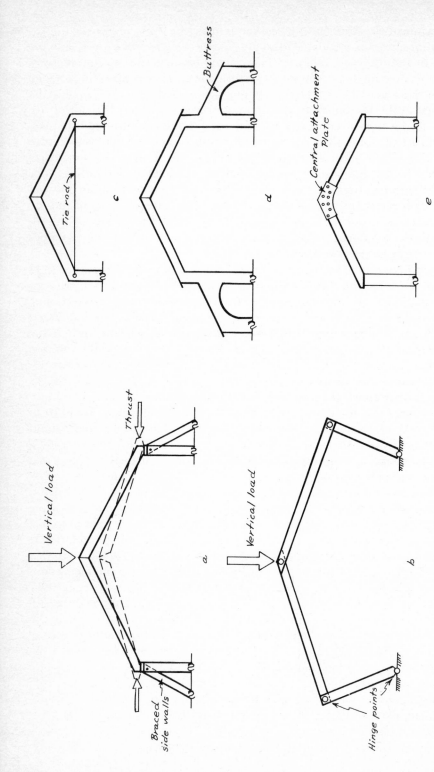

Fig. 7-2 Frame stability. (*a*) Failure mode of roof rafters without lateral restraint. (*b*) Roof frame without side-wall stability. (*c*) Rod-tied roof rafters. (*d*) Side-buttressed roof frame. (*e*) Curved-beam roof frame.

strong to carry all the roof loads to the gable ends of the house. Of course, the butting rafters push against each other and therefore must transmit a compressive force from one to the other. For this reason they must be directly in line; yet sometimes when the ridge plate is used, certain liberties are taken with the alignment of the rafters, and they are not actually in the same plane— a necessary requirement.

An alternative to the ridge beam is a bearing wall of some type that runs down the center below the ridge and supports the two rafters just as the beam would have. If such a wall is only supported on the ceiling joists, then these joists carry the full roof load, no truss action exists, and the roof structure is relatively inefficient and redundant.

Of all the roof-related structural problems, the vast majority are in some manner related to misunderstanding the simple propositions of stabilizing a roof rafter system. Figure 7-3 is a sketch of roof structure that illustrates some of the common errors associated with roof rafter construction.

The most dramatic omissions, so far as potential for catastrophic failure are concerned, involve the details of the way the tension tie (or ceiling joist) is installed and anchored. The problem may be twofold: (1) The attachment at the ends between the rafters (item 1) must be sufficient to transmit a tension force between one end and the other—the force that prevents the ends from spreading out. For an average-sized house, for example, one that is 30 feet across, this tension force may be on the order of magnitude of up to several thousand pounds. Since nail strengths range near 100 pounds, it obviously requires a large number of nails, so many that wood-splitting problems can become critical. In any event, six to ten reasonable-sized nails (10-penny or greater) are generally required for complete load transmission through the nailed joint. Several other alternatives are admissible. For example, in older buildings carpenters often cut wood to actually fit together in such a way that nailed attachments were avoided. In such cases roof rafters were "let" or set

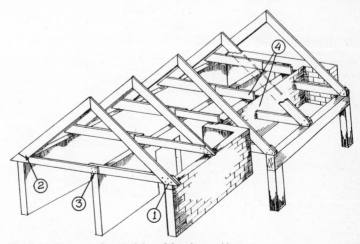

Fig. 7-3   Diagram of potential roof framing problems.

in a notch cut in the ties, as shown at ② of Figure 7-3. This joint detail presented several other problems, such as the difficulty of extending the rafters to provide an overhang. Other methods of making the attachment between rafter and tie ends include bolts, lag screws, or various types of sheet-metal framing anchors, that is, steel brackets that can be formed to fit between the two wood members and that are anchored by nails.

Since the tie tension must be transmitted from one rafter end to the other completely across the house, the tie must in some way be made continuous insofar as load transmission is concerned. This requirement is oddly complicating. First, a continuous piece of lumber the width of the average house, say, 25 or 30 feet, is extremely rare. This constraint means that two pieces have to be used and a joint has to be made at the center, most conveniently above a partition. Immediately, the same joint-attachment problem that exists at the rafter ends is reintroduced. Unfortunately, the need for a very extensive nail pattern is often overlooked, and in some cases each ceiling joist is simply toenailed to the partition cap plate with a single nail. This is obviously totally inadequate and results in a fairly common ceiling–wall-intersection plaster crack pattern along a central partition where such ceiling rafters join. When attic floors are installed on tie joists, the flooring is often nailed to the joist sufficiently to allow the tie tension to be transmitted partially in the floor deck.

(2) Another problem with maintaining force continuity in ceiling joists develops when the joists intersect abutting a beam. For example, suppose there is a bedroom that runs from front to rear below a peaked roof of a conventionally framed house. In order to avoid an exposed beam in the middle of the ceiling, the ceiling joist is framed into a beam that spans across such a room (see Figure 7-4). At the abutting intersection of joist and beam

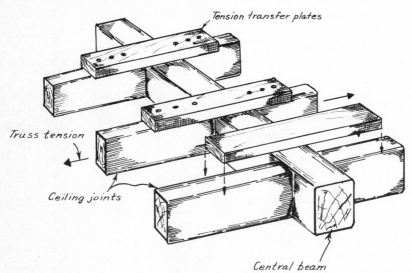

Fig. 7-4   Details of tension transfer plates at central ceiling beam.

a joint capable of transmitting a tension force is difficult to create. A few random toenails are not sufficient, but unfortunately they are commonly used for this purpose. A straight-line ceiling crack along the center of such a room is a signal that an inadequate attachment has been made at this point. The correct detail is to nail a board or metal strap across the top that directly connects the two joints. Some people who have encountered this problem have located a continuous plywood panel, either 2 or 4 feet wide, along this joint line. Properly secured to the wood framing, such a detail not only completes the tension attachment between ties but also stiffens the central beam and minimizes sag distress.

Still another problem associated with these tie members is created by an alignment requirement. Consider the view looking down on rafters with the joists below, as shown in Figure 7-5. If the rafters are kept in line and abutted, as shown in Figure 7-5, then the ceiling joists, if they are attached to the side of the rafters, must necessarily be placed slightly out of line so that they can lap at the center. The same situation occurs if the rafters are notched into the joists. The only way to have the joist directly in line is to lap the rafters at the peak, which is often given as a reason for using the ridge-plate detail discussed before.

Many houses have a porch space that extends to the underside of the roof tie joists. A Mount Vernon, colonial-type front is one example, but in some cases the porch is under only a portion of the roof, as shown in ④ of Figure 7-3. For several reasons it is often convenient to have the interior room ceilings above the porch ceiling; thus, there is a discontinuity in the tie joists along the line of the building front. In wood-framed construction, reasonable attachments can be made through a stud wall system, but in masonry construction it is extremely difficult to create the necessary anchorage. The results obviously can be disastrous and in the extreme lead to a complete roof col-

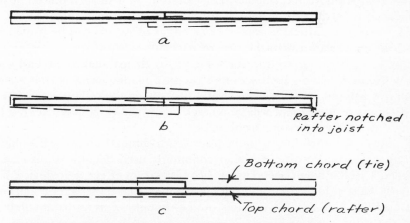

a

b

Rafter notched into joist

Bottom chord (tie)

Top chord (rafter)

c

Fig. 7-5 (a) In-line top chord with staggered bottom chords at sides and center. (b) In-line top chord, angled and overlapping bottom chords. (c) Overlapping top and bottom chord members.

lapse. Actually going into an attic and examining the details of such a structure may be unnecessary, for a telltale sign of such an inadequacy is a joint separation between the front wall of the house and the porch ceiling. The remedy in the case of such offset tie members is simply to install extensions of the house ceiling joists that run out over the top of the porch and anchor to the rafters someplace slightly above the bearing point.

In this and other examples given of inadequately joined roof structures, do not suppose that because a house has survived for a number of years without problems, is proof that such attachments are adequate. Not only does the question arise of whether a significant live load has ever been applied to a building, but also a problem of potentially variable nail-joint strengths is somewhat unique to roof structures. Roof structures in general, and particularly that part above any ceiling insulation barrier, cycle in temperature and moisture content far more than any other part of a house. The withdrawal strength of nails is an extremely variable phenomenon and is particularly vulnerable to the moisture content of the wood. Toward the end of a cold winter, roof timbers can be extremely dry and nail pullout forces may be one-half or even less the value at other times of the year. Thus, the issue is not only how much roof load has ever existed, but so far as attachments are concerned, when the load occurred with respect to wood-moisture conditions.

Open, peaked ceilings have always been a popular residential building detail. Since few house walls are buttressed in any way, it seems somewhat inconsistent to call such a ceiling a "cathedral ceiling"; still, this is a popular name. A span of any substantial length simply could not be constructed without (1) buttressed walls, (2) a ridge beam, or (3) a bottom chord tie, but periodically a small single room actually gets finished with a totally inadequate roof structure system. As explained in connection with Figure 7-2, the walls will eventually push out and the roof collapse; however, a small size allows several other, albeit marginal, load-transfer conditions to exist that collectively give roof support and stability. For example, in a small room the loads are sufficiently reduced so that the hinge effect discussed in connection with Figure 7-2e at either the center of or edges of rafters can be provided by a practical nail pattern. In the case of particularly short rooms, the side walls may be stiff enough to transfer some of the thrust load to the end walls. In any event, rarely do such serious structural inadequacies permit a room to survive without some movement and distress. If the ceiling is plastered, the first signs of movement will be a crack below the ridge line. Next, a bow in the side walls will become evident.

Obviously, introducing tie beams even at limited points will stabilize the roof structure; however, another commonly used detail is to install what is called a "collar beam" (see Figure 7-6). This is, in effect, a tie device, but one that is located high up in the ceiling—so high that the effect of spaciousness is maintained. Such collar beams can be thought of as a sort of combination of the ridge plate of Figure 7-2e and a tie rod or tension member. In any event, relatively substantial loads are involved, and not only member sizes but

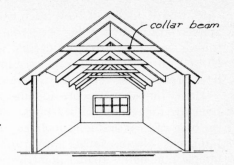

Fig. 7-6   Roof rafters with collar beam.

also attachments must be properly sized to ensure a complete and adequate roof structure.

From a structural standpoint, conventional peaked roof framing consisting of rafters and tie beams is in effect a truss—the rafters are the top chord and the tie joists are the bottom. Typically, when people refer to a roof truss they mean a self-contained truss structure that could exist totally independent of the rest of the house. Such residential roof trusses are divided into two classes, ones built of heavy timber members and generally spaced 8 to 10 feet on centers, and the recently developed metal-plate-connected roof "trussed rafters." These trusses are fabricated in a way similar to that of the floor trusses, made up of 2×4s connected with nailed or spiked metal plates, described in Chapter 6. For the typical residence, the diagonal truss members are 2×4s, while the chord members may be 2×4s or 2×6s, varying according to size, roof pitch, and lumber quality. Trussed rafters are set at 24 inches on center, and at this spacing with the complex of diagonal members, the attic space is almost inaccessible. If attic storage space or possibly even living space is considered of no value, then truss rafters are a reasonable, inexpensive roof framing system. On the other hand, the cost differential between conventional roof framing and these trusses, when prorated to usable attic space, may be a sound investment. While new-home builders may have a choice between the two roof structure systems, owners of existing houses do *not*. Obviously, there would never be any incentive to modify a rafter system to trusses, but the converse is not true. Owners of houses with trussed-rafter roofs poke their heads through an access panel and see the forest of truss diagonals taking up all that usable space, and desire for the space often overcomes reason. Some people have simply cut out some of the diagonals, particularly those toward the center of the span. Their argument is that they have not removed *all* the diagonals—only a few. Trussed rafters, to be competitive, are carefully optimized structures without any wasted or unnecessary members, and not only does each member have a load-carrying function, but also these loads are relatively high. Thus, trussed rafters simply never should be cut or modified without careful analysis, which generally dictates a substantial auxiliary structure to replace the removed truss members. In most cases where diagonals have been removed, the weakened truss has given ample warning that it has been wounded, by sagging and making strange sounds before any collapse occurs. In general, metal-plate-connected roof trussed rafters, except for an occasional truss damaged during installation, have proven to be relatively trouble-free.

Heavy timber trusses are and always have been a relatively expensive roof structure for residential buildings. When they are used, they are justified on the basis of their aesthetic qualities, and they are left exposed. In such cases, lumber is selected for its appearance, and the connections at the various intersection points (panel points) are most often bolted, all of which adds even more to an already premium cost. Very explicit standards govern the design of such trusses; moreover, it is one of the few areas of residential building construction dictated by anything approaching formal research. Because of this it seems surprising that heavy timber trusses would have any significant structural problems, but unfortunately they do. The common distress phenomenon is a splitting out of the timbers from a bolt toward the free end, as shown in Figure 7-8. There is some controversy, not only as to why this splitting should occur, but also as to a proper correction. Just by the nature of how heavy timber trusses are fabricated and assembled, it is sometimes virtually impossible to remove and replace any individual element. One solution to the splitting-timber problem is to install a small bolt across the timber depth that acts as a sort of clamp and prevents further splitting. The one serious disadvantage with this approach involves the expansion-contraction properties of lumber; specifically, that any such clamp arrangement across the grain will loosen as the wood shrinks and will release the load. Nevertheless, if the bolt clamp is applied and periodically retightened, it is a reasonable solution to timber-end-splitting problems.

Fig. 7-7 Exposed roof trusses.

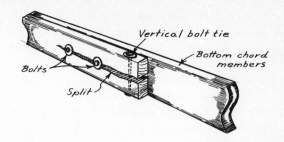

Fig. 7-8 Splitting bottom chord at bolt connection.

Ridge-Line Sags

The distress associated with any type of structural frame instability or inadequacy is easy to identify and therefore associate with its cause since cracks and movement very accurately pattern the deformations of the structure. For example, in an untied rafter system with plaster on the exposed underside, a crack will begin to open under the roof peak, widen at the center, and narrow and eventually disappear as it reaches the gable ends where an adequate tie exists. Similarly, most roof structure failures associated with wood deterioration due to either rot or insect damage so consistently produce distress patterns directly corresponding to the failure geometry, that the cause of the problem is easily identified. Unfortunately, there is another whole class of roof structure distortion in which the cause is surprisingly difficult to determine, and which often must be simply accepted as fact without any precise explanation as to cause. Such distress might best be characterized as a variety of curious bumps and sags at locations where one would expect to find straight lines and plane surfaces. Ridge-line sags and distortions to the plane between the ridge and eaves lines of the roof are the two principle patterns of this class of distress, but the combinations of possible causes to produce exactly the same distortion geometry are so many that it may almost be misleading to group them according to the final distress geometry.

In many houses it is difficult actually to see these distortions until they really become extreme. Almost all houses have a very slight sag in the length of the ridge line, but an observer standing on the ground and viewing the ridge from the side often has very little to use as a reference, and in general such a distortion may go unnoticed for years unless the observer has a particularly sensitive eye for distinguishing between a straight line and one with a slight curve. On the other hand, this distortion becomes very apparent to someone sighting along a ridge line from a gable end, and many homeowners working along the ridge installing an antenna or checking a chimney, return to the ground to report that their roof is sagging several inches. When a ridge sag exceeds 1½ to 2 inches, it is generally easy to notice even from the ground.

The explanation that a ridge sag was built into the house is certainly satisfying in that it is not associated with some failure mechanism, but at the same time few people believe that a ridge would be built with such an obvious distortion. Few home builders would welcome people climbing on the roof to sight along the ridge line to check for straightness, but the fact remains that houses were, and are today, built with a sag. The explanation, in part, is associated with a generalized explanation for sagging ridge lines and the methods used to lay out most pitched roofs. First, as illustrated on the end-papers, the roof structure *away* from the gable ends is either a rafter system or a truss, while *at* the gable ends the roof edge generally is supported on the extensions of the side walls, whether they are wood, frame, or masonry. These are very different structures and are fabricated in different ways. For example, gable-end stud framing is built up from the attic floor level and is cut to fit the "theoretical" roof slope along the top, that is, the pitch of the roof without any allowance for deformation. Whether the roof structure is constructed of rafters or trusses, there will inevitably be some deformation due to their own dead weight. Thus, the roof decking must span between an extremely rigid structure at the ends and a comparatively flexible one that will deform as much as ½ inch as the deck and roofing is applied. Fortunately, the decking tends to distribute the abruptness of this differential movement, and it is not until the second or third joist from the end that the full deformation exists. The result is a built-in roof-ridge sag.

In addition to the sagging that develops as a result of differences in stiffness between the gable ends and interior roof supports, there are other reasons why sags are built into roofs. In rafter construction, particularly ones that overhang the wall, a notch is cut into the joist where it rests on the wall. Very slight errors in locating this notch and eventually placing the rafter on the side wall can result in considerable variations in the ridge elevation, and it is to overcome such tolerance problems that many carpenters choose to install rafters with a ridge-plate detail. Somewhat analogous tolerance problems occur with trussed roof construction. Sometimes the gable ends are constructed before the factory-fabricated trusses even arrive on the job, and slight dimensional variations can produce what appears to be a sag. Recognizing this problem, it would seem reasonable that as many houses would have built-in ridge "humps" as sags, but since it is so easy to block-up on top of the gable ends to level out the roof deck, ridge lines tend to be straight or sagged down but rarely humped up. Another problem with trusses that creates the illusion of a sag occurs when the trusses are slightly misaligned, and the ridge is not a truly straight line even though it is horizontal.

The other construction error that produces many sagged ridge lines is caused by overload of the roof structure. It is a fairly common practice to build a small, horizontal projecting platform on to a roof for temporary storage of roof shingles or, more dramatically, bricks and mortar for chimney construction. All the shingles on a roof can easily weigh several thousand pounds, and if they are concentrated on one or two roof-framing members, permanent deformations can easily occur. When chimneys are on the gable ends of houses, the bricks and mortar are generally stored on exterior scaffolding; but it is surprising to see how many houses with interior chimneys have a roof-plane or ridge-line sag very near the chimney. When people review the construction sequence of a house, they find that bricks for the exposed part of the chimney were stored on a platform built on the roof, sometimes for several weeks.

Ridge-line sags that develop well after a house is completed can, of course, be associated with roof-frame instability; but when it is, it is most often accompanied by other distortion patterns, such as bowed eaves lines, that clearly define the cause. More subtle and more difficult to evaluate are distortions that result from wood shrinkage and long-term (creep) deformation of roof structures. Both of these phenomena allow sagging to occur because of the differences in structural characteristics between gable ends and roof framing. In other words, the sag is really just a differential movement between the ridged ends and the flexible, framed middle portion of the roof. If no gable ends existed, any vertical movement along the ridge line would be uniform, straight lines would remain straight, and without elaborate long-term monitoring there would be no way to tell that the roof ridge deflected.

The effects of wood shrinkage on ridge sags is grossly more noticeable on masonry houses than on wood-frame. On wood-frame houses, even though the shrinkage in studs in the end walls is slight compared with that in the depth of roof rafters, it does occur, and any mechanism that alleviates the differential movement between end walls and framing reduces sag effects. In masonry buildings the end walls remain a constant dimension, and anything causing roof deformations, including construction errors, creep deformation, shrinkage, dead-load deflection, overloads, and frame failures, will result in ridge sags.

Thus ridge sags are a special case. While it is extremely difficult to identify the cause of such sags, it rarely makes much difference simply because sags do not represent a very critical problem. Like so many other elements of a house, if the movement is either static or extremely slow in advancing, a roof sag can almost be considered merely an aesthetic problem. Some people consider sagged roof lines quaint and are not in the least disturbed by them. In the 1920s and early 1930s house designs that went under such names as "Manor Type," "Tudor," or "Dutch" actually were designed and built with a 6- to 8-inch sag in the ridge line. Other than to mimic old houses that naturally deformed, it is doubtful if anyone ever intentionally built roof-lines with a bow or had a practical reason for doing so.

In any event, other than examining a roof to determine if a sag is associated with a frame instabilty, the most reasonable approach to a ridge-sag problem is to monitor it and see if it is moving. Since the sag is really the result of a differential movement between the gable ends and interior roof framing, any monitoring need only measure relative movement. If a wire, string, or monofilament plastic line (e.g., fishing line) can be stretched between gable ends and kept at the same tension, then the movement can simply be measured between this line and the underside of the ridge. An easy way to maintain constant tension on a monitoring line is to run one end over a pulley and attach a small weight to it. Do not simply tie a string or even a wire between fixed points on the ridge because any horizontal movement of either the string or the roof will cause the string to deflect and the reading to be worthless. Expect variations of plus or minus ¼ inch per year. Movements greater than this may be important and should be examined by a professional. Do not try to jack a sag out of a ridge. The very nature of roof framing makes this difficult, and the possibility that some of the sag results from long-term, permanent deformation makes success unlikely. Furthermore, it is almost impossible to predict exactly where a roof would move if jacks were placed under the ridge and advanced.

If it is determined that a roof sag is excessive *and* moving at a rate greater than ⅛ to ¼ inch per year, then some correction is probably needed. Obviously, frame instability problems must be corrected by the methods already described; but for correcting the effects of long-term deformation, the basic roof structure must in some way be supplemented to reduce the stresses on the lumber elements. There are simply too many options regarding such supplements to be able to give specific rules, but certainly some of the alternatives that should be considered are the addition of knee walls, collar beams, sistered joists, or a series of central supports. Naturally, any supports between the roof rafters and ceiling joists must consider the partition geometry and floor framing constraints in the floors below—considerations that may become complicated and require an architect's or engineer's advice. When roof-ridge sags occur with metal-plate-connected roof trusses and it is decided that some stiffening is required, the options become even fewer than with tied rafter construction. An almost natural inclination is to add diagonal elements and attempt to create new intermediate bearing locations for the trusses, but this actually can introduce another whole new set of distress patterns and in extreme cases lead to a certain class of structural failure.

In addition to ridge-sagging problems, another generic type of roof deformity that is surprisingly frequent is a sag in the supposedly plane surface between the ridge and eaves line. Like the ridge, this roof distortion is sometimes difficult to observe. If gutters project beyond the roof eaves edge, it is impossible to sight along the surface of the roof, and in such cases the only easy way to spot such a deformation from the ground is to see a shadow caused by the sun. Many roofs are not orientated with respect to the sun in such a way that the sun's rays ever fall along the roof plane. In such cases a strong flashlight shone across the gable ends may define this plane sag.

The reason most often given for these sags is that the roof framing was originally marginal and that over a long period of time the rafters have simply deformed under the comparatively low stresses of dead load alone. In many cases this is true. It is a little difficult to understand exactly why builders often undersized rafters. In many houses built in the first half of the century, floor and wall structure was substantially oversized compared to current, acceptable practice, yet the roof rafters were grossly inadequate by modern standards. The explanation for this seems to be lack of appreciation for long-term, creep deformation coupled with an honest desire to apply rational analysis to roof-framing problems. It should be evident that snow will not in general collect on a pitched roof as deep as on a flat roof. As it builts up it will simply slide off, and thus the rationale follows that pitched roofs need not be structured for as great a live load, like snow, as a flat roof. Since wind loads are intermittant, most wood structures can carry such short-term loads with ease. This is a perfectly reasonable analysis—save for one thing. It just happens—call it inverse serendipity if you will—that when roof-framing members are sized for snow loads in the order of 20 to 30 pounds per square foot, they are simultaneously sized (unknowingly perhaps) to withstand the effect of creep deformation under their own dead weight. Unfortunately, there is little explicit data to predict wood creep phenomena, and while all designers and builders are at least vaguely aware of the problem, few can say with absolute certainty how much will occur at a given time, under a given load.

Roof-rafter sags, therefore are, perhaps in the majority of cases, due to long-term creep deformation caused by the dead weight of the roof structure. If this is true and the members are adequate for the live load requirements of the local code, a sagging rafter is, at most, only a cosmetic problem. The real dilemma is to be sure of the cause. Except in extreme cases, creep deformation in wood has very little to do with a dramatic, rupture type of failure. Unfortunately, there are other mechanisms causing rafter sagging that may be a signal for abrupt failure. If a wood structure has been seriously overloaded to the point of a rupture failure, it may, when unloaded again, partially return to its original shape and remain, in outward appearance at least, undamaged. Analogously, interior and therefore hidden damage can occur with some insect damage. Termites tend to leave a number of signs of their coming and going. The honeycomb patterns of termite damage are generally visible on the timber surface; moreover, termites almost always leave trails of sawdust that show their presence. Other insects are not as obliging, and particularly in the case of some wood-boring beetles and bees, there are few outward signs to indicate the extent of damage. As a general rule, any damage to a roof rafter that might effect the structure seriously would be toward the center of the member. If damage is visible only near the ends, any sagging is probably not related to internal insect damage.

If rafter sagging can be related to creep deformation, and if it can be tolerated aesthetically, it is probably best to leave it alone. On the other hand, if the sags are related to reduction of load-carrying capacity, then clearly something must be done. In most unfinished attic spaces it is comparatively simple to add extra rafters alongside the existing ones, but the problem is to make a connection at the base, along the eaves, so that structural frame stabilty will exist. In many cases this is impossible to do from the inside because there is not enough space on the interior. If the new rafters can be secured to the original ones and the remaining lumber is sound, then there is no problem. In some cases the lower part of the roofing and sheathing may have to be removed to allow access to the rafter ends.

As a practical matter it is almost impossible to try to force out the bow. Not only must any jacking to remove creep deformation take an inordinant amount of time, but there is very little to jack against. In one case of particularly long, severely bowed rafters, an owner installed a truss system just to add strength to the rafters. This truss consisted of a thin steel rod attached at the top and bottom and bent at the center to form a shape with the rafter resembling a bow. At the center, between the rod and rafter, a short block of wood was wedged. After six months these wedges fell out, and then it was discovered that they could be progressively wedged tighter to eventually force all the sag out of the rafters. The process took four years longer than most owners would care to work with any problem. Finally, knee walls are certainly admissible as a means of decreasing rafter bowing, but collar beams high up on the rafters do little good.

On rare occasions rafter bowing is a result of a dead weight of layers of old roofing materials. It is not too unusual to find a new roof applied directly over old roofing. This is not altogether a bad practice, but like so many other things, people sometimes take the position that if something works one time, then twice should be even better. Asphalt shingle-type roofing can weigh 4 to 5 pounds per square foot, and the accumulation of three or four layers of old roofing can create a serious overload. Furthermore, roofing materials can absorb reasonable amounts of moisture, particularly in older houses with poor vapor barriers. Under normal conditions this effect is negligible, but 10 or 15 percent moisture added to the weight of several old roofs can further aggravate an already bad situation. The answer is obvious: Never apply more than one new roof without removing the old one.

Metal-plate-connected roof trusses appear to be less vulnerable to roof-plane sagging than rafters, but the final proof that this is true may take years until the full effects of creep have had time to develop. Where roof sags are evident, it is generally between the points of intersection of the diagonal members (panel points) and involves deformation in bending of the top chord member alone. Stiffening the top chord can involve either installation of more diagonals or a "sistered" chord member simply nailed to the original one.

Flat Roof Systems

Low-pitched and flat residential roofs can be framed in several ways. Wood joists placed almost like a floor structure is certainly the most common method, but this can create a very serious ventilation problem. Another approach to framing nearly flat roofs is to space wood beams 4 to 8 feet on center and span between the beams with a "structural" wood deck. Of course, any deck spanning between joists or beams at any spacing is structural in the sense that it must transmit a load, but when longer spans involve the use of heavier deck, this deck is referred to as "structural deck," consisting of heavy tongue-and-groove decking, which is regularly described by its initials, "T&G deck." T&G deck ranges in thickness from 1½ to 4½ inches, and the width averages 6 inches. The thinner planks have one tongue-and-groove, while thicker deck often has two in the thickness.

This beam-deck system is fairly clean looking and is often left exposed. Aside from problems connected with moisture transmission, which will be discussed later in the section on roof insulating and venting, this framing method as a result of its own simplicity is relatively trouble-free. One of the few problems of any consequence is that the deck, unless it was initially oversized, is likely to permanently deform into a gentle sag. If there is any pitch whatever to the roof, a minor sag is only an aesthetic problem, but if a deck was originally set level, a sag may allow water to collect or "pond" over the bowed-down portion of the roof. This is one of those problems that is self-perpetuating. The roof deck originally sagged because it could not support its own weight over a long period, and the wood plastically deformed. Ponded water over the sagged areas naturally adds weight, which causes further permanent deformation to occur. Since any deformation is a relatively slow process, many people simply choose to ignore the sagging; but realistically at some point it will become critical and some sort of remedial repairs must be made. There is no hard-and-fast rule that defines exactly how much ponding can be tolerated, but anything above 1½ to 2 inches should be treated as a potentially serious condition. Since there is no way to jack the deformity out of the plank, the only alternative to eliminating ponding is to recontour the external roof surface. This inevitably involves removing the roofing and building up a new shape from the existing roof deck. Two methods are relatively standard. One is to use expanded polystyrene foam plastic panels as a filler to develop a new roof contour. The major problem with this is that conventional built-up roofs are sometimes difficult to apply over several inches of the foam plastic. On the other hand, it does add insulation to a roof system, which will result in real dollar and fuel savings. The other means of recontouring a roof is to place sleepers or tapered wood strips directly on the existing deck. A plywood deck is then placed on these sleepers and a conventional built-up roof system applied to the deck. With this procedure the stumbling block is the small space between the new and old deck. If it is unvented, it is a perfect place for moisture to collect; and, therefore, any wood in this space is a likely candidate for rot.

Since both these repair methods have their disadvantages, it should be evident that recontouring a flat roof is not a particularly easy or desirable repair, and it may even make people consider the wisdom of flat roofs in general. A few owners of flat-roof houses have found the roof-leakage and ponding problems so troublesome that they have actually added a conventionally pitched roof on top of the flat one. This is an admissible solution for only a limited number of houses, because certainly not all houses initially

Fig. 7-9   Tongue-and-groove decking.

designed and built with flat roofs can aesthetically tolerate a pitched roof. For those special cases where it is acceptable, it is generally a surprisingly simple matter to create the pitch by building stud walls at right angles to the joists and framing between these bearing supports with lightweight lumber. Since the space between the original roof surface and the new one is necessarily several feet high, it is a comparatively easy space to insulate and ventilate.

Many of the observations about ponding are true of all flat roofs and not just those framed with beams and structural deck. Still, roofs framed with joists tend to have fewer sags requiring massive recontouring of the roof surface.

Tongue-and-groove decks are not at all restricted to flat roofs, but the inherent problem of sagging on a highly pitched roof is of little consequence, and is generally simply ignored. Despite the visual appeal of T&G decking, comparatively few house builders are likely to use it in the future because of some of the difficulties of providing adequate insulation. This is somewhat of an anomoly, because it was not too many years ago that the insulation barrier provided by 4 inches of wood was actually considered better than average and was thus actually one of the criteria of selection. In any event, the constraints imposed by insulation may become one of the principal issues in the selection of a roof system, and certainly it can play a dominant role in the details and methods of repairs and remodeling.

Insulation and Ventilation

For several reasons it is almost impossible to discuss roof insulation without also addressing the problems of ventilation. Roofs have the most extreme temperature gradients of any element in a house, and therefore it is logical that they have the most insulation; but the very existence of this insulation increases the gradient and worsens the potential for moisture concentration within the roof space. In several different chapters the problems of moisture transmission and condensation have been discussed. In some ways the roof problem is analogous to that of insulating above a crawl space. An absolute, total vapor barrier is almost impossible to create, but the optimum location for such a barrier may switch from one side of the insulation to the other between summer and winter, according to the local climate.

Until the mid-1950s insulation in the roofs of houses was, if it existed at all, far more for show than for actual effect. The actual effects of a 2-inch-thick layer of insulation or batten loosely laid between joists on the ceiling of the top floor can hardly be measured, and we are only now learning the need for not only quantity but also quality of installation—that it be tightly fitting and free of holes, through which air can circulate.

The simplest roof to insulate is a peaked roof with an unused attic space. Insulation can be fitted between ceiling joists and the entire attic ventilated. Many local codes actually specify the quantity of air that must circulate within the attic space, and this is a requirement that is likely to be rigorously enforced. The need for this ventilation is in part a recognition that the vapor barrier applied above a ceiling is incomplete and also that between summer and winter the vapor gradient may actually change directions. From a heat-transfer point of view the circulating air may increase total heat transfer, because the increased air velocity can sweep across surfaces and carry more heat away than can stationary air. Many people theorize that in summer an attic space full of extremely hot air must be removed and substituted with the outside ambient air; but, except in rare cases, the stationary hot air actually works as an additional insulation barrier, and in certain climates with particularly damp summer night air some combination of scheduled venting of an attic space would be preferable to constant venting. Unfortunately, optimum conditions of air circulation in an attic space vary—according to type and orientation of the house, local climate, and time of year—to such a degree that any scheduled program would be extremely complicated and require expensive sensing devices as well as controls. Thus, the less than optimum pragmatism has been simply to specify that a certain ventilation be provided to let air circulate within the attic space.

The location and type of attic vents vary with the type of house and local practice. Three locations are typical: (1) gable-end vents or screened, louvered openings at the ends of the house, generally on the triangle formed by the ridge; (2) ridge vents, which are shielded openings running a significant part of the ridge line; and (3) eaves vents or screened openings in the soffit along the eaves line. Ridge vents are fairly noticeable, and in houses where the appearance of the roofline is important to the overall composition, many people find them unacceptable even though they allow uniform air circulation. Eaves vents sometimes get complicated by the details of how the rafters bear on and overhang the side walls. A very common complaint is that the ceiling insulation blocks either the vents themselves or the air-flow space just inside, between the stud plate and the roof inner surface.

Various types of manufactured vent devices are available that allow natural air circulation or forced air pumping either with electric fan units or with wind-powered fan devices. It is impossible to generalize about which vent method is the most suitable for any given situation; but eaves, ridge, or gable-end vents are most often selected to be installed at the time of construction, while the manufactured, local types are often installed after the fact as supplementary venting in cases where it is clearly demonstrated that more venting is required.

The control of moisture chiefly in the winter months in the attic space should be the primary criterion for modifying attic-ventilation requirements in more northerly climates, while trapped summer hot air should govern in dry, southern sections of the country. If there is a question about venting in a particular attic space, several simple experiments can be made to determine the effectiveness of any given system. Any moisture problem is most likely to develop in the winter, and particularly in the space covered by insulation. Thus, measuring the moisture content of ceiling rafters covered by insulation is a reasonable means of judging wintertime venting adequacy. Moisture contents as high as 12 or even 15 percent can be tolerated, but moisture-

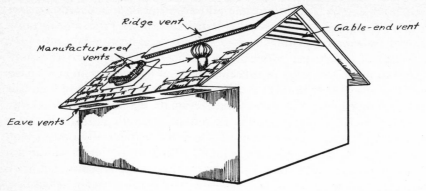

Fig. 7-10   Roof vents.

meter readings above these values imply the need for more venting. In summer, temperature-dominant situations, a thermometer can be taped to the ceiling, and the temperature differences between outside and ceiling can then be recorded for several different vent conditions. Such an experiment should be repeated several times to make sure that consistent conditions exist for each case.

A far more complex venting problem arises when the insulation must be placed in the roof between rafters. Such roof-insulation conditions occur in two different situations: (1) when an attic space is to be a living space, and (2) when a conventional room space has a peaked (or cathedral) ceiling. The generic problem is twofold: not only must the insulation be held away from the roof deck, as shown in Figure 7-11, but at both ends of this air space some means must be provided to allow the air to flow in and out. If, for example, the lower end is blocked by an attic floor, no air can enter; while if the insulation and ceiling are carried all the way to a ridge line, no air can flow out at the top. When people are insulating the roof in an attic space, the most practical venting arrangement is to install what is called a "knee wall," that is, a short wall several feet high toward the eaves line, and a collar beam a foot or so below the ridge. The roof insulation can then be made to run along these surfaces, and the remaining volume at the ridge and eaves triangles can be left open as axial vent spaces and the air eventually removed at either end. This approach is particularly accommodating in roofs with large intersecting

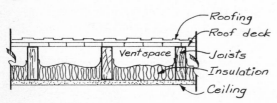

Fig. 7-11   Roof vent space.

gable details, because the two air passages at the top and bottom of the roof can be made to intersect such spaces, and the entire system thus can be vented.

When the side walls intersect the roof, and when aesthetics dictate that the ceiling run into the ridge as in the so-called cathedral-ceiling detail, roof-venting alternatives become few and complex. If the insulation definitely can be held 2 or 3 inches away from the roof deck, then ridge and eaves line vents are practical, but as soon as there are any intersecting rooflines or large gables, there are bound to be sections of roof that are not positively vented.

In a few older houses and many churches this problem was solved by installing a dummy ceiling below the roofline. Most often such a ceiling intersected the roof at the eaves, but was held below the ridge by a foot or so, thus creating a ventable space between ceiling and roof. The theory was that few people could ever be aware that the pitch of the ceiling is something slightly less than the pitch of the roof, and in some church reconstructions such a hidden space is a complete surprise to everyone.

These same problems apply to all roofs without peaks, and in particular to nearly flat roofs structured with roof joists. If batten-type insulation is used between the joists, then venting must extend to each individual joist space. This can become extremely complex and really be the dominant factor in establishing roof details. Among the many venting systems tried on flat roofs are the following: soffit and fascia vents; vents into parapet walls; and vents into a space created by "subpurlins," or small joists at right angles to the primary framing. All the methods are relatively expensive, and if they are marginal in any way, there are only a few simple methods of supplementing the venting system.

Since the mid-1950s several rigid insulation-board materials have become commercially available. An expanded foam plastic (polystyrene) is perhaps the most common and is often used as an insulation on the outer rather than the inner roof surface. Properly installed, such a material can solve many of the roof-insulating and -venting problems, particularly on flat roofs and roofs where the structure is left exposed on the inside. The common application is to nail wood strips or battens along the roof surface, place the insulation boards between these strips, and then add another lightweight plywood deck to receive the roofing material. This sounds simple and relatively foolproof, but like anything else there is the potential for some serious problems. For one thing, the foam plastic, even though it appears continuous, is not always a very good vapor barrier. Thus, some continuous vapor barrier is needed

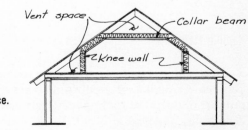

Fig. 7-12 Attic vent space.

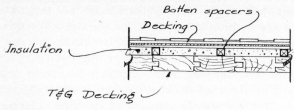

Fig. 7-13 Details of insulated T&G deck system.

on the top side of the ceiling deck. Since anything at this location will eventually be nailed through, there can be no true continuity to the barrier. Secondly, if leaks do develop in such a system, they may have no place to drain, and continuously trapped water can destroy the whole system. If a wood ceiling is left exposed, the general feeling is that the wood can breathe enough to allow excess water transfer; but under certain climatic and heating combinations this is literally impossible, and the wood will actually receive moisture rather than give it up.

Even a superficial examination of the venting and insulation problems associated with roofs makes it clear that they are sufficiently critical to be necessary and dominant criteria in both the selection of new roof structural systems and the process of reworking an existing roof. One word to the wise: There are many claims made for different types of insulation, particularly about one type being "better" than another. *Better,* in the context of insulation, requires some qualifications. If, for example, one insulation is said to have twice the insulating characteristics of another, the probable meaning is that for the same *thickness* of insulation one will have twice the thermal resistance (R value) as the other. In certain applications thickness may be critical, but particularly in roofs it makes little difference whether the insulation is 2 inches or 6 inches thick. From a cost standpoint insulation is priced almost as a constant with respect to conductivity, that is, resistance per unit thickness. There is, therefore, no cost incentive to use thinner insulation. The principal factors in selecting an insulation material should be durability; variation in resistance with moisture content (certain materials always absorb some moisture and in the damp condition lose much of their insulating properties); fire resistance (some materials will actively support combustion); smoke characteristics (particularly whether noxious fumes are given off as products of combustion); and finally, chemical interaction with other common building materials.

Roofing Materials

The top, water-repellent surface of a roof is and always has been a compromise between a number of conflicting criteria. This is evident just in the sheer number of different roofing materials that have been tried over the centuries. Availability and cost always have been dominant factors; nevertheless, even when people have had a variety of options, an optimum choice has not been clearly evident.

Roofing systems have always fallen into two categories: a continuous-membrane type, or the more common type, which is a collection of individual, overlapping elements that are placed to shed the water but that collectively are by no means waterproof. Thus, while shingles do keep the water out of a roof, they certainly would not do as a material with which to build a water tank, for example. The need for the individual, detached elements is simply that until fairly recently, there were no continuous-membrane materials that could withstand the constant, often abrupt, movements induced by the alternate cycles of heat and cold. In recent years, a few rather specialized plastic membranes have been developed that will completely seal a roof for a reasonable period of time; but in the past tar and bituminous compounds spread on paper-type materials and painted canvas were the only means of creating anything resembling a continuous roof surface.

The list of materials used in the flexible, water-shedding roof includes almost every material that is not water-soluble and a few (sod, for example) that are. Tile, slate, copper, lead, steel, turned aluminum, concrete, stone, wood, grass, asbestos, and literally hundreds of manufactured, composition-type materials have been tried. The requirements of appearance, cost, durability, installation, serviceability, and fire resistance are today the dominant factors in roofing selection. Unfortunately, it is difficult to convince an owner that he or she should invest in a roofing system that will last much beyond the average mortgage, and so as a practical matter composition shingles are most likely to be the choice for new and reroofing jobs in the majority of cases.

The two principal concerns in reroofing are (1) whether to remove the original roof, and (2) certain flashing details. Very few people would argue that more than one old roof should ever be left under a new one, although once in a while a roof with three or four old roofs beneath it is found. The number of opinions on how to reroof is exactly equal to the number of people consulted. Exclusive of cost differences the principal argument for leaving one old roof below a new one is that the old one will protect the house during installation; while the best argument in favor of removing the original roofing is that the roofing nails cannot fully penetrate two roof layers and still have sufficient anchorage in the roof deck. There is modest validity to both arguments, although neither can be said to be completely true—houses are regularly reroofed from the wood deck out, without serious water problems, and second roofs rarely blow off owing to insufficient nail anchorage. If the roof is removed, it is a good buy to add a new layer of roofing felt (paper).

On roofs with many complicated metal flashing details at edges, valleys, and chimneys, roofing over the flashing without completely installing new materials can lead to serious water-intrusion problems after several years. Copper, galvanized steel, and aluminum flashing generally survive thirty or forty years, but not often twice this time, so it is certainly prudent to replace flashing during reroofing. Particularly in the case of low roofs that run into wall surfaces where the flashing has been installed more or less concurrently with the wall-surface installation, it may be extremely difficult to remove and replace this flashing. The average owner may not be particularly inclined to climb around on a roof and inspect the details of the work; and the net result of the combination of difficulty and lack of inspection sometimes leads to the substitution of very strange details for proper flashing. The most common problem is that a roofer will simply cement a new section of flashing to the extension of an old, protruding piece. Either the cement or the old flashing eventually fails and directs water below the shingle. Before an owner agrees on a reroofing procedure, he or she should spend an hour or 2 at the library with architecture manuals that show flashing details, and then have a clear contractual understanding of exactly how old flashing will be reworked.

Typically at the edge of a shingled roof a short piece of flashing is laid back under the shingles. The idea is to prevent wind-driven water from working its ways back up under the shingle; furthermore, bending down a short section of flashing creates an edge that will allow the water to drip off (hence the name "metal drip") and not run back on the surface of a soffit. For some reason this edge is generally only a few inches long, and in many cases rot develops in the upper edge of this "drip." Thus, during reroofing it may be reasonable to install a much longer drip band that runs a foot or 2 back up under the shingling.

Inevitably there are penetrations in roofs. Plumbing stacks, forced-air vents from kitchens and bathrooms, flues, and chimneys all penetrate the roof and must be flashed around. In many cases, flashing around such objects serves no purpose other than to direct the water away from the projection; and if the water ever were to build up to any depth, it could flow into the roof around the edge of the flashing detail. It is for this reason that roofs tend to leak during the winter, when ice and snow build up on a roof and allow water to overflow the flashing edges.

The two most troublesome flashing details are around some chimneys and skylights. The common denominator between these otherwise rather different elements is that they both present a broad, flat surface against which water, flowing down a roof, can back up and overflow. Once a leak develops at such a location, a common procedure is to attempt to caulk any joints. Such a repair may last for a few months, but rarely does caulking of an open roof joint ever permanently seal a roof leak. The most satisfactory solution for a leak along the uphill (roof) side of a wide, flat roof penetration such as a chimney or skylight is to build a "cricket" on the high side. This is sort of a miniature gable or water deflector that prevents water from ever building up at the top of the flashing or from backing up under the shingles to flow in below the flashing. A cricket can be built up out of metal or rolled roofing.

The limitation of conventional caulking for openings in roof surfaces is twofold. As a general rule most caulking materials will simply not tolerate the violent environment of a roof. They are designed to seal openings that have movements of a small percent of the total width. On the other hand, roof joints regularly undergo movements roughly on the order of magnitude

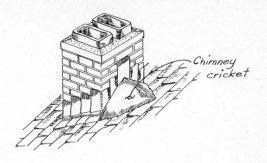

Fig. 7-14 Rooftop chimney cricket.

of their width. Recall that at any given joint the accumulated expansion or contraction of a good part of a roof surface may be concentrated. It is for this reason that properly designed flashing is purposely left free to hinge, slip, and bend across joints. In any event, the caulking material likely to be available to the average homeowner or repair person is simply not intended to accommodate such movements.

Another problem with many caulking materials is that, while they weather well with temperature and moisture variations, few are intended for permanent exposure to direct sunlight. Not only is there a tendency to dry out any liquefiers, but also some polymer compounds deteriorate rather rapidly when they are exposed to ultraviolet radiation. On old roofs some joint openings have been sealed for years with a black band of tarlike material, and people often try to repeat this successful detail by applying modern roofing cement compounds. The old joint was most likely sealed with natural tar or coal (tar) pitch, materials that are not commonly available today. If a roofing cement patch is to be made, it is good practice to cover the compound with a piece of rolled roofing or shingle to protect the patch material from direct sun and rain.

Many residential building defects can be tolerated and ignored without serious consequences; however, roof leaks are not only noticeable and inconvenient, but also damage due to leaks can be so extensive and severe that they must be repaired. The problem is to locate the source of the leak. Rarely does water come out directly below where it runs in, and it can flow a number of feet within the roofing and roof structures before it drips out into a room. Leaks in sloped roofs can generally be isolated most effectively by hosing the roof from the lower slope toward the top. When this is unsuccessful it may mean that the leak is the result of wind-driven water working its way back up the slope and into some opening. If this is true, try to associate the leak occurrence with wind direction and if possible repeat the sprinkling when the wind is blowing from the critical direction.

Leaks on flat roofs are particularly difficult to locate, and in frustration owners often have an entire roof reapplied to stop one leak source. Another means of isolating a leak is to dam up the water in selected areas and see whether the leak can be reproduced. If this is to be tried, a week or more waiting period between experiments should be allowed, because some leaks take a considerable time to percolate through a roof system.

APPENDAGES

Sales advertisements for houses invariably emphasize a porch, balcony, or patio; yet, after several years of occupancy, these areas all too often become nothing more than forlorn storage depots for unwanted junk, rarely visited by human beings. Obviously, many owners do use these areas, but the number who do not is significant enough to make one ask exactly *why* they are not used. The answers, in part, are that they do not function as conveniently as people suppose; they require relatively more maintenance than many other parts of a house; and finally, they are often subject to structural and distress problems, problems that can easily be ignored by applying the philosophy of "out of sight, out of mind." A patio that evolves, after a home is constructed, as an extension of the homeowners' normal living pattern is more apt to be used than one that is incorporated into the original design as a standard detail. The reasons for this slightly odd situation are rather involved; however, knowing why such areas are not used can lead not only to an understanding of how they relate to distress and deterioration problems, but also to methods of repair that can make these areas more serviceable.

The recurring problem of definition must first be considered. Despite what dictionaries say, one person's porch is another's balcony, is another's patio, is another's. . . . There seems to be no single collection of elements that can be said to differentiate between the definitions of *patio, balcony,* and *porch.* Take, for example, a patio. Some people think a patio to be an open-air, paved area on grade; yet, apartment dwellers call a walk-on rooftop at the fiftieth floor their rooftop patio. Another definition of patio is that it is open to the sky; yet put an arbor over the top, or even a giant skylight enclosure, and it remains a patio. Conversely, areas that go by the name of balcony and porch can just as easily be open to the sky and still maintain their right to be called balcony or porch. Finally, from one part of the country to another, the different names apply to different types of spaces. What may obviously be a terrace to a New Yorker is clearly a patio to a Carolinian, is a porch to a Georgian, is a balcony to a. . . . Rather than create a new dogma or perpetuate a shakey old one, it is best to describe the specific details of the space and how it is constructed rather than to use any of these names. Most of the problems that develop in these areas are related to their construction details and their relation to the rest of the house, and it will be on this basis that definitive distinctions will be made.

One of the rather odd problems that occurs with these spaces when they are designed and built as part of the original construction is related to the (compass) direction. With the rather rare exception of a house that is individually designed and built for a predetermined site, the porches and patios of most houses relate to a particular part of the house, while, in turn, the house relates to a particular compass direction only by chance. Thus, an area designated as a "sun porch" in the original design may be at the rear of a house, face north, and never see the sun. In a particular townhouse community the rear "patios" were surrounded by 8-foot-high brick walls to create privacy and assure security. These yard areas are livable when the houses face any direction but south, for then the yard is on the north side and never sees the sun. The result is a damp, mildewed yard where few plants will ever grow and few people will ever sit. As a general rule there are few building areas so enclosed and shut off from the sun, and a whole special set of deterioration problems result. For example, paving blocks or bricks in such a setting are much more subject to frost heaving, because their surfaces are relatively wetter and colder. There are no solar drying effects, and the high walls permit little wind to circulate to cause drying. Walls around such spaces exist in more adverse environments than commonly encountered, because both sides are cold and damp, the south side being shielded by the house, and the north side facing away from the sun. This almost perpetual dampness also contributes to certain brick and mortar deterioration in these walls.

In planning a porch or patio addition, direction should be carefully considered as it relates to both the sun and prevailing winds. These directional environmental factors also may be dominant parameters affecting distress characteristics as well as repair methods.

Since such appendages to residential buildings cannot be clearly defined by name alone, it is a little difficult to categorize them in some other orderly way. One method of categorizing them is in relation to their basic structure, as follows:

1 Decks built directly on earth and at grade level
2 Decks founded on earth but raised above the surrounding grade by a retaining-wall detail
3 Framed decks supported on low walls, columns, or piers and beam systems
4 Framed decks hanging or cantilevered off the house
5 Roofed and unroofed areas

Decks Built Directly on Earth at Grade Level or Surfaces with Some Type of Stone Pavers, Brick, or Poured-in-Place Concrete

A generic problem common to all decks founded on earth is the distortion due to ground movements, which can be divided into two distinct categories: settlement (downward), or heaving (upward). Most natural soils, particularly at locations away from any waterways, are naturally consolidated sufficiently so that they rarely "settle" significantly of their own accord. On the other hand, adjacent to a house where foundation excavations have been backfilled, it is almost the rule rather than the exception that some soil consolidations will occur with corresponding surface settlements. Such movements are likely to continue for a number of years according to how carefully the foundation fill material was selected and installed. Settlement characteristics in relation to both magnitude and time will be significantly altered by water conditions in the soils. Some of these problems have been discussed in Chapters 2 and 3. Placing any sort of paving on the ground adjacent to a house creates a different surface water environment and, therefore, a different set of distress conditions associated with settlements.

Once in a while an owner of a forty- or fifty-year-old house will discover that after many years a relatively level, planar patio abruptly begins to deform several feet outward from the building wall. Because it survived so long without any distortion, it is difficult to make a convincing argument based on foundation backfill settlement. What often happens is the following: The fill consolidates as a result of very low soil- and surface-applied loads to a relatively stable degree, and for many years the settlements, although continual, are negligible. Generally, any surface pavement is sloped in such a way that it drains water away from the house. After many years, the accumulated settlement is suddenly enough to change the drainage and allow surface water to collect near the building line. This water seeps into the fill soils that heretofore have been dry, and thus a whole new set of settlement conditions are precipitated. With each increase in settlement, more and more surface water is directed into the soils; and to the owner, it appears as an accelerating process. Very often such a condition is heralded by a wet-basement condition for the first time in the life of the building. It is the very abruptness of the appearance of water problems after so many years of dry conditions that is so puzzling and irritating, and it often leads owners to foolish conclusions and repair methods. The solution, of course, is to recontour the surface so that the water is again directed away from the foundation wall. Rarely is it necessary, as some suppose, to dig out, expose the foundation wall, and apply new waterproofing (see Chapter 2).

Incidentally, the age of forty to fifty years may, for a house, be the beginning of its winter of discontent. It is at about this time that a number of otherwise seemingly petty occurrences on the exterior combine to cause such problems as described above. For example, it is at about this age that gutters, downspouts, and downspout drains began to fail just as accumulated surface-water-flow conditions near a house become troublesome. All these simultaneous occurrences conspire to obscure the cause or at least complicate any synthesis process. Perhaps the problem is even further compounded by what may be called the "unisolution theorem." This is a human desire, perhaps for simplicity, perhaps for orderliness, which requires that the cause for any *single* problem be confined to a *single* element. As the number of rational explanations for any occurrence increases, the credibility of the analyses decreases. To the extent that this theorem is ever operable, it is least appropriately applied to water problems in and around forty- to fifty-year-old houses.

In any event, fill settlements and subsurface water conditions seem to be the chief causes of pavement subsidence near a house. Alternatively, the two mechanisms that cause pavement to heave are expanding damp soils brought about by freezing temperatures, and plant roots growing under the pavement.

For soils to be expansive when frozen, they must also be wet; and this is simultaneously the key to both the diagnosis of and the remedy for the problem. In well-drained soils, particularly those protected from above by a slab or pavement, the soils can be almost completely dry, at least dry enough to disallow expansive characteristics when frozen. In somewhat the same manner as described above in connection with water-induced consolidation of old fill materials, the process of frost heaving can begin somewhat abruptly after many stable years and then be self-perpetuating. After only modest heaving, perhaps as a result of an unusually cold, damp winter, the surface becomes uneven, drainage is not as positive as it originally was, more water flows below the pavement, and subsequently there is even more frost heaving.

Repair solutions for a severely heaved patio slab or pavement should include, if possible, provisions for positive surface and subsurface drainage. If there are lower elevations near the house, one simple solution is to lay the pavement on a bed of granular material, such as well-graded gravel or crushed stone, and to provide a path from the bed directly to the lower elevation. The path can be simply a buried path of the stones, or it may be a drainpipe. Once in a while people will fail to provide this drain relief; that is, they will simply dig down a foot or 2, install a gravel bed, and found the pavement on top. If the surrounding soils are very permeable and will drain any water that flows into the gravel bed, this is a fine solution; on the other hand, if the surrounding earth is a slow-draining material such as a dense clay, the excavation for the stones acts like a giant tub and actually traps more water below the pavement than might otherwise have collected.

Soil types and local topography may make it practically impossible to create a drain field below a paved deck area. Under such conditions the particular type of pavement, and whether it is continuous, becomes important.

In the yards of row houses with essentially the same soils, moisture, drainage, and drying conditions, pavement of individual slabs laid a few inches apart will displace both vertically and horizontally after only a few winters; while stones set with mortar joints between them, or continuous concrete slabs, survive far longer. Even then, any heaving is rarely as abrupt, simply because of the more continuous nature of such pavement.

In open, natural environments tree roots tend to spread uniformly with respect to the trunk, but in confined spaces around buildings and walls roots travel strange paths to reach water and nourishment. Many homeowners are familiar with how certain trees, particularly willows, maples, and some oaks, will zero in on a source of water such as a drain line and literally break through heavy drain tile to get at the water. Trees planted in the middle of paved areas send out roots below the pavement to reach water, and if they remain close to the surface, the pavement can be grossly upset and distorted. The sidewalks of tree-lined streets in older residential areas bear witness to this phenomenon, for rarely will such walks survive without heaving. The tree roots, of course, cannot get water below the streets and necessarily fan out toward open yards—yards separated from the trees by sidewalks. In those cities that place the sidewalks next to the curb and the trees in the yards, the sidewalks fare much better.

If roots do cause a patio slab to heave, the remedies are not easy. If left unattended, the slab is likely to continue to be pushed up, but unfortunately, short of removing the tree there is little that can be done. Trees simply will not withstand a disturbance of their roots, and any significant changes in the water supply within the drip line of the tree may not be tolerated—the tree will die. If grades and elevations permit, it is sometimes possible to raise the deck and build a framed structure on piers, for example, that will be unaffected by the roots and conversely will not affect the tree.

A common problem with slab-on-grade paved areas—patios, if you wish— concerns the pavement materials. Concrete, slate, and various other stones are common, but brick is a favorite because it can easily be laid and expanded by even the most untalented home craftsperson. Often owners in a fit of energy stop by the local building supply house for a "load of bricks." The trouble is that there are bricks and there are bricks, and what is good for a wall may not be good for a patio surface. Specifically, there is a generic type of brick called a "paver." Not only are pavers especially made to withstand the rigors of flat exposure to water, earth, and sun, but true pavers are a different size and are proportioned differently from conventional bricks. Most pavers are exactly half as wide as they are long, so that they can be set in various patterns, such as herringbone, without any mortar joints. Few standard building bricks can survive long as pavers; either the surfaces begin to chip and spall, or the bricks randomly break apart. Certain ground chemicals, particularly salt compounds, very actively deteriorate the bricks, and there is really no practical solution to the problem short of removing the bricks.

Decks on Soils Surrounded by Retaining Walls

Obviously, most of the problems already discussed in connection with paved areas on grade apply to this case, but several new problems develop in some applications. Incidentally, the name porch seems to be more acceptable when a patio is raised above grade and when it is surrounded by a retaining wall. Put a roof on it and it is almost certainly referred to as a porch.

A not uncommon way to build a porch alongside a house is to build a retaining wall, fill in the area with earth, and place a concrete slab partially on the earth and partially on the surrounding walls. Since the earth is installed before the walls are adequately braced by the slab, the tendency is to be rather gentle about compacting this fill material. The argument goes that the earth is really only a form to support the concrete during the curing process. This is a valid line of reasoning, provided the concrete slab is adequately reinforced to span the full distance between walls, for what happens almost invariably is that the earth fill settles and leaves a void below the slab. In turn, the slab, if it is not properly designed and structured, cannot span the full distance between walls and, accordingly, deflects. As a practical matter, a concrete slab would require a significant amount of steel reinforcing to be able to span an average porch width, say, 12 feet or so, and typical house builders are rarely inclined to provide such steel. The eventual result is a grossly deformed porch slab that eventually may even rupture if the settlement and, correspondingly, the slab deflection is great enough.

It is not uncommon to find such slabs deflected 2 and 3 inches. Often the movement has taken place over a sufficiently long time to permit some plastic deformation, and in such cases the deformation may not be accompanied by any cracking.

Solutions for such a situation are somewhat messy because they involve the installation of some concrete, but they can be relatively simple and not too costly. The basic objective is to provide additional support for the under-reinforced slab. A successful procedure has been to cut (or break) a slot in the slab, perhaps 10 inches wide from wall to wall. A trench a foot or so deep is then dug in the earth. Steel reinforcing bars are then placed in the bottom of this slot, and the entire void is filled with concrete. This, in effect, is a concrete beam that will help support the slab between the walls. An engineer can easily determine the dimensions of the beam, specify the steel reinforcing, and sketch the details of how the beam should bear on the walls. In some cases it may be appropriate to do a somewhat analogous repair by installing a series of vertical piers by cutting through the slab, digging down to good soil, and then placing concrete in these holes in the ground.

In addition to slab settlement problems, there are several other generic complaints with such porches. For one thing, it is the closest that soil fills come in contact with the rest of the house and, in particular, with the wood in adjacent floors and partitions. It is thus a natural path for a termite invasion. The first signs of these unwelcome visitors may be at a wooden sill plate below a door leading to such a porch. Almost as a matter of routine maintenance, termite poisons should be injected in the soils below such a raised porch slab founded on earth.

The walls surrounding such a porch are, of course, earth-retaining walls; however, they are retaining the interior earth fill rather than the exterior soils, as in the case of foundation (basement) walls. Thus, these walls are subject to many of the inherent defects of all earth-retaining walls (see Chapter 3). A somewhat unusual problem is associated with raised porches with concrete-slab decks. Typically, residential porch slabs are 4 to 8 inches thick, and in terms of weight and relative stiffness, such slabs are unique in the average residence. In effect, they dominate the structure of a building, and if they move in any way with respect to the rest of the house, massive cracking is almost inevitable. Aside from the contraction of the concrete during the curing process, the principal causes of movement are differential temperature conditions, freeze-induced movement, and settlements of support structure. Sometimes it is difficult to explicitly define the cause by viewing the resulting damage, but the phenomenon is frequent enough that some generalized patterns can be identified. When porches face south and are exposed to a full view of the sun, the slab can easily reach temperatures of 40 to 50°F above the surrounding walls and structure. While this is a significant temperature gradient between building elements, it is probably not enough to produce really gross distress if it were to occur only infrequently. However, it is likely to be repeated day after day, year after year. The very nature of a heavy slab resting on masonry walls causes recurrent strains that are unlikely to produce completely reversible movements. For example, if the slab were to be pushed away from the main house, wall debris could filter down into the resulting opening and prevent the opening from being closed. Similarly, repeated thermally induced movement may break a mortar joint in the support wall several brick courses below the slab-bearing elevation. When the slab shrinks back, it may not be able to drag the section of wall back with it. As a result, a permanent step or projecting ledge is created along the brick wall face. Such offset cracks may grow to ¾ inch owing to the cumulative movements of a number of years.

Porch slabs elevated above the surrounding grade, even though they are in contact with earth fill, rarely experience freeze-induced heaving, simply because the earth below them is dry and therefore not particularly expansive when frozen. Frost does, however, move such slabs. A fairly standard construction detail is to separate the slab from the house with a corklike material. Such joints are supposed to permit differential movement on the theory that the cork is flexible and will simply compress if the slab moves against it. Unfortunately, if water works its way into this joint and freezes, it can push the entire slab away from the house. This is not just a one-time occurrence. As the gap widens, within reason, more water can intrude, freeze, and push the slab out even farther. Because the slab is so massive and stiff, if it is properly anchored to its support structure, it may not move. In this case the house wall adjacent to the porch may actually be pushed in.

When a side porch joins a building at the basement area, the porch footings should be founded at the same depth as the basement foundations. This may require excavating another 6 or 7 feet, placing the footings, and then building a relatively deep wall from the footings to the slab elevation. Obviously this is expensive, and many builders choose simply to locate the porch footings deep enough to ensure frost protection, and then hope for the best. The best, surprisingly, is that porch walls often settle! If there is any attachment between the house and slab, such movements simply drag everything attached to the slab, such as house walls and parts of floors, along with it.

Framed Porch Slabs

Some of the incentives for providing a structural concrete slab that can actually frame between supports have been discussed. In recent years cost imperatives have been a strong incentive for the construction of wood-framed decks. In a few sections of the country steel decks have been popular, and for small porches or landings they still are used.

A porch detail that has been used for many years, in every part of the country and for almost every type of residence, is a wood deck structured with standard framing lumber and bearing partially on the house wall. The only significant variables are the details of the supports and the type of deck. Any wood exposed to the weather will eventually deteriorate. The modern practice of using lumber that is relatively more resistant to decay is at best a stopgap measure, for eventually the protective chemicals leach out and the conventional decay process begins. Paint, the traditional means of protecting wood, can be both an asset and a liability. Specifically, paint, which is rarely truly waterproof but only water-repellent, can seal the wood surface and prevent drying of trapped moisture. The first signs of deterioration appear in the wood around bearing points and in areas of restricted air flow, which are likely locations for rot.

The first issue concerning deck selection involves whether water must run off or through the deck. If the space below the deck is unoccupied and properly ventilated to ensure drying, deck planks can be spaced with approximately a ½-inch gap between them. On the other hand, when the water is to spill off the deck, a continuous, pitched surface must be created. Perhaps the most common porch decking material is a tongue-and-groove flooring very similar to conventional, interior flooring except that the edges are slightly rounded. This flooring is not set tightly together, because it must accommodate a great deal of expansion and contraction, and necessarily some water always works its way down along the tongue and into the groove. Because almost no air can freely circulate in such confined, damp spaces, the tongues are the first rot casualty—many times they literally disappear within the first several years.

In any exposed wood deck system, builders have always recognized that another particularly vulnerable place for rot is where the deck bears on the support lumber. During the first quarter of this century, when the majority of houses were built with a wooden porch, it seems that almost every carpenter had a different scheme for protecting or separating this joint to minimize rot. Heavy tarred building paper was laid on the support joist top edge, various combinations of contoured wood strips were used to separate the deck and joists, and in some cases special galvanized steel washers were inserted below each deck board. Most of these methods were experimental, and of course, it took many years to validate any particular detail—a time beyond the working life of most of the carpenter-experimenters. The result is that the porches rotted out at about the same rate as those without any special detail between the deck and support lumber.

Once in a while a wooden porch deck was required to be truly waterproof, in which case roofing details were sometimes tried. Another solution was to cover the deck with a heavy canvas material and then enamel the surface in much the same manner as cabin roofs of wooden boats are "canvassed." This method provided a surface that not only was reasonably durable and waterproof but also could tolerate a good deal of foot traffic. If canvassed decks were carefully and regularly maintained, that is, painted every year and any holes patched, they lasted almost indefinitely; however, when a hole remained unattended for one or two seasons, it was amazing how extensive and dramatic the deterioration could become. Once water penetrated below the membrane, it could not dry out, and large areas rotted out completely in one season.

Like all wood-decay problems, there is only one really practical solution, to remove and to replace any rotten wood. Thus, rather than concern yourself particularly with repair methods, it is perhaps more appropriate to consider the best alternatives to replacing a deteriorated wooden porch deck. Certainly, lumber treated especially for exterior service should be used, but beyond this the don'ts are probably more important than the dos. Specifically, plywood does not make a very good exterior porch deck, and even exterior grades will eventually start to delaminate near the edges. Many owners attempt to replace a slightly elevated wood porch with a concrete one. The typical approach is to place low masonry walls on spread footings founded just below the surface. The interior is then filled with earth and a slab placed on top. This method is almost guaranteed to maximize future distress. For one thing, it involves increasing the backfill and therefore the soil horizontal pressure against the foundation wall, thus creating the potential for wall cracking if not total collapse. Secondly, the installation of new earth, high up on an exterior wall, is an open invitation to termites; and even if the soils are poisoned, the potential will continue to exist after the chemicals have lost their effectiveness. If the house has a basement, then part of the walls may be founded on the fills at the original foundation excavation, and differential settlement is almost inevitable. A very determined owner, having recognized the potential for these problems, may decide to build a new concrete structure and do it completely properly and avoid the pitfalls. There is no question that such a porch can be installed without creating problems, but this is one of those situations where the difference in cost between the marginal way and the guaranteed problem-free way is so great that alternatives really should be considered.

The support structure for raised porches is most often either masonry piers or wood columns. In older homes brick-masonry piers are typically 12 inches × 12 inches square, because this is an easy dimension combination for building brick piers. Each side can be a stretcher plus a header brick, and each course can alternate the position of the brick, as shown in Figure 8-1. Such a pier, by any judgment, theoretically should be adequate to easily support a part of a wood porch, and, in fact, it does work; however, the surprising thing is how oddly distorted such a pier almost inevitably becomes. Forty to fifty years appears to be their undamaged service life, for after this

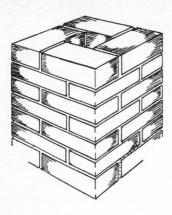

Fig. 8-1 Brick pier bonded coursing.

they seem to deteriorate rapidly. There appears to be no single reason for this, but it is extremely rare, even in the most carefully built houses, to find such masonry in completely sound condition. In part the deterioration may be attributed to such factors as exposure to weather on all sides, proximity to the earth, continuous horizontal movement induced by the changing dimensions of the porch, and sometimes marginal foundations; but even all these acting collectively hardly account for the magnitude of distress commonly encountered. Fortunately, though brick piers lean, tip, crack, split, and have deteriorated mortar and brick, they generally are so obviously distressed that some repairs are made before complete collapse occurs.

The attachment detail between the porch and house varies with the type of house construction, that is, wood or masonry, and with the particular framing system used on the porch. In some cases piers are located next to the house as well as out in the yard, and the porch is thus supported completely independently of the house. In many respects this is the best design, because any problems with the house will not affect the porch, and vice versa.

If the house is masonry and the porch is wood, then the typical support detail at the house wall is to bear the wood joists or beams into the masonry in slots or "joist pockets." As soon as any holes of this type are left in the masonry, essentially the weather integrity of the wall has been violated, and a leak potential exists. Conversely, the joist fitting into the masonry pocket creates a dark, damp, unventilated enclosure that is an ideal location for rot and decay. The only practical alternative is to build a ledge on the masonry for the joists. In such cases the problem of horizontally attaching the porch to the house is generally solved by nailing a metal strap to the joist and anchoring the strap back to the masonry. Even galvanized steel will eventually fail, and then such a deck can literally be pushed off the house with a single shove. In one group of row houses with back porches originally secured in this fashion, almost every one in a block fell off the wall ledge following very modest earth movements during some nearby heavy construction. A more suitable original detail and remedy to rusted strap anchors is a series of anchor bolts tying the porch to the wall.

People seem constitutionally incapable of leaving an open porch alone, and almost invariably one owner will eventually enclose the porch. The first hurdle involves the floor slope. Most porches are sloped several inches in their width to assure positive water drainage. On an open porch filled with summer furniture such a slope may never be noticed, but in an enclosed room it is not only apparent but also virtually intolerable. Often the process of enclosing a porch is a very long-term, progressive project that continues through several owners. If this change does last through several owners, the original config- uration may become obscured or forgotten. Thus, not infrequently new own- ers become aware of a sloped floor in a room projecting from the side of the house, attribute the slope to settlement, and become involved in a major reconstruction program before eventually realizing that it is a built-in slope for what was originally an open porch. The simple way to level such floors is with the tapered sleeper system, discussed in Chapter 6.

In porches enclosed as interior spaces, still another generic distress problem may occur at the wall-corner intersection between the main house and the porch. In the majority of such cases a substantial crack develops at the wall corners and along the ceiling line. A variety of reasons account for these cracks. As explained earlier, foundations for porches are generally not as carefully sized and founded as those for houses. Not only are they often high up in fill materials and above frost lines, but they are also rarely sized for much additional load. Such additional loads as can easily be added in the process of enclosing the space are walls, roof, and interior finishes. Porch framing requirements are less stringent than those for typical interior floors, primarily because no deflection (stiffness) criterion exists for plaster wall and ceiling finishes. Finally, if the porch is old, the structure may be deteriorated by rot, particularly at support points. As if all these conditions were not enough to assure crack distress lines along the intersection between the old and newly enclosed space, the abrupt change in environment of the porch and the corresponding moisture and temperature adjustments inherent in such a transition almost guarantee some discontinuities along the intersection lines.

Remodelers, either explicitly or intuitively recognizing the potential for differential movement between the old and new construction, regularly do not rigidly attach the new wall to the old. Insofar as finishes are concerned, this is not an altogether unreasonable detail, but at the same time there may be structural incentives to provide some means of transferring loads, partic- ularly lateral (horizontal) loads such as wind, between the two building ele- ments. There are several easy "slip" attachments that will allow movement in one direction, such as vertical, and yet maintain alignment in another. For example, steel angles or a channel section can be bolted to the wall to allow movement up and down and in and out, and yet not side to side. Of course, both the exterior and interior finish details must take this into account, and some sort of flexibility or sliding finish detail must also be provided.

A standard deficiency with wood porches in general and wood-supported porches in particular involves not so much the size and condition of structural members as the details of the attachments between these members. The most

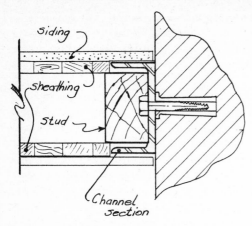

Fig. 8-2   Plan view of slip joint.

critical attachment points are along the line between the porch and the house (Figure 8-3Ⓐ) and at any post supports (Figure 8-3Ⓑ andⒸ). The supports to the house seem plagued by two problems: (1) the problem of making a secure attachment to the primary house structure and yet still providing a weatherproof and waterproof exterior surface; and (2) the problem of lateral-load transfer. Specifically, while there is generally not enough exposed vertical surface on the average porch to allow significant wind forces to develop, people moving around a porch can actually create significant horizontal loads.

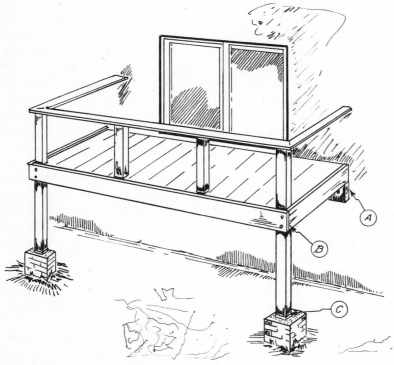

Fig. 8-3   Framed-elevated porch.

Thus, it is not uncommon to find porch floor joists resting on a perfectly adequate vertical support ledge with little or no positive attachment to resist any horizontal forces. Such porch structures do collapse, and this inadequacy is often a contributing factor—the joists simply slip off the support at the house.

Projecting wood porches are sometimes added as either an afterthought or an option to a standard house design. In such cases siding may be continuous across the area of support, and rather naively a support ledge or "ledger plate" is attached *through* this siding to the primary structure. Realistically, this attachment is almost impossible to justify from a structural point of view, because almost no attachments can provide the needed support if they must extend through several inches of siding, insulation, and sheathing before reaching an adequate structural member. If there are questions about the suitability of existing or planned attachments of porch to house and porch to posts, an experienced contractor, an architect, or an engineer should be consulted. On the other hand, common sense should be able to identify a wholly inadequate attachment. For example, at post supports a perimeter beam may be only lightly nailed to the top of the post, and the post just resting on a concrete base support. Since a few really determined shakes could easily dislodge such connections, it should be obvious that they are inadequate. Most lumberyards have a variety of metal post attachment fittings for both the upper and lower joints. When selecting such hardware it is difficult to "overdesign"; thus, the rule should be to buy the best available.

Jumping on a floor or pushing against a wall may not sound like a very scientific test of the adequacy of a building, but to compare a known, adequately structured house to another in this way is not a totally unreasonable approach. Nowhere is this more applicable than in judging the adequacy of certain porch structures and their railings. By running and stopping very abruptly, a fairly substantial lateral load can be produced. Do this on a porch and feel how much it moves and how long it continues to vibrate. There is certainly no hard-and-fast rule by which to judge the importance of the movement, but it is certainly legitimate to require that it feel *firm* or perhaps *substantial*. Some may say that this is trying to engineer by the use of language, yet any casual observer has a reasonably consistent understanding of when these words are applicable. Somewhat the same criterion can be used as a measure of the adequacy of a porch railing. If it does not feel like it will support the really determined push of several people, it probably will not. Incidentally, it should provide this support, and in fact, almost every building code requires that railings support a horizontal force of 50 pounds per linear foot for their entire length. If someone tells you to stop shaking the porch or the railing because you might knock it down, you can be almost positive that it is structurally inadequate and that some corrections are needed.

The question of railing adequacy is applicable to both exterior porches and interior rails dividing floor levels and at stairways. The lateral-load specification also applies to interior railings; and while a failure may allow a person to fall only a few feet, injuries can be severe. Interior rails are sometimes so grossly and obviously inadequate that insurance coverage may even be in question; railing adequacy is certainly a matter to be taken seriously insofar as life safety is concerned. A modern standard "dividing" rail in some houses consists of 1-inch or even smaller square steel posts spaced 4 to 6 feet apart with thin steel "pickets" between. Sometimes these posts disappear into a hole cut in the flooring, in which case they may stop well short of any substantial wood support. Other details have a square base several inches across, which, in turn, is screwed to the floor. Such details are completely inadequate and will only support a fraction of the specified load. Builders do not install rails of this type particularly as a money-saving device, because they are relatively expensive and not really cheaper than a structurally adequate rail. Strangely enough, it seems that it is one of those details that is so common that people just suppose there is no alternative. Even when people fall through these rails they passively lick their wounds and reinstall exactly the same railing in the same manner. Since the code load requirement is 50 pounds uniformly applied along the top edge, a rail just a few feet long must withstand several hundred pounds total horizontal force. The average adult certainly cannot push much more than this, and thus should *not* be able to push down a rail by hand. This test was recommended to the prospective buyer of a home, and when the entire rail was easily ripped out, the builder defended the weakness of the railing by arguing that it was purposely made flexible so that people could easily see how fragile and weak it was and therefore would not lean against it! Simply put, a house should withstand any bare-handed attack, and if any part wiggles, breaks, or shakes when pushed, pulled, or jumped on, then something is wrong!

Balconies

Relatively small porches, built off the interior structure particularly at the upper stories of a house, fairly consistently are called balconies, although some people may still refer to them by such names as sun decks, sun porches, or if the deck is tiled, patios. Whatever the name, this particular class of appendage is relatively small, easily structured, and braced so that the question of purely structural adequacy is rarely an issue.

The most serious problems involving balconies almost always have to do with water leakage. Two areas of potential leakage exist: (1) where the structure attaches to the house or extends from it, and (2) at the doorsill. Presumably the details of preventing water from running in at the doorsill should have been solved in design, but there are genuine difficulties inherent in extending a balcony from conventional, wood floor structure that make it oddly difficult to prevent water from entering over the sill. The basic problem is that wind-driven water can blow back under a sill set at the porch level, and the solution is to create a few-inches-high step-down between the interior floor level and the back edge of the porch. This sounds simple enough, but if the porch is just an extension of the interior floor structure, which it often is, such a step means cutting into the primary structure at what may be the very point of maximum stress. Recognizing this, builders may be inclined to build a step-up-and-over-type curb, but most codes discourage this sort of detail on the basis that people can easily trip over it, particularly on the way out. Thus, without relatively complex structure at the floor extensions, the only practical alternative is modest metal flashing partway below the doorsill, with primary reliance on carefully caulked joints. As the caulking deteriorates or the joint moves excessively, water is bound to find a path into the interior. Repairs are often complicated, because it is difficult to know how hidden flashing is located. The best procedure is to dismantle the sill if possible and reinstall it in a bed of mastic.

If floor joists extend through the wall to support the balcony, metal flashing details can become extremely complicated and expensive. Again, the only alternative to proper flashing is caulked joints; but very few caulking materials are designed to accommodate the movements as the joist expands and contracts, and after a few years an easy water path to the house is opened. Because the details are so variable, there are no hard-and-fast rules of repair, but simply recaulking old joints is at best only a temporary fix. One very important consideration is to remember that in such cases water can run down and around the bottom side of the joist and create a permanently damp place, a place conducive to rot. Therefore, water intrusion is not the only consideration, and protection of the structure is equally as important.

Garden Walls

Exterior, free-standing masonry walls are built for many different reasons, and strangely enough the original builders often have a special feel and concern for these walls. It is hard to know exactly why people seem so especially attached to such walls. Perhaps these walls remind some people of childhood and recall Robert Louis Stevenson's famous poem about garden walls, or it may be that garden walls give people a special sense of security, a sense of being enclosed in their "own land." Walls can be built as a screen, to retain earth and allow level changes in a terrace effect, for purely decorative reasons, for security, and for some, simply for the love of building walls. Drive through an Italian or Spanish section of a city and you will see backyards full of "masonry works"—masonry paths and walls that seem to have been built more for the love of building than for functional, utilitarian purposes.

Regardless of why such walls were originally built, they must be maintained if they are to survive. As time passes, yards change usage, and owners come and go, the original incentive for the building of walls sometimes is lost. As walls become useless, owners often lose interest in them. The inevitable result is that yards have old, forlorn walls in various stages of disrepair. Unfortunately, distress and deterioration of garden walls is not in the least restricted to old walls; in face, certain distress problems are more apt to develop within the first year or two.

Masonry deterioration is the most common problem found in exterior walls. Regardless of whether the masonry is stone or brick, the general process remains more or less the same. The environmental differences between interior and exterior masonry walls are obvious and have already been discussed in detail in previous chapters. In many respects, however, garden walls (i.e., low exterior walls exposed on all sides) are subjected to a relatively more destructive environment as compared with house exterior walls, than are exterior house walls when compared with interior walls. Garden walls are literally partially buried in the earth, and they are therefore vulnerable to the moisture and chemicals in the earth. Unlike a basement wall with one side that is left exposed to drying, a completely exterior, free-standing wall can only dry the buried base by sucking up moisture within the wall to a level above grade, much as a lamp wick draws up oil. With this moisture gradient, sometimes called "damp rise," come earth chemicals, principally salts, that can, under certain conditions, cause both brick and mortar to completely disintegrate. The mechanism is somewhat analogous to that of water expansion during a freeze-thaw cycle. Specifically, salt compounds migrate through the permeable body of the brick; but according to the type of brick and method of firing, they can become trapped in a plane behind the face of the brick. If these trapped salts reach a certain concentration level in the presence of water, they can become expansive, and according to the brick strength, they can cause the brick face to spall off in almost exactly the same manner as the faces of freeze-damaged bricks.

Masonry mortar under the very best of conditions will deteriorate with time when exposed to certain chemicals commonly found in soils; furthermore, with poorly formulated, mixed, and applied mortar, which is nearer to the rule than the exception in average old masonry work, it is surprising that exterior walls survive as well as they do. The standard mortar problems related to ground chemicals involve softening of the mortar near the grade line, which leads to the disintegration process described in the case of basement brick walls.

The harsh environment is not in the least restricted to the wall base. The tops of walls are most often flat, and if they are also only exposed masonry units, another easy water path into the wall interior exists. In conventional building walls the surface is meant only to shed water, and it is almost impossible to make brick masonry waterproof in the sense that a tank to hold water can be made of brick masonry. Actually this *can* be done, and many sewer lines in older cities as well as cistern-type structures are of brick masonry, but these special cases require a level of brick and mortar quality as well as craftsperson expertise that, for practical purposes, does not occur in average residential construction. The problem, of course, is that on flat, exposed masonry the water can collect and work its way into the interior. In many very old applications designers recognized this particularly vulnerable surface and either "capped" the wall head or contoured the brick so water would easily flow off. Garden wall caps run the gambit of materials, but long sections of stone, precast concrete, tile, and metal are common. Contoured bricks are an ideal solution to the top-water problem, but today such specially shaped bricks must be made more or less by hand, and the cost has become almost prohibitive. In the past, when all bricks were handmade, a different shape did not affect cost and was the easiest solution.

The solar environment of garden walls at first seems to be analogous to that which causes parapet wall problems, discussed in Chapter 4. But there is another situation that can be even more damaging, and that is one of no sun at all. For example, garden walls near the north wall of a house may *never* be exposed to the sun, for they are shaded by the house from the south and, of course, the sun never falls on the north side. Thus, a wall that already is in a particularly damp environment may never have an opportunity to be exposed to the drying effects of the sun. Under such conditions damp rise from the earth may meet moisture flowing down from above, and all the deterioration processes in masonry that are related to water will occur. One interesting perspective on the relative effects of moisture and sun on exposed masonry can be had by examining walls on both exposures at a particular house. If the walls were clearly built at the same time using similar materials and techniques, the principal differences after a few years will most likely be those caused by the differences in sunlight and moisture conditions.

Many garden walls retain some amount of earth, and yet rarely are they designed as true cantilevered retaining walls. Given enough time, the walls begin to tip, and eventually they will simply fall over if unattended. Tipping is a generic problem with exterior walls, and horizontal pressure from earth fill at level changes is not the only cause of this class of movement. When walls surround a garden, the earth on the garden side is apt to be regularly dug up and loosened. In addition, the garden-side soils are often saturated

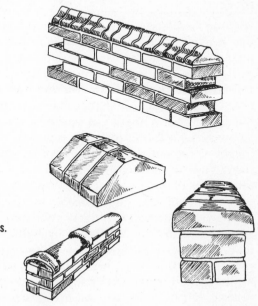

Fig. 8-4   Garden wall caps.

with water both from rain, which can easily flow into the cultivated soils, and from gardeners watering plants. Such differential conditions between the two sides produce gradients in moisture and soil below the footings that allow the walls to tip.

When trees are planted close to a wall, the roots can easily grow beneath the footings and both heave and tip walls. In long walls, particularly ones running east and west, tipping is attributed to the differences in moisture produced by the sun drying. This is a rather difficult argument to establish by any analytical means, for while the differences from side to side are easily identified, they produce such slight variations that it is almost impossible to explain any tipping on the basis of differential moisture created by solar drying. The proponents of this argument can, however, point to a number of cases when east–west walls are tipped and nearby north–south-running walls remain vertical. The actual mechanism may be more related to freezing phenomena. The sun-sheltered, northside earth will freeze and push the wall horizontally against the warmer, unfrozen soils on the south side.

The inadequacies of foundation excavation fill that allow general subsidence near basement walls can, of course, cause garden walls to tip. The best design practice would require that the wall footings be founded below any fill materials. But people who build walls after a house is completed either cannot distinguish easily between fill and original soils, or the extra wall height seems hardly worth the possible benefits. The result is that walls running near a house are rarely founded on original soils and, perhaps worse, they may even be located across the transition zone between fill and undisturbed materials, therefore guaranteeing the potential for differential settlement and tipping.

One standard method of minimizing tipping problems is to zigzag the wall so that, in effect, the wall is buttressed by returns at direction changes. In addition to certain aesthetic considerations, Thomas Jefferson probably had this in mind when he built his famous serpentine walls, which snake across the lawns at Monticello and the University of Virginia. Certainly buttresses work, but in certain situations buttresses can actually increase wall tipping. In extremely poor soils an exterior wall is sort of a balancing act, and if nothing differential or changeable exists from one side to the other, it will remain vertical. A short wall introduced at right angles, designed to provide a buttressing effect, is different from one side to the other. In poor soils the weight of the buttress wall plus the added soil pressures on the projecting footing top surface may be enough to actually push the buttress down and force the wall to tip.

A somewhat analogous situation occurs when true cantilevered retaining walls are founded on extremely poor soils. Such walls are designed with an asymmetrical footing, as shown in Figure 8-5. The intent is to extend the footing further into the hill below the higher soils so that the resulting soil pressures on this "heel," will offset (the moment from) the horizontal earth pressure and maintain the wall plumb. This is always somewhat of a delicate balance, but in good soils the margins between the movement one way or

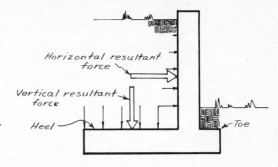

Horizontal resultant force

Vertical resultant force

Heel

Toe

Fig. 8-5 Cantileavered retaining wall.

another are so great that tipping rarely occurs. In poor soils the wall is similar to the person trying to keep an unbalanced canoe upright in the mud at the shore: It was obviously easier to maintain a balance in the mud than when the boat is floating in water.

Whatever the cause of tipping, the one certainty is that the problem will worsen with time. Just by being tipped, a wall has more weight on one of its sides than on the other, and in all likelihood, the process will continue. There are several fairly reasonable methods of righting a tipped wall short of tearing it down and completely rebuilding. It may sound too simple to work, but one means of straightening a tipped wall is simply to push it back. It may take quite some time—perhaps weeks, possibly days—but with a steady pressure against the wall the soils can actually be made to "fail" and allow the wall to be moved back. Some people saturate the soils on the side in the direction of motion, and it may help to dig out part of the soil to relieve any excessive load. Once the wall has been returned to its original position, something must be done to stabilize it, and, of course, the method depends on the original cause. One fairly standard method for holding retaining walls in the vertical position is to fix the wall to a soil "anchor," which is a plate buried deep in the earth and tied to the wall with a bar or cable.

Different combinations of masonry buttresses are regularly used to hold walls upright, but this method can be very expensive and space-consuming. In some cases wood or steel piles are drilled or driven in to hold a wall, but for the average residential case, this may be an excessively complex solution. Still another practical means of plumbing a tipped wall is to drive wedges into a mortar joint line near the base. Once the joint has snapped free, continued driving will force the wall into a vertical stance. The mortar joint can then be packed with a stiff, low-shrinkage mortar compound, and after it is completely cured the wedges can be removed.

Obviously, most of the masonry crack-producing mechanisms exist at exposed walls; however, there are a few phenomena that are somewhat unique. Because the walls must cycle through a full range of temperatures between summer and winter as well as on a daily basis, exposed walls obviously move far more owing to thermal effects than do house walls. There are certain crack patterns that are clearly attributable to thermally induced movements. In Chapter 4, the cracking at the edge of parapet walls are described. This is the condition in which intersecting parapet walls expand against each other to accommodate this movement and eventually push the corners free of the walls below. Intersecting garden walls have this same movement condition, but they are free to slide at their footings or tip at the corners. Thus, there is never any crack evidence of this problem with walls intersecting at right angles. Unfortunately, many times garden wall intersections are rounded off into a 5- or 10-foot-radius curve. In such curved walls, a standard crack pattern develops near the point of tangency (Figure 8-6). The explanation is simple: The curved intersection is too stiff. Certainly, the entire curve can be neither translated over nor tipped, and the crack develops to compensate for the thermal movement.

Recognizing the potential for movements, designers locate expansion joints in garden walls at much closer intervals than in conventional building walls. So that the abutting walls will not get misaligned, a common practice is to build an intersection joint that will allow movement in the direction of the walls by slipping in and out of a slot and yet prevent any relative lateral movement between the walls. Certainly in theory this is a reasonable solution, but in practice it can have serious drawbacks. As soon as this "slip joint" is made tight enough to maintain alignment, it is also tight enough to trap water, which can freeze, expand, and completely destroy the joint. Attempts to caulk the joint openings are likely to trap water on the inside, where it also can freeze and expand. There is not an absolute consensus on the best slip joint, but most agree that free drainage and small internal voids are the best means of preventing any serious freeze-related problems. A few steel rods in horizontal holes, wrapped in a flexible material such as roofing felt, will generally suffice.

Internal voids in the masonry of a house wall rarely have any meaning, and, of course, CMUs have intentional voids. With this experience as a precedent, garden walls were built with various combinations of hollow-masonry

Fig. 8-6 Garden wall with rounded corner.

units. In general, the results have been relatively unsatisfactory, but in very random, sometimes inconsistent ways. The problem seems to involve two dominant mechanisms: (1) damage due to expanding ice trapped in voids; and (2) moisture-expansion incompatibility between clay-fired bricks and some CMUs. A fairly typical brick and block retaining-wall combination is to have the block on the earth (retaining) side and brick on the exposed side (see Figure 8-7a). Even though voids exist in the block cavities, apparently they can drain easily through the exposed surface of the block, and this design in general seems to survive freeze-thaw cycles. On the other hand, the block side varies in moisture content from complete saturation to extremes of dryness, and while brick and block expansion characteristics are relatively compatible for thermally induced changes, in the *extremes* of moisture they are comparatively incompatible materials. In a house, brick is generally used on the exposed and therefore wetter side; and in such an environment the fundamentally different moisture properties of brick and block have little significance. In some cases retaining walls built of this particular design have cyclically moved back and forth until they simply fall apart. Once in a while this materials combination survives completely undamaged for many years; and the best explanation seems to be that although the system does not work in extreme situations; that is, in extremes of moisture differences and extremes of moisture-expansion incompatibility, should any of these conditions vary significantly, the wall might survive. Since these conditions can

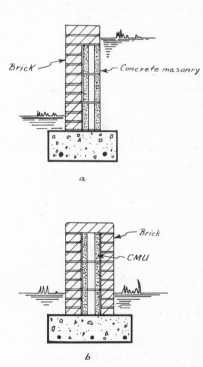

Fig. 8-7 Masonry garden walls. (*a*) Exposed brick face with CMU toward earth. (*b*) Brick exposed both sides with interior withe of CMU.

never be defined a priori, however, this may not be the best wall design available.

Figure 8-7b represents a wall system that the designer wanted to be particularly thick for appearance and functional reasons—it was low and used as a sort of continuous bench. The exposed surfaces were brick ; the interior was block. Not only were moisture conditions symmetrical, but also the block was not necessarily the wettest component, and apparently this design did not fail as a result of moisture-expansion cycling. Instead, after the first winter the wall literally lay in pieces—completely demolished by expanding ice trapped in the interior block cavities. The rebuilding procedure in this case was to remove the top brick and fill the voids with concrete, a procedure that proved completely satisfactory.

Steel reinforcing in walls is an intuitively appealing, strength-increasing component; and when properly sized and installed, it can significantly increase the load capacity of any wall. There are, however, some pitfalls in its use. Most of the problems relate to trying to fit too large a bar in too small a space and in not completely filling any voids around reinforcement bars. Masonry mortar joints typically range from ¼ to ½ inch thick, with the majority of modern joints at ⅜ inch. This is true for most joints, including the collar joint between withes of brick. Even when ⅜-inch-diameter bars are used in such joints, the entire bar cannot be completely encased in mortar. Even worse, fairly sizable voids are often left near the bars because of the difficulty of working mortar around them. Two types of problems can result from such bar-installation methods. Water can collect in the voids, thereby creating the potential for freeze damage. In addition, if water can regularly flow in and around steel reinforcing, the likelihood of serious rust problems exists. Steel reinforcement bars embedded in concrete always rust, but under normal circumstances an equilibrium condition is reached and maintained in which the iron oxides (rust) on the bars protect them from the relatively small amounts of water, and particularly oxygen-rich water, that work their way into the body of the concrete mass. In masonry walls continuous voids around reinforcing can actually work like conduits, through which water can actually flow past the steel. Under such conditions, serious corrosion problems can occur unless fairly elaborate precautions are taken. Such precautions may include: either reducing the size of the reinforcing or increasing the mortar joint thickness; requiring that the reinforcing be galvanized, as is true with most horizontal-joint reinforcing; or finally, pump-grouting under a slight pressure any vertical joint in which reinforcing is placed. Unfortunately, such procedures are not too common in the home-building industry; and as a practical matter, it is better practice to try to solve construction problems using methods typical to the industry rather than introducing perhaps better, but nevertheless different, building techniques. If walls are to be reinforced, standard methods should be used, such as conventional joint reinforcing and, in the case of vertical reinforcing, setting the steel in a large cavity that can be easily and completely filled with concrete or mortar grout.

Repair methods for exposed, garden-type masonry walls must, of course, be so tailored to the particular cause of distress that it is impossible to generalize about a universally adaptable solution. In the special case of garden wall repair, perhaps even more than in other cases, a survey of what has and has not been successful in the area is a first priority in planning a repair program. Two special considerations must be kept in mind, however: Remember that freeze- and salt-distress resistance of bricks vary considerably; and just because a brick looks the same as another, it does not guarantee that the two share the same physical properties. Most bricks are actually given a name by the manufacturer, and in specifying a brick that has been proven to work in garden walls, one should use the particular name. Secondly, most distress to masonry garden walls is a very time-related phenomenon, and proof that a particular wall system is working should not be based solely on one or two years of observations.

Chimneys and Fireplaces

Pick up a book on the homes of average families in colonial times and the illustrations will almost certainly show a grouping of furniture arranged around a fireplace that covers half the wall. At that time, and until late in the nineteenth century, the fireplace was almost the central, dominant feature of a house. The owners knew how to work it and, equally importantly, how it worked. The fireplace and chimney were regularly maintained; and as the size of a house grew with additions, either the size or number of fireplaces grew. The local craftspeople knew how to build the system, and particular masons were noted for their ability to build a fireplace that drew particularly well and lasted a long time.

Fig. 8-8   Brick in garden wall.

Today, fireplaces are a luxury in new homes, and until very recently, they were almost a liability to heating a house. They really were used more for decorative effects than for cooking and heating.

The details of how a fireplace and chimney are proportioned, sized, and built seem much more akin to witchcraft than to science. The depth of the firebox in proportion to the size of the opening must be related to the shape of the smoke chamber above; and everything must relate to the size, height, and location of the chimney. Modern codes define many of the proportions, but only to assure a system that works, and not one that necessarily works optimally. There are a number of old references to fireplace and chimney construction that consider most of the dominant variables; and when these are followed, really dramatically better fireplace performance results. Conversely, when the simplified modern code requirements are not adhered to, correspondingly bad performance almost always occurs. Poor fireplace performance is not just irritating, it can be extremely dangerous, particularly when systems sometimes draw out the smoke and sometimes do not.

Perhaps the best references on fireplaces were written in the first quarter of this century, at a time when the old mechanics who knew the art joined with practical engineers to produce a good blend of art and science. If an owner has problems with fireplace performance, these references are still available in most public libraries, and others are being republished as part of a nostalgia-energy-conservation format. Unfortunately, an improperly operating fireplace is not something that can be easily rectified, and in extreme cases, all or part of a system must be taken down and rebuilt.

In addition to housing the flue for the fireplace, most chimneys also house the exhaust stack for heating and hot-water furnaces. Do not assume that this must be true. Today furnaces are often located to optimize air distribution in ducts, which generally dictates a fairly central location. On the other hand, fireplaces, and therefore chimneys that are often built as options are generally located toward the ends of houses. Finally, many modern homes have an anomaly—a fireplace and electric heat. In any event, since the early 1950s, prefabricated, metal-encased stacks have been readily available for home use. Such stacks may run through interior partitions, and the average occupant, viewing the upper floor levels, can have no idea exactly where the stack runs through the house. To the extent that these commercial stacks deteriorate, the only solution is rather complete replacement. Active masonry stacks do have various, relatively standard distress characteristics that are worthwhile considering.

Smokestacks, simply as a structural component of a house, start off at a disadvantage. In most cases, they are an isolated element, a part and yet not a part of the structure. For example, there are certain restrictions about how wood floor and roof structure can bear on masonry, and in many cases the chimney is actually completely free of both floors and roof. Obviously in wood-framed buildings, the walls are independent of the chimney, and in some cases even masonry bearing walls have little or no anchorage to the chimney. In light of this obvious discontinuity in a house, it should not be surprising in the least to find a number of rather typical distress characteristics surrounding a fireplace and chimney system. It is certainly the rule rather than the exception to find plaster cracks in ceilings and walls more or less radiating from the fireplace-chimney wall. The exact crack patterns are a function of the details of how the chimney is structured with respect to the wall. Every combination possible has been built—(1) the chimney standing actually away from the outside wall as in early Virginia houses; (2) the chimney completely exterior to the shell yet against the continuous exterior wall structure; (3) the chimney built half in and half out of a slot in the wall (the masonry of the chimney may or may not be exposed in such cases); (4) the chimney against the outer wall but built on the inside of it; (5) the chimney actually built well within the interior toward the middle of the house, which is common in early New England houses; and finally (6) all combinations of the above as chimneys move in and out at each floor level. In other words, there is the generic class of chimney that has the same relation to the structure at each floor, in the simplest case a straight, uniform-thickness chimney, and the class that steps in or out of the wall according to fireplace arrangements.

Crack patterns are generally very symmetrical in relation to the chimney; for example, an almost universal ceiling crack pattern found in houses with the chimney half in and half out of the wall is a pair of cracks beginning on both sides of the chimney and running out into the living room ceiling. Such a pattern is likely to be repeated in the room above if the chimney stays in the same relation to the structure. Sometimes this double crack is replaced by a single crack more or less centered on the fireplace opening. Another very standard chimney-related crack pattern is a separation crack along any edge of the chimney–wall-intersection lines. These can be both on the inside and outside of the house or at one location only. The most singularly frustrating thing about this whole class of cracks is that they are so unpredictable. The very randomness of these cracks is perhaps why they so universally exist—no one can say for certain when and why they exist—and therefore no one has devised methods of construction that will guarantee that they will not occur.

A completely different class of distress in chimneys is related to the fact that chimneys and fireplaces are paths for hot gases, gases that range in temperature from 400 to 1000°F. The most noticeable example of this hot-gas-related distress occurs near the top and appears to be largely according to the details of the chimney liner and how the cap is arranged. Historically, the firebox was lined with a fire-resistant brick, not necessarily a "firebrick" in the modern sense, but simply a brick that would not disintegrate after a few exposures to flame. Further up the chimney gas temperatures were low enough that more or less standard brick could be used, and in some cases the only concession made to the heat was to parge the surface with a mortar stucco. As time went on, specially fired clay pipes, almost like ceramic tiles, were used as liners. These liners had two advantages: (1) presumably they could better withstand the temperatures; and (2) since these pipe sections were long, there were far fewer mortar joints—the weakest link in a chimney exposed to hot gas. For the most part these ceramic flue liners retain the gases and are very durable, but near the top they tend to deteriorate more rapidly than elsewhere. There are various arguments as to why the environment at the top, where the gas temperature is lowest, should be so destructive. In part it is because the wind can create turbulence and drive the gases against the walls of the liner; also, the liner can be suddenly cooled by rain and wind. The brick and mortar on the outside of chimneys near the discharge point are often deteriorated by the alternate heating and cooling.

Unlined chimneys naturally fare much worse than lined ones, with the worse damage, again, near the top. Varying with the dominant wintertime wind direction, which drives the gases against one particular wall, the mortar and brick on one side will deteriorate and cause the top several feet to lean. In older sections of cities this chimney leaning is so repetitious for mile after mile of houses that it almost looks like it was intended. In London, England, with its almost contant wind direction of west to east, seventeenth-century paintings of the city neatly show all the chimneys leaning in the same direction.

Oddly enough, there seems to be no universal rule that can predict whether they lean to windward or leeward—the direction is related to the particular cap detail. This is not unanticipated, because the cap determines how the gases can swirl around the top of the masonry as well as how the interior is protected from wind and rain. In short, the upper several feet of a chimney will eventually deteriorate if left unattended. Generally, owners are unaware of the progressive nature of this deterioration, and when a brick lands in their yard they are convinced something catastrophic suddenly has happened to the chimney.

There is, of course, a catastrophic occurrence that *does attack* chimneys, and that is lightning. The physics of lightning are not completely understood, and even less well defined are the details of how lightning can be so oddly destructive. To just remind an owner of the tremendous amount of energy discharged when lightning strikes does not begin to explain the bizarre things lightning can do. Lightning can literally blow a chimney apart! Sometimes it seems to pass well into the stack before it does serious damage. Other times it will knock a few bricks off the top and nothing more.

The chimney repair process is complicated and necessarily expensive. Certainly as preventive maintenance, a homeowner should make several repairs that will extend the life of a chimney. The exterior mortar should be repointed as soon as noticeable deterioration begins. Also, the top section and possibly two sections of flue liner can often (but not always) be replaced with relative ease. In cases where the entire liner has failed, some of the manufactured metal flues may be considerably easier to install than to completely replace the original, ceramic liners. Local codes may be restrictive even with respect to repairs, and certainly should be consulted.

Conclusion

Diagnosing residential building distress, devising suitable methods of repair, and even carrying out the repairs may be more a matter of a little careful thought than of any special background knowledge or mechanical skill. Play the detective; think about things. All the propositions involving the structure of the average house are relatively simple to understand, and an excessively complicated explanation is often a tip-off that it misses the mark. For the average person, comparative analysis is the simplest and most foolproof; if the cause of a crack is puzzling or if a particular remedial method is in question, examine other houses that are roughly of the same age and type of construction. Finally, do not make the mistake of substituting words for ideas. The language of construction and names of components may be unclear, but since the ideas are simple, they can be thought of simply and therefore understood.

GLOSSARY

Abut To nearly touch or touch along a boundary line.

Abutment A structure principally designed to resist lateral loads, a buttress-type structure.

Acoustics (1) The physical science dealing with sound. (2) The characteristics of a material or a space related to sound transmission.

Adobe An air-dried brick of earth or natural clays used in Southwestern United States and Mexico.

Angle iron A common name for a mill-rolled steel-bar section shaped like an L.

Arcade A covered passageway or walkway with at least one side composed of a series of arches.

Arch The symmetric, rounded shape at the top of an opening in a wall. Most often refers to masonry construction where individual units are wedged together to transmit forces across the span of the opening.

Flat arch An arch whose bottom line or soffit is straight and horizontal. Also called a "French and Dutch arch."

Segmental arch A round arch with bottom outline less than a semicircle.

Balloon frame A type of timber wall framing in which the studs are run continuously and pass floor construction without an interruption.

Band course, band molding In masonry and wood construction, a long projecting horizontal element on a wall plane.

Banister Corruption of baluster or small columnlike posts repetitiously in line to support a handrail.

Base course In masonry, the lowest course of a wall or pier.

Bat (1) In masonry, a part, generally half, of a broken brick. (2) Building insulation in a long strip and wrapped in a baglike container.

Batten A narrow board covering the open joint between other boards.

Bed joint In masonry, the joint on which the masonry is laid in mortar, the horizontal mortar joint.

Belt course See **Band Course.**

Bench mark In surveying, the datum elevation or reference mark for measuring elevations and locations.

Bent A rigid frame, most often generally in the form of an inverted U.

Berm A long bank of earth adjacent to a building or structure.

Board foot A unit measure of lumber 1 inch thick × 12 inches × 12 inches. Abbr.: B.F.; b.f.

Bond   (1) In masonry, the stacking arrangement of masonry units so that they overlap joints and lock together. (2) The mechanical or chemical attachment between two adjoining surfaces.

Brick nogging   The filling with brickwork between heavy timber framing.

Bridging   Bracing, generally cross diagonals, set between joists to help distribute loads between adjacent members.

Cantilever   A projecting beam supported at one end only.

Centering   The construction support below masonry or concrete temporarily installed during the curing process.

Chair rail   An applied wood or plaster band on an interior wall at chair-back height, designed to protect the wall surface.

Collar joint   In masonry, the joint between adjacent wythes of masonry units.

Coping   The exposed cap or top course of a wall.

Corbel   A bracketlike, cantilevered projection from a wall surface, generally of successive courses of masonry.

Dado   Interior wall covering from the floor to chair-rail height, often consisting of vertical wood strips.

Drip (line)   A narrow, projecting surface at the top of a vertical wall opening designed to prevent water from running back under the soffit and thereby forcing it to "drip" off.

Eaves   The edge of a roof that projects over an outside wall.

Efflorescence   Salt compounds that leach out of the face of brick or mortar and deposit on the masonry surface.

Failure   The limit criterion at which a structural element or mechanical system no longer meets its intended service requirements.

Fascia   A horizontal band at the eaves line.

Gable   (1) The end wall of a building below a pitched roof. (2) Spaces projecting from a pitched roof, generally including an end window.

Header (beam)   The short beam between joists to support an intermediate but interrupted joist.

Hip   Of a roof, the high line of intersection of two roof planes; a sloping eaves line.

Intrados   The underside, bottom line, or soffit of an arch.

Jamby   The side of a window or door frame or the side of a window frame.

Lintel   The structural member spanning a wall opening.

Mastic   An adhesive that remains soft and elastic.

Moment   The products of a force times the distance from the force to a line. A measure of the rotational effects of a force about an axis.

Ogee   A molding shape consisting of part concave and part convex curves.

Party wall   The dividing wall between buildings or land parcels.

Paver   A brick, tile, or stone unit especially intended for surfacing an exterior walk- or driveway.

Pent roof   A roof of a single, sloping surface.

Soap   A thin brick, cut or molded, to be used more like a tile for facing a surface.

Soffit   The underside surface of a projection or wall opening such as below a roof overhang, window, or door opening.

Soldier course   In masonry, bricks repetitiously laid with their long faces vertical. Particularly used above wall openings and as decorative bands.

Stress   An internal force per unit area in a structural member. An important criterion by which the load-carrying capacity of a member is judged.

Stringer   The structural side rail of a stair.

Temper   The mixing of mortar to a proper consistency. (Re) temper, adding additional water to mortar after the initial mix to maintain its workability.

Terne (plate)   A coated steel roofing material in which the coating is lead and tin.

Water table   (1) The level of water in soils. (2) A projecting surface on walls located near the grade line.

Weep Hole   A small opening in a masonry wall for drainage, often only an omitted head joint in the mortar.

Withe   (1) A single width of masonry units. (2) A cavity within a masonry wall equal to the width of the units.

Wrought iron   (1) A ferrous material manufactured by a specific process involving pressing or hammering and rolling. (2) Referring to products supposedly made from wrought iron.

INDEX

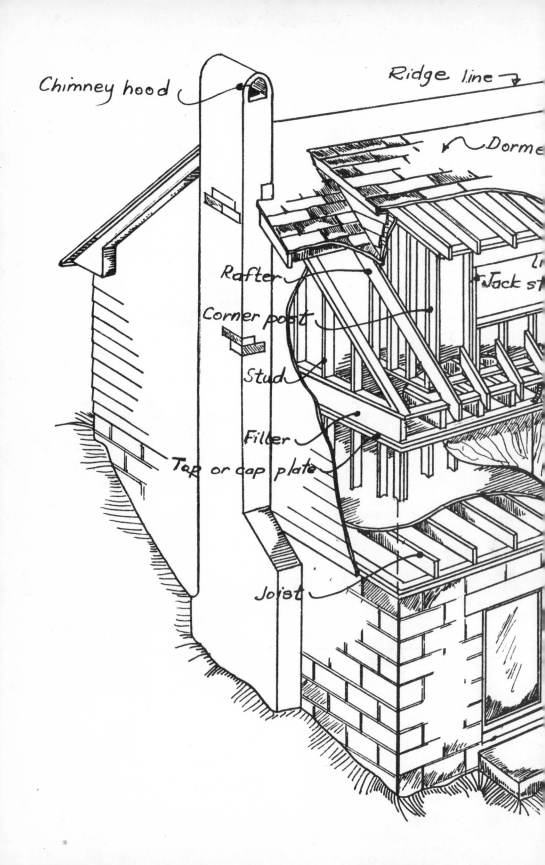

Chimney hood

Ridge line

Dorme

Rafter

Jack st

Corner post

Stud

Filler

Top or cap plate

Joist